LINCOLN CHRISTIAN COLLEGE AND SEMINARY

Lee Ellis shines the spotlight on human behavior and offers powerful tips for leaders and team members alike. This book is a must read because it helps us understand and manage ourselves as well as all of our relationships with others.

Laurie Beth Jones, author,
Jesus CEO and *The Path*

Lee's coaching and teaching on how to build relationships and get better results have been a great help to my team. He's pulled together some very powerful concepts into one book and then summarized them in each chapter with an easy-to-use Coach's Clipboard. Now everyone can benefit from the expertise of this great leadership coach.

Rex Adams, president,
BellSouth Long Distance

Lee Ellis has worked with our team and also trained our trainers to apply many of the concepts in this book with great success. He brings a wealth of knowledge and experience on the subjects of leadership, teamwork and talents. I know this book will be a valuable resource for individual and team development.

Bill Burke, president,
The Weather Channel Companies

Lee is a first-class individual, whose wisdom and experience make him well-qualified to assist those of us who want to be better leaders. He has helped me and our team. I'm proud to count him as a friend.

David M. Ratcliffe, president and CEO,
Georgia Power Company

Leading Talents, Leading Teams *is the leadership book for today's professional environment. In a business landscape that has been cluttered with immoral management, Ellis develops the importance of integrity as a common thread that is woven through all the essential topics in leadership today. The book combines cutting edge research with sound, down-to-earth practical examples that make the book immediately useful to*

the practicing executive. If you plan to read just one book on leadership this year, I enthusiastically recommend this one.
Archie B. Carroll,
Professor of Management and
Robert W. Scherer Chair of Management,
University of Georgia,
author, *Business and Society*

I first met Lee Ellis in a North Vietnamese Prison. Leaders emerged of course and Lee was among them. He seemed to understand, better than most, what was required to maintain harmony and cohesion in that naturally tense environment. Now Lee has written a book that captures many of the principles that made that complex prison organization work. Anyone seeking a better understanding of how to lead and manage others, in any kind of organization, will profit from this book.
General Charles G. Boyd, U.S. Air Force Retired,
President and CEO,
Business Executives for National Security,
Washington, D.C.

LEADING
TALENTS,
LEADING
TEAMS

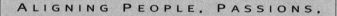

ALIGNING PEOPLE, PASSIONS,

AND POSITIONS FOR

MAXIMUM PERFORMANCE

LEE ELLIS

NORTHFIELD PUBLISHING
CHICAGO

© 2003 by
LEE ELLIS

Edited by Adeline Griffith

All rights reserved. No Part of this book may be repro-
duced in any form without permission in writing from the
publisher, except in the case of brief quotations embodied
in critical articles or reviews.

Library of Congress Cataloging-in-Publication Data

Ellis, Lee, 1943–
    Leading talents, leading teams: aligning people, passions,
and positions for maximum performance/Lee Ellis.
        p. cm
Includes bibliographical references.
ISBN 1-881273-29-6
1. Teams in the workplace. 2. Ability. 3. Manpower
planning. 4. Organizational effectiveness. 5. Leadership.
1. Title.
    HD66 .E425 2003
    658.4'02–dc21

1 3 5 7 9 10 8 6 4 2

Printed in the United States of America

CONTENTS

108092

❖

ACKNOWLEDGMENTS

Throughout my life, I've been blessed by the encouragement and support of many talented people. That has certainly been true in the process that led to the completion of this book, and I want to acknowledge some whose contributions stand out.

My dear wife Mary has stood by her man even when he kept hiding out in his basement office for an engagement with another chapter. I appreciate her patience, loving support, and good critique during this writing period. I'm looking forward to more time together and promise to get busy on that long delayed and growing list of honey-dos. Meredith, the last one still somewhat in the nest and a talented writer in her own right, has been encouraging and a practical help in putting together the drafts. Thanks also to our other adult children, Pat, Kristy, and Lance and their spouses, for their faithful support.

My parents, Leon and Molene are no longer with us, but they contributed enormously to the development of my character and my talents. I am especially grateful to them and to my brother Robert and his wife Pat and their family. They were so faithful during my five and a half years as a POW. I acknowledge and regret the pain they suffered because of my situation. I love and appreciate them more than words can express. They kept the faith and worked tirelessly to keep our cause alive and make sure we were not forgotten.

I'm especially grateful to Larry Burkett who brought me on board at Christian Financial Concepts to develop a "test" that would help young people find their career direction. That was the beginning of a new career for me that ultimately led to this book. His support and that of our Career/Life Pathways team enabled me to gain a knowledge and experience base with assessments. Thanks to Bob Yarbrough for his wisdom and encouragement and Mike Taylor for his insights and practical help in the development of our assessments.

Special recognition goes to our original research team, Beth Pinson Elder, Bette Noble, Dr. Garnett Stokes, Dr. Cheryl Toth, and Dr. Bridget Boyle. They ensured academic excellence and were totally supportive of our immediate practical needs for assessment. All of us on the team had a common heritage in that we were taught/encouraged by Dr. Bill Owens, the former chairman of the Institute for Behavioral Research at the University of Georgia. Although retired, "Doc" and his wife Barb continue to be a source of inspiration to me.

This book would not have been possible without the support of my teammates at RightPath Resources. I can't say enough about Sue Clark who has faithfully and freely dedicated her many creative talents for all the graphics. More than that, she's been there as a helper and friend every step of the way with ideas and assistance to make sure this book was finished. Jerry Mabe, my business partner, has helped in countless ways through ideas and wisdom. He supported my work on this book even when there were other pressing RightPath projects on the agenda. Gary O'Malley and Jane Hart also contributed ideas and encouragement that helped shape the direction. Hugh Massie of RightPath Australia provided encouragement throughout. Thanks, team.

Our customers and clients have played a key role also. They have been a source of great encouragement and friendship. And of course, they provided the platform for many of the examples and stories in the book. There are some great companies with great leaders in this country, and we have been blessed to work with some of the best.

Laurie Beth Jones's books and her friendship have been an inspiration. Thanks for sharing The Path and our common walk. Don Jacobsen is also a fellow traveler who never misses an opportunity to encourage me along the way, especially in my writing. Dan Walker and Steve Humphrey, who make up my accountability group, are special friends who also pushed me along the trail with their encouragement and prayers. This past year many friends at First Presbyterian Church in Gainesville have prayed and goaded me along the way to just "get it finished." Thanks, gang. It is.

This book has afforded me the opportunity to work again with Adeline Griffith, a fantastic editor who's also been a friend and source of encouragement. Thanks, Adeline, for sharing your talents.

I especially want to acknowledge the support of my friends at Moody Publishers who came up with the idea for this book and then believed in me enough to wait for five years to see it happen. My heartfelt thanks to Greg Thornton and his team for supporting me so faithfully in this effort.

Finally, I want to acknowledge my Heavenly Father, who has showered me with blessings of goodness and mercy all the days of my life.

❖

INTRODUCTION:
When Leadership and Teamwork Were a Life-and-Death Matter

It was the beginning of my third year as a POW in the communist prison system of North Vietnam, the night of November 21, 1970, and I was resting in the arms of the POW's best friend: sleep. For us sleep was an escape from the reality of the camp and the pain of our loneliness for our homeland and families.

Suddenly we were awakened as the building shook from the explosions of a nearby air strike. The North Vietnamese thundered back with a barrage of antiaircraft artillery and surface-to-air missiles.

In the early years of our captivity, these sounds caused some anxious moments. I worried about the pilots on the strike, praying that they would not join our ranks. I worried that a stray bomb or missile might come through the roof. But, most of all, I feared the law of gravity. I knew that what goes up must come down, and the barrage of antiaircraft fire and surface-to-air missiles (SAMs) could just as likely land in our camp. But that night the noises associated with the attack were an exhilarating and welcome sound.

It had been over two years since there had been any bombing

up North, and the consensus among the POWs was that the war could never be won as long as Hanoi and the Communist leaders were given sanctuary from the direct impact of the war. To think that the bombing had started again was a great encouragement. We knew it might be the beginning of the end of the war.

Unfortunately, we would soon learn it was not to be; the light at the end of the tunnel was still a long way off. This air strike had been a onetime event, a diversionary tactic for a raid on the Son Tay POW camp some twelve miles away. Son Tay had been my home for the previous two years, but we had relocated to Camp Hope only a few months earlier. The move was a key step in the North Vietnamese leadership's strategy to improve their international image by improving our treatment.

The raid that night was incredibly well executed but the camp was empty. Many in the U.S. called this raid a failure, but you could never convince the POWs of that. For you see, it turned out to be the greatest unifying factor that ever happened to the prisoners in North Vietnam.

The raid caused a knee-jerk reaction by the Communists, and within two days they moved almost all of the POWs (about 530 at that time) into downtown Hanoi, to an old French prison we called the Hanoi Hilton. Most of us had spent time in the Hilton in the early years, but then we were either in solitary confinement or in rooms of four or less people.

To really appreciate the impact of what the Son Tay raid did for us, you have to remember that in those early years of our POW experience the camps were always maximum-security environments. Communications with other rooms were strictly prohibited by the camp rules and enforced by armed guards in the hallway. If you were caught communicating, the consequences were usually severe.

Establishing and maintaining communications was a constant struggle between our captors and us. They tried to prevent it, but we were just as determined to succeed. We would take almost any risk in order to establish and maintain contact with other POWs.

Intuitively, we knew that communications were essential for

effective resistance. Perhaps just as important, they provided a pipeline of encouragement and a sense of unity. In those early years of captivity, our communications were limited and simple, but they were the veins and arteries that kept us going and pumped life into our efforts to survive and return with honor.

As a result of the Son Tay raid, we were all together in one camp and, for the first time, in rooms of forty to sixty guys. What an experience that was! It was more exciting than any Christmas one could imagine. There were a few old friends we had known before but mostly people known only by name on a long list of those we had memorized.

We had no books and very little outside information for several years, so each person was like a special gift. We talked, and talked, and talked. But as the newness wore off, our senior ranking officer (SRO) realized that a plan was needed to organize our communications and our resistance efforts. Equally important, he realized we needed a way to make productive use of the long hours of the day.

The challenge was how to maintain harmony and unity among fifty-two aggressive, independent, hardheaded, and egotistical pilots and crew members. In our new home, we were cooped up in a room that was about thirty-five feet by sixty feet, or about 2,100 square feet—the size of a typical middle-class house. To have harmony with this group would be a challenge under any circumstance, but under the stress of life in a POW camp it would require teamwork like none I had ever seen before.

Teamwork was not a new thing for me. As an athlete at a very small high school, I lettered in four sports, so I had spent a lot of time on teams. As the quarterback on the football team, I had learned to appreciate the results that could come when eleven people simultaneously execute their unique assignments on the snap count. Yet, I had never been on a team that would be as critical to my life as the one I shared with fifty-two men in Room 4 of Camp Unity of the Hanoi Hilton.

We were blessed that our ranking officer was a visionary who understood how to organize teams and use the talents of the people around him. Under his leadership, we developed a team that was so effective that the next two years in that room were a time of encouragement, learning, and growth for us all.

Talents and teams in the workplace

If teamwork can bring that kind of experience to a roomful of POWs in a communist prison camp, then just think what it could do for those who want to work together in an office, on an assembly line, or even in a family.

As you can imagine, being locked in the room with someone on a twenty-four-hour, seven-day basis for more than five years gave me a whole new perspective on understanding and working with others. We had no choice but to trust and respect each other and to be a team that was totally aligned toward the same goals. In those dirty and dark cells, teamwork was the key to survival. Many of the insights that helped us survive relate directly to the issues of talents and teams in the workplace, and I'll share as we go along.

Companies large and small are also in a fight for survival. The pace of business in the information age of the twenty-first century demands that every organization develop new and better ways to improve the way they lead and manage their people resources. Teamwork is more critical than ever as a means to faster decision cycles, faster execution, better customer service, and flatter organizations. The experts say it will be talents and teams that ensure economic viability in the increasingly competitive world economy.

In our company, RightPath Resources, we provide consulting and training in the area of human capital management to companies from the biggest (Fortune 100) down to small family businesses. From this vantage point, we see the struggle that is taking place as leaders and employees at every level try to deploy teams and improve the process of hiring, developing, and retaining talented people. Our role and passion is to provide solutions that bring alignment and maximum performance for the greatest benefit to all parties.

The goal of this book is to share with you my experience, our research, and the foundational truths that can change the way people are employed and managed in corporate America. So, let me ask you the following questions.

- Is it your goal to maximize your talents and improve your relationships?
- Are you interested in becoming a better leader?
- Would you like to gain new insights on how to unleash the talents of people and align them toward a common goal?
- Are you committed to building high performance teams?

If you have answered yes to these questions, you and I have a great *alignment* of purpose, and this book is written for you.

The coach's overview

There are many ways to present a book such as this, and while accumulating materials over the past five years I've considered many of them. Since the focus is heavily on teams and you (the reader) and I have similar goals, why not approach this from a team perspective? If you will allow me to be your coach, I'll share with you many of the insights that we use in coaching senior executives, first-line supervisors, team leaders, and team members.

If you are the kind of person I think you are, then you probably have two questions right up front. Where are we going? How are we going to get there? You want the big picture, so here is a snapshot. This book is broken into five sections that follow the same general logic we use in consulting and training.

S E C T I O N 1

Section 1 introduces *talents*, explains why they are so important, and considers why it is so difficult for us to be objective about ourselves and about others. This material provides the foundation for understanding individual differences. We will take a soft subject and deal with it in a very technical and business-oriented way.

SECTION 2

Section 2 unveils *specific talents* (strengths) and struggles and gives examples of each. You'll see how strengths and struggles are typically two sides of the same coin. This is the longest section because it's the foundation for understanding human behavior, and there is a lot to cover. The good news is that much of it is about you (and people like you). There is also information to help you understand all those people who are different from you among your teammates, friends, and family. By the way, I recommend that you take the free online profile before you read this section. See the instructions in Appendix H.

SECTION 3

Section 3 looks at *teamwork and team issues*. We'll examine the power of individual differences for both unity and diversity in team building. Also, we'll use individual differences to analyze teams and actually diagnose problems and provide solutions. By applying the knowledge you gained in Section 1, you'll never look at teams the same again.

SECTION 4

Section 4 is about *leadership*. There have been many great books on this subject, but this one is going to take a different approach than most. I'll be your coach, and we'll deal directly with the key issues of leadership in corporate America today. You don't want to miss this one, because it's fresh from the experience of working with more than ten executive leadership teams while writing these chapters.

SECTION 5

Section 5 takes us into *personal growth and development*. Knowing you don't just want to learn good information and then toss it in the bottom drawer, there has to be application. Your contribution to better teamwork and leadership can come only through personal growth. We'll deal with the barriers you will want to overcome to be the top performer you want to be.

Now that you know where we are headed, I hope you are excited about the journey. But if you are like most of us, you're operating at warp-8 speed and don't have time to sit down and read for long sessions. With that in mind, we have tried to package the chapters so you can eat this elephant one bite at a time. Even when the chapters need to be a little long, they are perforated like a graham cracker so you can break off just what you can digest at the moment.

Additionally, at the end of each chapter there is a *Coach's Clipboard* to help you reflect on the material and make it more personal. The whole idea of the Coach's Clipboard is that you use it to coach yourself to a higher level of performance and, along the way, be able to coach others as well. Finally, you'll find extensive support material in the Appendices.

Today everyone wants to impact the bottom line, and I suspect that you're no different. This information can have a significant impact in many areas of your life. When it does, there will be an upswing not only for profits but also for you personally and for all the players and coaches on your teams.

INDIVIDUAL DIFFERENCES:
Understanding How to Understand Self and Others

After twenty-five years as an Air Force officer/pilot/leader and as an educator, I retired and lit the afterburners in a new direction. This new focus has been in the area of human capital management, with an emphasis on the areas of career guidance, hiring, team building, and leadership development. The major emphasis of this business has been on identifying and understanding individual differences—how each person is wired. You may be thinking that sounds a little touchy-feely for a crusty "young" colonel but, believe me, it's scientifically based and has powerful applications.

Are you involved in leadership? (We all are in some way.) What about hiring, redeploying, or training? Do you coach, teach, manage, or work with a team in any way? Are you married? Have children? Then you can understand the challenges of working with people.

If you could have one tool that would make a substantial difference in every area of your life, a good understanding of individual differences would be that tool. This knowledge can facilitate change and get results. It can revolutionize your hiring, development, and retention, and it can turn a failing marriage into a successful partnership. It can give you insights into your children's behavior. Trust me. If you will soak up this material, it will powerfully affect your life and everyone around you.

So you'll know where we're going, here's an outline of Section 1.

Chapter 1. Talents: *A Treasure Worth Finding*
Chapter 2. Struggles: *The Dark Side of Talents*
Chapter 3. Objectivity: *Seeing Reality*
Chapter 4. Measuring Talents: *Understanding Assessments*

❖

TALENTS:
A Treasure Worth Finding

Talents and teams—lessons learned in the Hanoi Hilton

I am an observer of people—one who is almost driven to try to understand how individuals are different, why they behave the way they do, and what makes them tick. Typically, passions like this also come with a related talent and, as you might suspect, mine is assessing/reading (understanding) people. Looking back, I can see that this gift was always present, but it didn't get much development or attention until after the Son Tay raid when I was moved in with fifty-two other men.

As the youngest POW in Room 3 of the Hanoi Hilton[1] I watched, listened, and learned in a unique and challenging environment. Just imagine this group of highly competitive, achievement-oriented, opinionated aviators being locked up together twenty-four hours a day for years at a time. Thanks to great leadership, superb training, military discipline, and strong character, we were able to stay united as a team and resist our captors. But the thing that helped pass the time and made it bearable was the incredible array of talents in the group.

You would think that the screening and training programs

of our common profession would have pushed us out like peas from a pod. It's true that our values were similar in areas like commitment, sense of responsibility, attitude toward military service, and our passion for aviation. But who would have imagined that in this group we would see so many different interests and talents emerge?

In this group there were musicians, architects, linguists, craftsmen, educators, literary experts, poets, historians, politicians, farmers, aeronautical engineers, college wrestlers, gymnasts, a meteorologist, a lawyer, a jockey, an actor, a world-class skeet-and-trap shooter, electronics wizards, a rodeo bull rider, and a masters-level bridge player. In addition, there were experts in almost every special-interest category imaginable: travel, wines, cars, auto racing, rifles, pistols, physical fitness, movies, religion, and others.

Almost all the guys were college graduates, so there was no shortage of intellect. There was one fellow from Stanford, one from MIT, and a number from West Point, the Naval Academy, and the Air Force Academy. This strong educational background came in handy, because in this controlled and austere prison environment about the only area open for achievement and development was our minds.

At the direction of our senior ranking officer, we organized classes and activity groups to get people involved in some area of self-improvement. We memorized poems, attended classes, and had a first-rate choir; and one fellow even organized a Toastmasters Club. By the way, there were no books and no "legal" pencil and paper. If you wanted training aids, you had to be creative, and it helped to be stealthy when you were outside near the guard shack.

The days grew busy with planned activities. In addition to my duties as a covert communications officer, I took Spanish, German, and intermediate French classes. I spent thirty minutes a day in "language lab" speaking with two other guys, and I taught beginning French. One of the most creative classes I took was differential calculus. We worked problems on the concrete slab floor, using pieces of broken brick for chalk.

Looking back, I learned many lessons in that room, but

there are two that are most relevant to this book. The first is that on any team of people there will be a rich treasure of talents. Second, great leaders are able to draw out individual talents, link them together, and achieve a level of success that far surpasses what the group could do with each person working alone. We were fortunate to have had a leader who knew something about talents and teams. His example made a big difference in Room 3, and I think these lessons will help you, no matter what situation (or "room") you are in today.

Square pegs in square holes—conventional wisdom about talents that isn't conventional

We all know that old saying about putting the square peg in the square hole. But did you know that this is one of the most neglected pieces of wisdom in our culture and, in fact, in every culture around the world? It's unfortunate that the individuals who choose careers and the employers who do the hiring typically ignore the principle that gives the highest likelihood for successful employment.

The responsibility for mismatched talents begins at home. Studies show that the people who have the most influence over career decisions are parents. Yet sadly, the guidance from many parents is not based on sound wisdom but misguided or twisted criteria. Many children are pushed to follow their parents' careers. Others are pressured into fulfilling their parents' unfulfilled dreams. Many parents try to aim their children toward the high-paying and "hot" jobs or careers of the day. Underneath most career problems, we find that wrong thinking and a distorted view of success overshadow common sense.

Recently, while teaching a career development course in a large company, I was reminded of the powerful and often negative influence of parents. A young lady on the verge of tears related how her parents only cared about money and constantly criticized her for not entering a higher-paying career field. As a career counselor, I had seen parental pressure as a critical issue that people must deal with in career planning, so I used this opportunity to make a point. I asked the twenty-two participants to raise their hands if their parents still interfered or inappropriately tried to control their career choices. Twenty out of twenty-two of these *adult professionals* raised their hands. This provided an alarming insight into the continuing problems of career planning (talent management) in our society.

Turning our focus now to twenty-first-century corporations, we see that most are not applying the square peg wisdom to the hiring and teaming process. Many executives and managers still think that a person with a good work ethic or a good education should be able to do any job he or she is assigned. Of course, the person can, but he or she may not do it with a high level of performance, and that makes all the difference in a highly competitive world.

In corporate hiring, we see two obsolete mind-sets that override the talent model. The industrial model treats people like machines: hire them, plug them in, and expect them to operate effectively. The problem is that the individual's shape (square, round, or other) is not taken into account, and talents and passions are wasted. Similarly, the military model says that the trained and motivated person should be able to do anything. Just give the orders and it will happen. Neither of these approaches is able to maximize productivity or job satisfaction. So, whether it's at home or at work, conventional wisdom is not commonly applied to talent management.

Talents point the way to maximum performance.

The wisdom of using individual talents as the key criteria for making career/work choices is not a new idea. Some 2,400 years ago, the famous Greek playwright Aristophanes pointed the way when he said, "Let each man [or woman] exercise the art he knows."[2] In the first century A.D. when writing to the Romans, the apostle Paul took a similar line: *"Since we have gifts that differ according to the grace given to us, let each exercise them accordingly."*[3]

Philosopher/writer Johann Von Goethe put it similarly when he said, "The man who is born with a talent which he is meant to use finds his greatest happiness in using it."

More recently, some unknown sage has offered perhaps the best advice for parents who are guiding their children: "Our job as parents is not to mold them; it's to unfold them. God has already given them their shape."[4]

For those who want solid data that *talents* trump all other criteria, Gallup holds the cards. The Gallup Organization, well known for conducting public opinion polls, is also one of the leading management consulting firms in the world. For more than twenty years, they have collected data on workers, managers, and the workplace by surveying a million people and over 80,000 managers in more than four hundred companies.

Gallup's research conclusions are presented in a landmark book published in 1999 entitled *First Break All the Rules: What the World's Greatest Managers Do Differently*. The authors, Gallup consultants Marcus Buckingham and Curt Coffman, use Gallup's extensive research to document the value of understanding and using talents as the focus for matching people to positions. They conclude that great managers "select for talent . . . not simply experience, intelligence, or determination."[5]

Buckingham and Coffman also point out, "You cannot teach talents. You must select them."[6] A major conclusion from Gallup's research is captured in the authors' definition of talents: "Any recurring *patterns of behavior* that can be productively applied are talents" (emphasis mine).[7] They go on to say, "The key to excellent performance, of course, is finding the match between your talents and your role."[8]

I was thrilled when I first read these few simple lines of obvious truth. Gallup's research, once and for all, validated my own long-held view and the often-ignored conventional wisdom about matching people to jobs. Furthermore, their conclusion that *talents are behaviors* provided solid confirmation from a reputable outside source to the concepts that we felt so passionately about and upon which we had built our company, RightPath.

**Talents are the key to organizational
and personal success.**

Using statistics and numerous illustrations, Buckingham and

Coffman provide compelling data that when people are using their natural talents they are more productive, easier to manage, and experience greater feelings of success. Just as important, the Gallup data shows that profitability increases in organizations in which people's talents are recognized and developed.[9]

The evidence is mounting that the most successful companies are those that value and develop the talents of their people. Southwest Airlines, known for its unorthodox "fun" environment and the only major airline that showed a profit for 2001, has as its number one item in its formula for dealing with employees, "Give people freedom to be themselves."[10] (The implication is that you don't try to remold them.)

In his best-selling book, *Job Shift*, Ken Bridges says, ". . . We are finding that the most successful organizations are made up of people doing what they like to do and believe in doing, rather than of people doing what they are 'supposed to' do."[11]

In a similar vein, Peter Capelli, writing for the *Harvard Business Review*, concluded his article on the challenges of retaining talent with the following words. "One thing is for sure: as the early years of the new century unfold, executives will be challenged to abandon their old ways of thinking and adopt more creative ways of managing, retaining, and, yes, releasing their talent. Those who begin this difficult process now will be one step ahead of the game."[12]

Note that Mr. Capelli did not say remolding talents; instead, he used the word "releasing," which implies that they would be released (sounds similar to unfolded) to find a good match.

A recent McKinsey & Co. study underscored the importance of human treasure when it concluded that "the most important corporate resource over the next twenty years will be talent."[13]

And, Secretary of State General Colin Powell (former Chairman of the Joint Chiefs of Staff) highlighted the importance of talent to organizational success when he said, "Organization doesn't really accomplish anything. Plans don't accomplish anything either. Theories of management don't much matter. Endeavors succeed or fail because of the people involved. Only by attracting the best people will you accomplish great deeds."[14]

Talent mismatches cause problems for everyone.

Now ask yourself if you would be attracted to a work environment where your talents are likely to be mismatched and then remolded or one where they are matched and unleashed. The logic seems basic, doesn't it? But just because conventional wisdom seems so obvious does not mean that it's always easy to follow. I know from personal experience.

Throughout my military career, I was fortunate to lead some of the most talented people in our society, and they were pre-eminently responsible for my success. During my tenure as a commander of one of the Air Force's elite flying units, our pilots were hand selected for their outstanding record. Additionally, each had a minimum of 1,000 hours of instructor time in the T-38 supersonic jet aircraft we flew. They were superb as flight instructors, but for another project I made the mistake of thinking that they all could do everything well.

One year, for the annual charity drive (the military version of the United Way Campaign), I picked an officer who was a top pilot and a fine fellow, but he was not a promoter. As the campaign launched, our pledges came in quickly, but the amounts were well below our goals and achievements of previous years.

Each week, at the stand-up briefing, I slumped in my chair as the wing commander reviewed everyone's status; we were below rock bottom. With the pledges in, there was not a good way to go back and redo the process, so we just bit the bullet and tried to move on and repolish our reputation with other successes. I take full responsibility for that painful failure. However, it taught me an important lesson about the relationship of talents and success. From then on, I made sure that the talents of the person matched the requirements of the assignment.

I'd like to take the previous example and apply an analogy training to illustrate how you can practically apply the conventional wisdom of talents. If I were to rate the captain on his natural talents as an instructor pilot, I would give him a 6 on a scale of 1 to 10. With all of his training and experience, he performed at a level of 9—one of our best.

But, in looking back at his nature (which I should have

thought about), his talent for promoting and generating enthusiasm for the charity project would be about a 2 on that
scale. Even if we had provided extensive training (which we did
not) and he had improved the same three units that he did in
his flight training, he would still have been only a 5 on our
10-point scale. Average performance in some areas is normal,
but when it's a key responsibility it's not sufficient to keep the
team competitive.

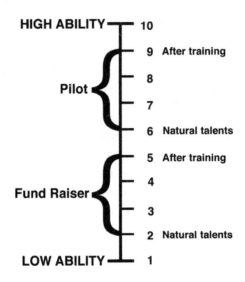

The problem with any talent mismatch results from the
corollary to conventional wisdom. When we match people to
jobs in which their primary work does not exploit their natural talents, we condemn them to a future somewhere between
failure and mediocrity (1 to 6 on our 10-point scale). When this
happens, we set up a lose-lose situation in which the individuals and the organizations suffer.

The principle we want to remember is that by matching
the individual talents to the tasks everyone benefits. For the
campaign the following year, I picked the right talent (about a
natural 7 as a promoter), and our unit quickly exceeded its
goals. That time, everyone came out winners.

Another way to illustrate the value of matching talents to
tasks is to think of swimming upstream and downstream. When

people are using their talents, it's like swimming downstream. Going with the current (your natural bent) is efficient and fun. After a long day of work you may be tired, but you feel good because you've been going with the flow and you've traveled quite a distance. You know you've been highly productive; and, just as important, those who are watching are cheering your progress.

On the other hand, when people are mismatched, it's as if they are swimming upstream. Can they do it? Of course they can, but it requires much more energy, is stressful and exhausting, and the progress is slow. And when the sun rises the next day, there is little excitement about getting back in the water.

Regardless of whether we use Gallup's research or simple illustrations with square and round pegs, scales of 1 to 10, or river swimming, the message is the same. People generally achieve their highest productivity and work satisfaction when they identify and use their unique talents. Author Pearl Buck put it this way: "The secret of joy in work is contained in one word—excellence. To know how to do something well is to enjoy it."

Yes, joy, satisfaction, and excellence at work are the natural outcomes when you lead (unfold and release) talents—yours and others.

Talents indicate a spiritual connection.

If, as Gallup concludes, our talents are primarily natural, then they are given to us at birth. This seems to indicate, at least for those of us who have a spiritual outlook, that talents are divine gifts that provide insights into both calling and career direction. And with the gifts come special responsibilities for developing and managing them for a God-ordained purpose.

In addressing this, the apologist and philosopher Os Guinness points out the danger of ignoring the call of our talents: "Crises created by a contradiction between successful careers and satisfying work are even more fateful. For when we set out in youth and choose careers for external reasons—such as the lure of the salary, the prestige of position, or the pressure from parents and peers—we are setting ourselves up for frustration later in life if the work does not equally suit us for internal reasons, namely our giftedness and calling. 'Success' may then flatter us on the outside as 'significance' eludes us from the inside."[15]

Reflecting on my days as a career counselor, I could fill this book with stories of individuals who chose to follow a path other than the one dictated by their talents. These are painful stories of men and women who chased after someone else's dream, who lived the lives their parents wanted, or who sought only the pot of gold at the end of the rainbow. (See the poem "RightPath" by Sue Clark in Appendix A.)

Equally, I could write about the stories of fulfillment for those who followed their talents and passions, which are almost always connected. Those who desire success and significance will do well to discover their own life path through the calling of their talents. Likewise, great leaders are able to identify talents and help individuals unfold and unleash them for everyone's good.

Coach's Clipboard

Key Point: The key to most of your talents is in your natural behaviors—your natural bent.

Action Items
1. Are you applying or denying the conventional wisdom of matching talents to tasks? For yourself? With others?

2. What talents are you ignoring that need to be unfolded and released?

3. Whose talents do you need to encourage and help release today?

1. In the early years (1965–1970), men were kept in solitary confinement or small groups of two to six people. After the Son Tay raid in 1970, the North Vietnamese moved us back into the Hoa Loa complex (Hanoi Hilton). This time we were in a section that had formerly housed Vietnamese prisoners. We called this compound Camp Unity, because most POWs were together for the first time.

2. Aristophanes 450–385 B.C.

3. Romans 12:6, NASB.

4. Unknown source.

5. Marcus Buckingham and Curt Coffman, *First, Break All the Rules: What the World's Greatest Leaders Do Different* (NY: Simon & Schuster, 1999), 67.

6. Ibid., 88.

7. Ibid., 71.

8. Ibid., 71.

9. Ibid., 37.

10. As quoted in *National Religious Broadcasters* magazine, "The People Department," May 1998.

11. William Bridges, *Job Shift, How to Prosper in a Workplace Without Jobs* (Boston: Addison-Wesley, 1995).

12. Peter Capelli, "A Market-Driven Approach to Retaining Talent," *Harvard Business Review* (January–February 2000).

13. McKinsey & Co. Study presented by Delloite and Touche Partner at SHRM Conference Keynote, October 1999.

14. General Colin Powell, *18 Lessons on Leadership* (tentative title), "Lesson 8"

15. Os Guinness, *The Call* (Nashville: Word, 1998), 150,151.

C H A P T E R	2

❖

STRUGGLES:
The Dark Side of Talents

You already know that the strengths from our talents are the keys to success at work. Now, we'll examine the concept of struggles and see how they affect work and relationships. As you'll see here and in the chapters ahead, struggles are typically tied to strengths. The better you understand this connection, the more objective you'll be about your own struggles and the better you'll be able to understand yourself and others.

Talents—a two-sided coin

As a rule, the key to success at work is to have maximum involvement of our talents and minimum exposure in areas in which we are not as talented. Strengths represent a person's best talents, and they are usually the ones we feel compelled to use. When we use them, it feels natural, it feels right, and we know that we are going with the flow.

However, there is another side to this talent coin that you may not have dealt with. It's natural to think of talents as being strengths, but we find that for every strength there is usually a corresponding struggle. For discussion, let's take the example of someone with a talent to work accurately with details for extended periods. This talent might be essential for someone who is a diamond cutter, an editor, a design engineer, or an accountant.

We know that this talent for accuracy and detail also encompasses certain strengths, such as those listed below, but look at the struggles that usually go with these traits. Note that I said "struggles." They may or may not be weaknesses.

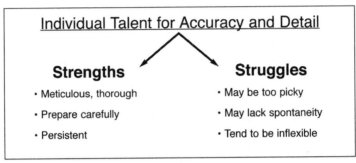

Individual Talent for Accuracy and Detail

Strengths	Struggles
• Meticulous, thorough	• May be too picky
• Prepare carefully	• May lack spontaneity
• Persistent	• Tend to be inflexible

© 2002 RightPath Resources, Inc.
All rights reserved. Used with permission.

If you read objective reports about high-profile leaders, you'll see that they all had struggles that went with their talents. For example, one of Winston Churchill's biographies had the following to say about his strengths and struggles when he took over as First Lord of the Admiralty.

"Churchill rose to this challenge with incomparable vigor and self-confidence. These characteristics were precisely the ones to which he owed both his failures and his successes as First Lord. For as Admiral Bacon said, Churchill's vices were simply his virtues in exaggerated form. Dash became rashness. Assurance became cocksureness. Churchill's overflowing energy was difficult to harness. His overwhelming faith in himself closed his mind to the opinions of others."[1]

(Note: Because Churchill was an amazing historical character and also a good example to study for insights into the strengths and struggles of leaders, I will refer to Churchill several times. Churchill was a great writer; however, for an objective perspective on his personality, be sure to read someone other than Churchill.)

You can see that struggles are usually a natural by-product of strengths, so they function as two sides of the same coin. Understanding this link enables us to see talents more objectively and more predictably. This knowledge has huge implications for talent management and team relationships, because it allows us to have realistic and balanced expectations about human behavior.

Understanding struggles at work

A key finding of the Gallup research referenced earlier is that great managers focus on an individual's strengths and ignore the accompanying struggles as much as possible. That seems to go against much of the effort in corporate America to improve weaknesses. This emphasis on strengths recognizes how difficult it is to change the behaviors that accompany our talents. Great managers realize that changing human behavior is like diverting the course of a deep river—difficult and very costly—so, for work assignments, they capitalize on talents and go with the flow.

Overcoming struggles that result from non-talents

When we talk about struggles, we think first of areas of non-talents. They don't have to be weaknesses, but developing them is not easy and they are never going to be our strong points.

Reflecting on the previous example (the talent for being accurate and detailed), it is possible for this person to become less picky, more spontaneous, and more flexible. However, it will be a difficult assignment, and certainly you would not want to put that person in a job in which his or her success depended primarily on *overcoming* those struggles.

We use the word "overcome" in relation to struggles because it fits so well. In fact, on several occasions, people have actually used the word *overcome* to describe the process it took for them to achieve those behaviors. Three individuals from different locations, who held doctorate degrees, challenged our profile reports in the same area. They said that they should have scored in the Methodical/Structured range, rather than the Spontaneous/Unstructured range. As we discussed it with them, they all said words to the effect: "I have struggled with being disorganized, not detailed, and too spontaneous, but I 'overcame' those problems."

What they were saying is that their drive to achieve their doctorate degree was so strong that they did what was needed to reach their goals. We asked them if they were still "overcoming" in these areas and they replied that they were, to which I said, "Now, you have validated that you are spontaneous, because your basic nature goes with the characteristics of that trait, and you have to struggle to be methodical and organized."

The first time this happened, I had the feeling that the word "overcome" was significant. The second time was an "aha!" experience, because I knew this person had helped me see clearly the difference between a strength and a struggle. If being methodical had been her real talent, she would not have had to "overcome" her spontaneous traits in order to achieve her goals.

Struggles from strengths overdone

During one of our corporate team session my business partner, Jerry Mabe, had an insight that further enlightened our understanding of struggles. He pointed out that there are really two kinds of struggles, and they both cause blindness. We can be blinded by darkness: the non-talent struggles like those described above. We can also be blinded by brightness: the overuse or overextension of our strengths. A cursory review of history indicates that many famous leaders have fallen, not because of their non-talent struggles but because of the misuse of their strengths. Because our strengths are responsible for so many of our successes, it's easy to over-rely on them to our detriment.

Most of us have experienced this "blindness of excess" from a confident, quick-minded, decisive person who has been "right" so often that he or she quit listening to anyone else's ideas. Or maybe you know a kind, supportive, helpful, soul who helps everyone and can't say no to anyone, until one day he or she physically and emotionally wears out. We are all susceptible, because the consequences from overdoing our strengths can be like the frog-in-the-kettle story.

The heat increases just a little at a time and the frog is boiled before it realizes it.

Once, during a session with a group of senior managers, I was explaining that most people identify with their strengths but sometimes push back on their struggles. This led to one of the saddest and funniest (sounds like a paradox) remarks I had ever heard about struggles. A middle-aged man at the end of the table looked over his glasses and remarked, "I know where you got this list of struggles in my report. You called my first wife. I heard about these every week for years."

Understanding struggles as the key to relationship

In the same way that an understanding of talents (strengths) can point the way to better success at work, an understanding of struggles—ours and others—can guide us to better relationships. Here's a common example to illustrate the point. Consider two very different people that we run into on almost every team: Tom and Betty.

Tom is a highly engaging extrovert who enjoys having fun so much that at times he's the office "entertainer." Also, he tends to talk too much, gets overly optimistic, often doesn't finish what he starts, and thrives on being the center of attention. He is, however, a good match for his work and very productive.

Tom's struggles irritate the reserved Betty, because when he's around it's difficult for her to get any work done. His struggles can exasperate her, and she doesn't see how they link to his talents.

Of course, Betty also turns off the engaging Tom at times. She can be cold and distant, and when she does speak up her words can be curt or negative. Her approach comes across as secretive and even quietly self-righteous. She never shares much about her life and really seems not to trust anyone. She also is a good match for her work and is a top performer.

You can see that these two are like night and day—oil and water—and they definitely don't seem to go together. The irony is that they desperately need each other and can make a great team if each can do two things. First, each must learn to accept the other person "as is." Second, they must adapt in order to align some of their own behaviors to work better with each other. As you might suspect, aligning our behaviors with others can be a very challenging undertaking, so we'll go into more detail in later chapters.

Remember that strengths are the focus for succeeding at work, and struggles are the focus for improving relationships. Anticipating and understanding struggles is key to leadership, teamwork, and all relationships, because struggles are the main source of problems.

Coach's Clipboard

Key Point: Expect a struggle for every strength. Remember that it's the struggles that stress relationships.

Action Items
1. What areas have been a struggle for you in performing your work? How do they relate to your non-talents?
2. What struggles do you have that irritate others and undermine your relationships?
3. How can you align your behaviors to work better with others?

---

1. Piers Brendon, *Winston Churchill: A Biography,* (NY: Harper & Row), 62–63.

CHAPTER 3

OBJECTIVITY:
Seeing Reality

If you are going to be an effective manager of talents—yours and others—objectivity will be vital to your success. Objectivity begins with you because, until you have an accurate view of yourself, there's little hope that you will see others clearly. The difficulty of seeing ourselves as we really are inspired Scottish poet Robert Burn's memorable line: "O' wad some power the giftie gie us, To see oursel's as ithers see us!"[1]

Objectivity is also essential to your ability to process decision-making information accurately. Furthermore, few things can undermine a leader's effectiveness quicker than a lack of objectivity. Without it we are likely to find ourselves on the slippery slope of credibility—that insidious place where words say the "right" thing but our decisions and actions shout something different.

Objective: Of course we are. NOT!

It's time for a gut-check on your toughness. If you are like many of the leaders I meet in the corporate setting, you're not too keen on the touchy-feely approach. So let's assume that you see yourself as being logical, objective, and maybe even tough minded.

You like dealing with reality. You want the truth no matter how challenging it is. You like to lay things on the table and let the chips fall where they may—none of that rose-colored-glasses treatment. You want bottom-line management information so you can make accurate decisions and get good results.

With that in mind, I know you would want me to tell it to you straight. The truth (bad news) is that you are not totally objective, and it's causing more problems than you realize. The good news is that you're not alone. We all have this problem. Stay with me and let's examine the *objective* logic behind those statements.

Granted, we may be as objective in our approach as we can be, but we are limited, especially when it comes to self! The problem is that our brains (our logic processing units) rarely receive completely accurate data to use in developing opinions and decisions. We process our perspective through the *filters* of our experiences—both good and bad. In addition, we view events, situations, and people through a *lens* that is somewhat out of focus.

Filters from the past limit objectiveness.

Our experiences often serve as filters that remove part of the reality (truth) from the data we are processing. The result is that we don't objectively experience people and situations, and this usually leads to mistaken judgments and bad decisions.

Recently, I met a person whom I disliked, initially, but after getting to know him better we became friends. The initial turnoff was because my filters were picking up on some of his characteristics that related to a bad experience I'd had with someone else.

These filters of past experiences can affect our mind-set in very powerful and illogical ways. A good example is the filter of many senior citizens who lived through the 1930s and still hold on to their Depression-era mentality.

An elderly couple next door still saves string and keeps stacks of empty coffee cans and Cool Whip containers in the basement—just in case they might need them. Another senior citizen who gets three retirement checks still conserves his money by recycling dental floss. In my mom's case, the shortage of food during the Depression years was her filter. Although during her last few years there was just her and her caregiver, and she no longer had a vegetable garden, she refused to let us disconnect her *two* freezers that added to her power bills each month.

Some of the most prominent filters in business today relate to gender, race, and generational differences. Some people who grew up in the 50s may have strong filters that cause bias toward women leaders and "generation X" geeks.

Some whites view blacks through filters of stereotypes and lifelong racial prejudices. Some blacks operate with a victim-mentality filter and see every missed promotion as being racially motivated. And although we all know these statements are true, they may offend some readers because of filters that prevent objectivity on these sensitive subjects.

Our self-view distorts the lens through which we view others.

Just as the eye uses a lens to collect and format images on the optic nerve, the mind seems to have its own lens. And, just as a distorted lens in the eye causes vision problems, our ego distorts the way we perceive others and ourselves.

This distortion usually comes from one of two twists. We tend either to be generous to ourselves and critical of others or critical of ourselves and generous to others. The following schematic can serve as a frame of reference to examine both of these distorted perceptions (Person A and Person B), as well as reality (Person C).

OBJECTIVITY

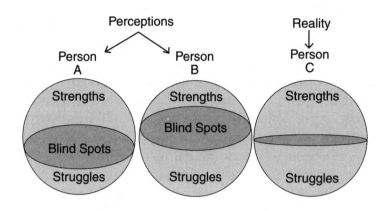

© 2002 RightPath Resources, Inc.
All rights reserved. Used with permission.

Person A: Generous to self and critical of others

It is likely a basic instinct of the ego that causes most of us to be overly generous in our self-evaluations, as in *Person A* above. Marriage counselor, conference speaker, and author of more than fifteen books on relationships, Dr. Gary Chapman provides insights on this phenomenon.

He says that at the first marriage counseling appointment he usually separates the couple and has each list the problems with his or her mate. Typically, they have no problems coming up with a long list of areas that need improvement. Sometimes one person will fill a page and ask for another one to continue the list.

Next, he asks them to write a list of their own short-comings. Guess what? This list is usually much shorter than the first, and some people even turn in a blank page.[2]

For most of us, it's natural to see ourselves as generally having it together (being right). This mind-set also makes it quite natural for us to see those who are different as being wrong. We also tend to focus on their struggles and ignore or discount their strengths. There seems to be a principle operating that if you overestimate yourself you likely will underestimate others, especially if they have different talents.

Person B: Tough on self and generous to others

There is another smaller group of people who relate to *Person B*. They hold themselves to an impossible standard of perfection and give others the benefit of the doubt. This burden can severely limit a person's freedom to be all he or she can be. A nagging self-critical perspective can prevent a person from stepping out into new areas, even with reasonable risks. It also can make it difficult to relate to others because of fear that one might be seen as incompetent. The principle here is that if you underestimate yourself you probably are overestimating others. Like those in Situation A, this individual needs to somehow clear the lens and get a more objective view.

Person C, Reality: We all have strengths, struggles, and some blind spots

Person C represents the outlook that we need in order to see situations and others from an accurate and balanced perspective. This approach recognizes that none of us have it all together and that we all have some great strengths and some serious struggles. With this outlook, we are better able to see some of our own issues and realize that there are some blind spots that need a good dose of sunlight before awareness and growth can take place.

Likewise, when we go into relationships knowing that others don't have it all together, we can anticipate their struggles. With this outlook, we are better prepared to encourage their unique talents and not be so disappointed when their shortcomings emerge.

Blind spots are a major problem for all of us. One of the most difficult and challenging responsibilities we encounter is helping people see and acknowledge them. This is especially true in corporate coaching. Although leaders may recognize their blind spots, they severely underestimate and discount them. Because people are so blind to some of their struggles, it's natural to deny their existence. Rather than argue with someone, it's better to replay a real-life example and ask that person to analyze the behavior and its consequences.

At a leadership development session a very confident and competent young man posed a personal question during the break: "What does it mean when someone is nice to everyone except you?" Having insights into his behavorial profile, I suspected he might be referring to his wife.

Taking a chance, I responded privately, "It probably means that you are too controlling, and this is your wife's passive-aggressive way of letting you know. What do you think?"

With an expression of shock and pain, he responded, "You know, I think you may be right. I do tend to be controlling, but I hadn't thought of it that way."

A controlling nature is one of the most common and most troubling blind spots among leaders, so much so that we'll discuss it from several perspectives in the course of this book. For now, let me just say that insight into your blind spots will give you a dose of reality and open your eyes to a more objective understanding of yourself and others.

Attributing motives and character problems to others destroys objectivity.

Our lack of objectivity toward self and others goes beyond just what we see and don't see (blind spots). Our distorted lens often puts a negative spin on the behaviors and actions of others. One writer helps us understand it with this simple example. "Have you noticed? Anybody going slower than you is an idiot, and anyone going faster is a maniac."[3]

My friend and fellow coach, Dr. Jim Street, explains this type of negative bias/spin from a psychologist perspective: "There is an old saying that we judge others by their actions and ourselves by our intentions. Social psychologists refer to this as the 'Fundamental Attribution Bias.' What they mean is that we are prone to attribute the questionable behaviors of others to a character flaw or negative personality trait, but we attribute those same behaviors in ourselves to our circumstances. In other words, we do not extend the same benefit of the doubt to others that we extend to ourselves. If I am late, it is because

I had to let the dog out and she wouldn't come in and then the phone rang and it was my old college friend and then the car wouldn't crank and then I got into a traffic jam. But, if *you* are late, it is because you are not dependable."[4]

By reflecting on your own actions and words, you'll probably see that you suffer to some degree from this same lack of objectivity. We seem to wear one set of glasses to view others and another to view ourselves. This biased perspective results in inaccurate management information and causes problems in truly understanding ourselves, which in turn causes problems in relating to others.

A lack of objectivity causes unrealistic expectations.

This inability to see others apart from our own filters and biased lenses sets us up for unrealistic expectations in our relationships. When we expect one response or behavior and get another, it often leads to disappointment, hurt feelings, and even anger.

Unrealistic expectations tend to reduce the room for error (grace) that we give others, thus affecting our ability to provide encouragement, patience, kindness, and forgiveness. Typically, our attitudes and reactions cause a reciprocal response from the other person, and before we know what is happening a conflict is brewing.

Awareness is the way, and courage is the entrance fee to gain an objective viewpoint.

An up-front awareness and recognition of the problem is the best way to prevent the perils associated with our filters and biased lenses. We must be on guard, constantly checking our lens and filters to see what biases or twists is being imparted to incoming information. In an article in the June 2002 issue of *Harvard Business Review* ("A Survival Guide for Leaders"), Ronald A. Heifetz and Marty Linsky emphasize the creative role that doubt plays in objectivity: "The absence of doubt leads you to see only that which confirms your own competence, which will virtually guarantee disastrous missteps."

By anticipating that it is going to happen, at least we know to be on the lookout. And if we are questioning ourselves, then we are being courageous enough to face this fallibility.

The courage to be honest about ourselves requires humility, which raises a question: "Should strong leaders be humble?" The answer is a resounding "Yes!" if they aspire to improve their objectivity and become more effective.

Coach's Clipboard

Key Point: No one is totally objective, but objectivity is essential to managing self and others. We must have the courage to honestly face reality.

Action Items
1. Identify an experience in your life that is still filtering your perceptions and undermining your objectivity. How can you take a more objective view about that experience?
2. Are you more like Person A or Person B described earlier?
3. What can you do to see yourself and others more objectively?

---

1. Robert Burns, Ode "To a Louse, on Seeing One on a Lady's Bonnet at Church."
2. Gary Chapman, Ph.D., *Communications in Marriage* audiotape series.
3. Attributed to George Carlin.
4. James Street, Ph.D., former professor of psychology, pastor, and executive coach, adapted from *The Fundamental Attribution Bias.*

❖

CHAPTER 4

MEASURING TALENTS:
Understanding Assessments

A quick review

So far, we've talked about how important individual talents (strengths) are for work success. I used the analogy of swimming downstream (good job match) versus swimming upstream (bad match). Dr. Phil McGraw, psychologist, consultant, and author, compares a bad talent match to rolling a boulder uphill and a good match to pushing the boulder from the top of the hill down the other side.[1]

These illustrations give a good picture of why talent management is so important for career planning for both the individual and the employer. Matching talents to tasks not only increases performance and productivity, it also reduces stress, improves health, and increases job satisfaction.

We also have noted that our struggles are typically related to our strengths. They are part of the package but maybe not something you want everyone to see. And we noted that these struggles do emerge as some of the key irritants that undermine our relationships.

Get ready to "lock on!"

Now we are going to explore the technical aspects of measuring talents. The underlying science is important for several reasons, not the least of which is that many people still think of this subject as being "soft." If you are one of those, let me challenge you to hang on. Yes, we are going to talk about human nature but in a very objective (there's that word again) and measurable way.

You will see that a study of talents can be very much like math or science: realistic, statistical, predictable, and (yes) quite objective. It is this scientific approach that makes this information so useful for individuals, teams, and organizations.

I recognize that most people don't have time to explore details anymore, but I want to ask for your indulgence. I'd like for you to lock on long enough for a brief explanation of how we measure talents. *Lock on* is an expression that is used both literally and figuratively in the military. In target acquisition, when you lock on, the system blocks all other targets and outside distractions and completely focuses on the target.

As the building communications officer in one of the POW camps, my job required that I lock on for up to an hour at a time to receive signals (flashing sunlight reflections) coming from a crack in a door more than one hundred yards away. Believe me, it took all the discipline I could muster to stay focused on some of those detailed messages. But if you will lock on for just a few minutes, you'll have the foundation for understanding talents in a new and objective way. And these concepts can make a powerful difference in your life, professionally and personally.

Understanding a talent scale or graph

The array of commonly occurring behavioral talents can be plotted on graphs the same as physical characteristics. To illustrate how graphical information can be helpful, let's take the example of weight and analyze how it might affect a person's career choice.

The graph below represents weight increments on the horizontal axis and numbers of people on the vertical axis. I've also inserted some associated male sports occupations at representative weights typical for the average participant. Let me clarify that this example is for illustration only and is not based on actual data, but you can see that it's close enough to make the point.

If we plotted the actual weights of people, we would see a bell-curve distribution that resembles the spread below. Most weigh between 100 and 320 pounds.

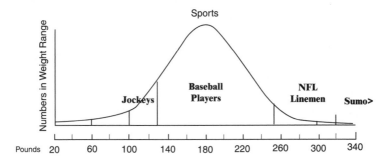

You may recall that the bell curve at one time was used to assign grades on very difficult quizzes on which no one came close to getting all the problems correct. It is actually based on the occurrence of differences in nature. Whether it's weights, heights, shoe sizes, or SAT scores, they all fall out on a frequency distribution with very few at the extremes and an increasing number as you approach the mean (also the midpoint in a standard population) from either direction.

You can see that the weights of baseball players cover a wide range that is more typical of the general population. Size is not such a critical factor in that sport. However, there are important career fields at the extremes of both ends of the spectrum where size is very critical.

Jockeys, who usually weigh less than 120 pounds, fall on the far left of the continuum. The good ones seem to enjoy their work and make a lot of money. On the far right side, we find NFL linemen weighing, on average, about 300 pounds and sumo wrestlers weighing as much as 400 pounds. Now these big folks also enjoy their work and make a lot of money. In sports, size is a kind of talent, and there is a place for those who are light and heavy. So we see that these very different talents are really neither good nor bad, but there is an advantage for certain size talents in certain sports.

I chose size to illustrate the talents from the extremes of the continuum to make it much easier to see that there can be a bad match (or fit) between the person and the job. Assume for a moment that you are a sports recruiter and someone who weighs 300 pounds walks into your office and says, "Where can you use my talents?" Would you consider sending him or her to an interview for a jockey?

Likewise, if a college student who weighs 115 comes in and wants to play in the NFL or be a sumo wrestler, you would try not to laugh but would steer him or her in another direction. These extreme and physically obvious examples illustrate the important principle for hiring and career planning that we discussed in Chapter 1—about matching the person to the work.

Unfortunately, most of our talents are not as obvious as weight; and, you can't necessarily identify them by someone's educational degree, work experience, or interests. What is needed is a way to objectively measure talents and array them on a continuum like the bell curve above. This behavioral information can be used to assist in matching people to positions so they won't try to swim upstream in the key elements of their work. In addition, behavioral insights can be especially helpful for mentoring, coaching, and individual development.

For teamwork situations, this kind of information helps each individual see and appreciate the different talents of others. It also will help leaders and coaches predict and plan for each person's struggles.

In the following chapters, we'll use a behavioral tool that research, development, and experience have shown to be valid and reliable. This tool depicts four factors (eight traits) of behaviors to explain talents (strengths) and the struggles that go with them. Let's take a closer look at the factors that we'll be using.[2]

Introducing the factors and traits

The following are the four factors validated in our personality research. Each is arrayed across a continuum (actually a bell-curve distribution) with Left, Right, and Mid-Range scoring regions. For each factor, the left side and right side of the continuum depict opposite traits.

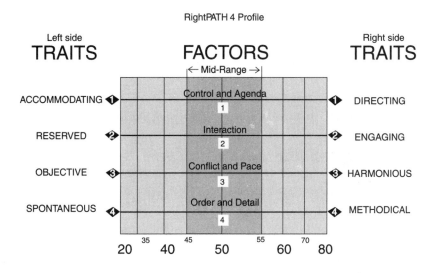

RightPATH 4 Profile

© 2002 RightPath Resources, Inc.
All rights reserved. Used with permission.

Now the good thing about having standardized scores (bell curve) laid out on mathematically defined ranges is that they allow you to see how people are different in a graphic and measurable way. As shown in the following illustration, no matter in which region a person scores on the graph, two-thirds of the world is going to be different. For those who fall clearly on either the right side or the left side, one-third will be somewhat different and one-third will have strengths and struggles that are their mirror opposite.

RightPATH 4 Profile
BEHAVIORAL CONTINUUM

	1/3	1/3	1/3	
1	Accommodating	Mid-Range	Directing	1
2	Reserved	Mid-Range	Engaging	2
3	Objective	Mid-Range	Harmonious	3
4	Spontaneous	Mid-Range	Methodical	4

Mirror Opposites

© 2002 RightPath Resources, Inc.
All rights reserved. Used with permission.

Using the graphic, we can see in factor 4 that highly structured Methodical people will experience one-third of the population as somewhat less structured and one-third as their mirror opposites: very unstructured and spontaneous. These spontaneous opposites with their less focused approach to details, schedules, rules, and procedures can be a source of irritation for those who are highly structured and methodical.

Of course the reverse situation is equally common and usually causes a similar response. The talents of these opposites complement each other and they can make a great team, if they can accept and value the other person's traits equally with their own. (Interestingly, opposites do often attract, so it's very common for Methodical people to marry Spontaneous people.)

Trait intensity shown below is another important characteristic related to this type of graph. Note that as the scores move outward either left or right from the midpoint of the graph the behavioral traits grow stronger. So, someone who is on the Directing side with a score of 60 may be assertive, but the person with a score of 75 may be so assertive that he or she tends to become controlling. Likewise, in the opposite direction, someone with a score of 40 may be compliant and a person with a score of 25 may tend to be passive. Keep in mind that stress usually intensifies the traits, so someone with a score of 60 may look like a 75 when the conditions are right.

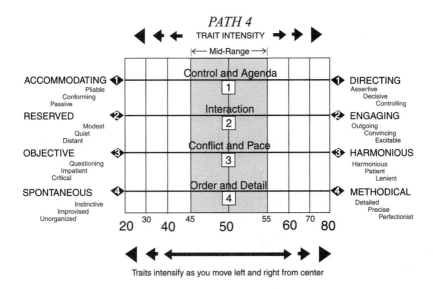

PATH 4

◀◀ ← TRAIT INTENSITY → ▶ ▶

|← Mid-Range →|

ACCOMMODATING ❶ — Control and Agenda [1] — ❶ DIRECTING
Pliable / Conforming / Passive — Assertive / Decisive / Controlling

RESERVED ❷ — Interaction [2] — ❷ ENGAGING
Modest / Quiet / Distant — Outgoing / Convincing / Excitable

OBJECTIVE ❸ — Conflict and Pace [3] — ❸ HARMONIOUS
Questioning / Impatient / Critical — Harmonious / Patient / Lenient

SPONTANEOUS ❹ — Order and Detail [4] — ❹ METHODICAL
Instinctive / Improvised / Unorganized — Detailed / Precise / Perfectionist

20   30   40   45   50   55   60   70   80

◀ ◀ ◀━━━━━━━━━━━▶ ▶ ▶

Traits intensify as you move left and right from center

© 2002 RightPath Resources, Inc.
All rights reserved. Used with permission.

One more point to remember. Every person will have a score or "home base" on each of these four continua. One senior leader called it the "happy place," because it's where one likes to hang out. Also, the score that is farthest right or left from the midpoint of 50 will have the greatest impact on a person's behavior. Thus, on the graph above, the third factor score of 34 will have the most obvious impact on this person's behavior.

Congratulations! You did lock on and now you should have a good grasp of how behavioral talents are measured. More importantly, I hope you understand how the graphs and the three ranges (Left, Right, and Mid-Range) can help us understand individual differences in a meaningful (and very objective) way.

We are about to release the brakes, light the burners, and take off for the fun stuff as we look in depth at these eight traits in the next eight chapters. But, there is one more important area to cover. Before actually flying, pilots have to become familiar with the guidelines in the operating manual. So here is a rundown of the guidelines you'll need to know as you begin to apply this knowledge.

Guidelines for Using Personality Assessments/Profiles

1. **They measure typical behaviors—normal traits.** The factors reveal recurring patterns of behaviors common to normal people and are not designed to diagnose deviant behaviors or mental health problems.

2. **A person's scores tend to remain stable over time.** People are capable of adapting to meet the needs of new situations; however, they typically revert to their natural behaviors (happy place) when the need to adapt goes away. Knowledge, experience, and values can cause people to adapt or moderate from their natural behavior on a more permanent basis.

3. **There are no bad or good scores/profiles.** There can be a bad job match but not a bad or good profile. Every score/point on the continuum represents important talents. All points have strengths and struggles.

4. **They don't identify personal baggage.** No one grew up in a perfect world, and we all have acquired some baggage from painful or disappointing life experiences. Usually when you see someone acting beyond the boundaries of normally accepted behaviors you are seeing their baggage—a reaction to pain from the past.

5. **They should not be used to put people in boxes.** Humans are very complex and multitalented. Additionally, people have an amazing ability to adapt to various situations. Behavioral profiles are guides to understand people's most obvious talents but not to restrict them from opportunities to develop new talents.

6. **Decisions should never be made solely based on profiles.** Behavioral assessments provide powerful insights for working with people and can be very helpful for decision making. On the other hand, they are just one piece of data and should be considered along with other sources of information and experienced-based judgment.

7. **Leadership can come from any profile.** If you study leaders at all levels from president to principal and general to

Girl Scout leader, you will see that there are many ways to lead. It is the knowledge of and comfort with oneself that has a major impact on a person's leadership effectiveness.

You've mastered the nitty-gritty of this tech manual. However, there is one last briefing item before we leave the briefing room for the flight line.

Leaving your biases behind

If you are like most people, you tend to have a bias toward your own behavioral style. For example, if you are easygoing and accommodating, then you probably value those traits more than those of someone who tends to be opinionated and pushy. Likewise, if you are more dominant or assertive, you may tend to value those behaviors and be judgmental of those who are more compliant and passive.

Regardless of your tendency, I'm going to ask you to set aside your biases and judgments to gain a more objective view of yourself and others. It won't be easy, but the rewards are huge. Ideally, you will come to understand those who are different from you and see their traits as being just as valuable as yours are. After all, those who are different are your teammates. Their talents contribute to your work and life success. And more than likely some of those "different people" who can irritate you the most are living under your same roof!

Coach's Clipboard

Key Point: Talents (natural behavior) are measurable, so behavioral profiles can be used to predict strengths and struggles with a high degree of accuracy.

Action Item
Before going forward, review the graphs and make sure you understand the technical details covered in this chapter. This will help you understand the information on the traits in the chapters ahead.

1. Phillip C. McGraw, Ph.D., *Self Matters* (NY: Simon & Schuster, 2001), 32.
2. The RightPath Profiles come from unique instruments. These factors may be similar to those of some other personality assessments, but they are not exactly comparable. For example, the RightPath Spontaneous traits are different from what is meant by spontaneous in the MBTI™ .

❖

INDIVIDUAL DIFFERENCES—
Understanding Self and Others

Before going any further, let's agree to deal with objective truth. If there is any element of wishful thinking or wanna-be mentality hanging around in your cockpit, get rid of it now. Remember, you want objective management information, and it starts with being real about yourself.

If you have not already taken the free online profile that came with this book, I recommend you do so now, before proceeding to Chapter 5. If someone else is using it, the "Home on the Range" block at the beginning of Chapters 5, 7, 9, and 11 will be helpful.

Once you know your traits, you'll be able to gain an objective view of your strengths and struggles. Let me encourage you to appreciate your unique design: value your home base or roosting spot on each Behavioral Continuum. It's absolutely the best spot for you. If you will accept and use your associated talents to the fullest, you will find the greatest joy in life and the most success at work.

Remember the following ideas as you go through these chapters. Your strengths are your best talents for your work. You may need to overcome some of your struggles enough so that you don't get in trouble at your job, but you are never going to remake yourself. Struggles are usually the source of your conflicts with others. By working on yours and accepting or overlooking theirs, you'll improve your relationships.

Chapters 5 to 12 present the personality factors and traits. Chapter 13 discusses how to use this information in career selection and job matching.

Chapter 5: *Directing Traits*   **Chapter 10:** *Objective Traits*
Chapter 6: *Accommodating Traits*   **Chapter 11:** *Methodical Traits*
Chapter 7: *Engaging Traits*   **Chapter 12:** *Spontaneous Traits*
Chapter 8: *Reserved Traits*   **Chapter 13:** *Matching Talents/*
Chapter 9: *Harmonious Traits*   *Traits to Tasks*

For more information on these and other assessments, see the contact information in Appendix G.

CHAPTER 5

DIRECTING TRAITS

FACTOR 1
Control and Agenda
Dominance

Accommodating	Mid-Range	Directing
Compliant		*Dominant*

© 2002 RightPath Resources, Inc.
All rights reserved. Used with permission.

Where's your home on this range?

To make the next two chapters covering this factor more relevant, look at the bullets below and choose the range (Left, Right, or Mid-Range) that you think might fit you best.

Think back over your entire life, consider your natural tendencies, and decide which series of words is most like you. If you are sure that you have natural tendencies to act in both ways, depending on the situation, then place your mark in the Mid-Range.

☐ **ACCOMMODATING**   ☐ **MID-RANGE**   ☐ **DIRECTING**

- Fit in
- Process oriented
- Cooperative
- Cautious/Practical

- Take control
- Results oriented
- Competitive
- Bold/Strategic

The Control Continuum

As you can see, this continuum encompasses two very opposite drives that relate to controlling the agenda and making decisions. Those who fall on the left side (Accommodating/ Compliant)[1] are naturally motivated to fit in with the established agenda and to accommodate others. People who fall on the right (Directing/Dominant) are just the opposite; for them, fitting in is difficult. Their natural drive is to take control of the agenda and direct everything toward achieving *their* own goals.

As with the other personality factors in the following chapters, we'll take an in-depth look at both sides of the continuum, beginning with the Right Side first. Also, keep in mind that we use two similar assessments (RightPath 4 Profile and RightPath 6 Profile). These have different but similar names for the Left-Side and Right-Side traits. I'll footnote these at the beginning of each chapter and then use them somewhat interchangeably in the descriptions. Remember that neither side is good or bad. Both sides have strengths and struggles.

A reminder about the Mid-Range. You will recall from the previous chapter that one-third of the population falls in each range (Left, Right, and Mid-Range) on the personality continuum. Mid-Range indicates a flexibility that allows the individual to operate with either Left-Side or Right-Side traits, depending on the situation. This does not mean that they will be lukewarm in the factor but that they can more easily adapt to exhibit traits from both sides of the continuum. So, if you exhibit strengths and struggles equally from both sides, you probably are somewhere on the Mid-Range of this personality factor.

Right Side—Directing/Dominant

Control and Agenda

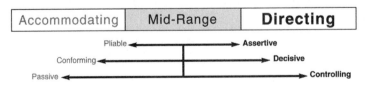

© 2002 RightPath Resources, Inc.
All rights reserved. Used with permission.

As you would expect, Directing personalities naturally are driven to control their environments. They assume authority, and they are comfortable giving direction to others. They especially like to get results—the quicker the better. They are self-assured, often expressing their strongly held opinions in a very direct manner.

Be careful not to automatically assume that they are extroverts. Even though they may be outspoken and have strong verbal skills, they are likely to be as introverted as they are outgoing. As we will see in Chapters 7 and 8, Extroversion/Introversion is a completely separate factor that relates to our interest in and energy for relating to strangers.

The following is an overview of the strengths and struggles associated with the Right-Side, Directing personalities. Note the relationship of the strengths to the typical struggles.

Directing/Dominant Traits

Strengths	Struggles
Results oriented	May lack relationship skills
Assertive, initiating, set agendas	May be controlling and pushy
Decisive	Don't listen, defend ideas
Speak directly, frank	Bluntness can be offensive
Like multiple projects	Overcommit what others can do
Like challenge, competitive	Avoid routine and details
Confident, self-assured	Self-centered and egotistical
Quick minded	Impulsive
Visionary, see big picture	Overextend expertise, resources
Independent	May struggle being just a team member

For a better picture of this trait, consider the following well-known people who exhibit behaviors representative of this group. Examples include media personalities Sam Donaldson; Lucille Ball; Barbra Streisand; Rush Limbaugh; Dr. Robert Schuller; Oprah Winfrey; and her frequent guest psychologist, Dr. Phil McGraw. In the military, of course, we've had generals like George Patton, Douglas MacArthur, and Norman

Schwarzkopf. Directing personalities in government would include Prime Minister Margaret Thatcher and presidents John Adams, Teddy Roosevelt, Harry Truman, and Richard Nixon. There are many prominent ones in sports as well: Joe Namath, Hale Irwin, Arnold Palmer, Michael Jordan, and coaches Mike Ditka and Bobby Bowden.

DIRECTING STRENGTHS

Results oriented. These people want to make something happen and they'd like it done quickly. If they are in charge, they don't hesitate to make decisions and get things moving. They use their strong will and directing nature to push ideas and projects along toward a quick victory. If they are not in charge, and progress is lagging, they will push for a decision and action. If it doesn't happen, they may disengage or just look for another opportunity where they can have more of an impact on getting results.

Confident, bold, adventurous, daring, and in control. Directing personalities are rarely short on confidence. They typically assume that they see the best solution and that they will prevail in any undertaking. Is there an obstacle in their way? Not to worry! They are attracted to challenges like a bear is to honey. If you want to get them engaged, just lay out a problem and say something like, "That's probably too difficult" or "No one has ever done it."

A good example of the Directing mentality comes from the supposedly true story of the lady who ignored the warning and pushed her baby stroller onto the escalator. Her surprised sister-in-law followed her up and cautiously inquired, "Didn't you see that sign that says no strollers on the escalator?"

The Directing personality mother replied, "Yes, but that's just for people who don't know how to take a stroller up an escalator."

I gained another insight into this personality while watching an interview with Steve Fossett, the explorer and Chicago stockbroker. His confidence, courage, and pioneering spirit typify the Directing personality. In 1997, he was on a second attempt to go nonstop around the world in a balloon. As he was about to climb down into the gondola/cockpit for launch, a TV journalist asked him if he was scared or nervous about the undertaking. Fossett replied, "Oh, no, not at all. I'm in complete control."

I about fell out of my chair when he said this, because as a pilot it seemed to me that he had virtually no control over where that balloon was going to go. He was at the mercy of the winds aloft, and as it turned out they took him where he hadn't planned to go. But in Fossett's mind he was in control, because it was his decision, his plan, his balloon, his cockpit, and he believed he could subject all to his control. (In 2002, Fossett was successful, becoming the first to circle the globe nonstop in a balloon.)

As I look back, I can relate to Steve Fossett's outlook. My first career included one of the riskiest jobs in the world, yet I felt very much in control as long as my hand was on or very close to the "control" stick. As a matter of fact, the day my aircraft was shot out from under me I still felt in control as I steered my parachute, made my landing, and called for my wingman to strafe two hundred yards north to cover my escape to a nearby river.

But within a minute, I was surrounded, captured, and stripped to my undershorts. There, standing in a rice paddy, half naked, and surrounded by people who would like to chop off my head, I suddenly realized that I didn't have much control over anything. Furthermore, for the next five years, about all I had control over was my mind and my will.

Jerry Mabe, my business partner and president of Right-Path, points out that highly directing people do not see themselves as being out of control until they experience a *total* loss of control. Until then, they typically see themselves as either in control or soon to be back in control.

Fast paced, multitasked, visionary, with strong opinions. Their minds work quickly, so they prefer a fast pace, and they need multiple projects to keep them engaged. They are focused outward and seem to have an extraordinary strategic or visionary talent: to see over the horizon and plan for the future.

They love to develop or build, and this strategic view allows them to envision what the finished product should look like.

Primarily generalists, they are ready with an opinion on any subject. If you ask a question, you are going to get an answer that they feel strongly about, although they may not have thought about it before. The expression "sometimes wrong but never in doubt" describes this group quite well.

Leadership oriented, power sensitive. Directing personalities have a keen sense of awareness in areas related to leadership, money, and power structures. They naturally feel most secure when they are leading, because they trust themselves and tend to be somewhat distrusting of others. They also know how to use their power to protect their territory. They abhor a power vacuum, and if there is one they will naturally fill it with their own influence.

Secretary of State Al Haig gave a classic example of this trait on the day that President Reagan was shot. Haig, a former White House chief of staff and Army general knew full well that he was not the next in line of succession, but it was perfectly natural for him to step up to the mike and say, "I'm in charge." He sensed that the country, and especially our enemies, needed to know that leaders were in place and that power was not lacking in Washington. Haig wanted everyone to know that everything was under strong control, and at that moment his natural drive to take charge and project power emerged.

Theodore Roosevelt, who saw himself as a twentieth century gladiator, once said, "I did not care a rap for the mere form and show of power. I cared immensely for the use that could be made of the substance . . . While president, I have used every ounce of power there was in the office."[2]

Assertive, competitive, want to be number one. These Directing/Dominant personalities typically have a clear edge in fields in which drive to overcome opposition and difficulty and the ability to handle rejection are key characteristics of success. After profiling hundreds of successful outside salespeople, we found that the common traits are assertiveness, ambition, and a desire to achieve results—all characteristics that correlate highly with this group.

All the traits are competitive in some areas. However, the Directing/Dominant group takes winning seriously in every endeavor. It doesn't matter to them if it's checkers or war. They have but one goal: to defeat all opponents and be number one.

DIRECTING STRUGGLES

Egotistical, self-centered, and insensitive to others. I know that may sting, so let me clarify and say that this is their nature and not their values. They may have overcome this struggle somewhat, but remember that the same ego that powers their significant strengths also feeds their struggles.

In team development sessions, we separate people into groups that share the same traits for the "Awesome Traits Exercise." The assignment is for each group to present their trait as the most awesome for success in their role. This is a powerful experience for everyone, because there is nothing as insightful as experiencing personality differences in the flesh.

Because of their cocky attitudes, the awesomeness of the Directing groups is sometimes overwhelming. In what was couched in humor, one group actually said, "We are the best and most awesome because we are the ones who tell you little people what to do." Almost everyone laughed, but we all knew that this is not far from the way many of them see the world. It's also typical for them to claim strengths of other traits that they really don't have. That's not unexpected, because their strong egos tells them that they are good at everything.

The exercise also requires participants to share some of the common struggles of their group. They typically admit to being self-centered, controlling, impatient, and opinionated. What they don't acknowledge, and probably don't even realize, is that the self-centered person takes from others in order to feed his or her own ego. Like a giant magnet, this person often pulls from others to meet his or her own needs.

Those in this group who have real courage accept that their egos are a serious struggle and work the problem by shifting their focus from themselves to others. They learn to observe the body language of others to see whether their spirits are being lifted (encouraged) or burdened during their interactions. They also enlist confidants who will give them honest feedback on how they are affecting others.

Inability to be wrong—look out for the progression in D Major. One of this group's best talents is an ability to operate decisively and with confidence. They typically build a track record of successes, and these further stroke their egos, which in turn adds to their already high confidence. But no one can be right all the time, and when they are confronted with being out of step they often have great difficulty accepting it.

Perhaps you have heard it said about powerful leaders, "There's a graveyard just outside his (or her) office for those who dared to confront him (or her) with the truth." Of course, if you continually shoot the messenger, pretty soon there will be a stack of dead messengers and no more messages. A good indicator of those with a dysfunctional, dominating personality is that they keep their nonchallenging people and run off those who question their ideas or try to hold them accountable to walk their talk. [3]

Observing this a few years ago, it occurred to me that what I was seeing was a Progression in D Major: a very discordant and dysfunctional characteristic of Dominant people. How far the progression goes depends on the individual's level of dysfunction. You can probably think of employers, famous politicians, high-profile coaches, and even religious leaders who went down this scale. Note the progression below of what happens when they are confronted with an unacceptable reality about themselves.

STEP ONE   **Deny.** *"That's not true." "I wouldn't do that." "It never happened." "They're wrong."*

STEP TWO   **Defend.** *"They just don't understand the situation. Under the circumstances, it was the right thing to do."*

STEP THREE   **Demonize.** *"They are out to get me. They are disloyal, jealous."*

STEP FOUR   **Destroy.** *At this point the evidence of the "unacceptable" reality is so strong the only tactic left is to try to eliminate the messenger.*

After watching many leaders over the last thirty years, I've observed that the outwardly confident but inwardly insecure dominant and controlling person is the most likely one to be caught in this type of extreme denial.

To prevent this progression, the main defense for all personality types is humility and a concern for others. Humility does not imply weakness; rather, it indicates a true confidence and feeling of self-worth that is strong enough to openly admit, "I'm not perfect; I made a mistake" or "I'm wrong and I respect you enough to listen to what you have to say." Or, just as important, "I don't have it figured out and I'm open to your suggestion." Humility can be difficult, but it's incredibly powerful.

Poor listeners. The number one struggle shared by this group is that when it comes to listening they are more awful than awesome. Of course, this revelation is no surprise to everyone else, because they have experienced it many times.

Since Directing personalities have high confidence and often a good success rate to back it up, their instinct is to think they are good at anything and everything they undertake. But when they are honest, they admit listening is a problem. It's not that they don't have good intentions; it's just that there are several overriding issues.

First, listening requires that you yield some degree of control to the other person. You have to give up control of your time, because you don't know where they are going and how long it will take.

In the "Awesome Traits Exercise," one senior leader commented on behalf of her Directing group: "You don't understand how hard it is for us to listen. Our minds just can't slow down enough to stay with you." Another typical response is, "Sometimes I have a hard time hearing what you are saying because my mind has jumped ahead to my response." Or, "If I disagree with you, I'm thinking about how I'm going to convince you that I'm right and you are wrong."

Directing personalities love a significant challenge, and becoming a good listener will challenge every ounce of their being. That's because it will require some degree of mastery over all the other struggles of this trait.

To become a good listener requires having humility and patience, setting aside strongly held opinions, being sensitive to the thoughts and feelings of the other person, and much more. The task is difficult, but the payoff (results) will bring dividends at work and at home that are truly awesome.

Ideal Work Environment. They work best when they can decide, direct, build, develop, create, lead, conceptualize, control, and initiate solutions.

Managing the Directing personality. They don't like to be managed, so give them turf and something to control or they will try to take over yours. Give them challenging goals, adequate resources, and clear boundaries. Then stay out of their way.

Keep in mind that their unique talents can make this group difficult to manage. They aren't afraid to rock the policy boat, kick in the door of the front office, or pick up and leave. Because they tend to be aggressive, it's easy for them to ignore boundaries and walk right onto someone else's turf. If they sense weakness, they'll try to take power—even from their leaders.

A good management practice with Directing individuals is to expect them to overstep their bounds and be watching for it. When it happens, reestablish their boundaries and move quickly to get their attention (and remember that they don't understand subtlety). Be clear and direct and don't overlook the one thing they understand best: power!

Coach's Clipboard

Key Point: Directing/Dominant people should keep in mind that success is a team effort and that it is important to really hear what others have to say.

The coach says, *"Listen up, and give more respect to others' opinions."*

---

1. RightPath 4 Profile™ uses Accommodating–Directing.
   RightPath 6 Profile™ uses Compliant–Dominant.
2. Philip B. Kunhardt Jr. and Peter Kundhardt III, *The American President,* CD 5, Track 3, HarperCollins Publishers, 1999.
3. For more insights into the impact of these leaders on their companies, see *Good to Great,* by James C. Collins (NY: HarperCollins, 2001), Chapters 2 and 3.

CHAPTER 6

ACCOMMODATING TRAITS

FACTOR 1

Control and Agenda

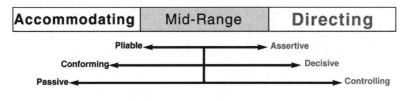

© 2002 RightPath Resources, Inc.
All rights reserved. Used with permission.

Now we move to the other end of the control spectrum and look at those who are much more willing to accommodate someone else's agenda.

As you will see from the strengths and struggles below, the Accommodating[1] traits are nearly opposite from the Right-Side Directing personality group. They are much less concerned about power and who is in control and are more interested in fitting in with and supporting the established agenda. Shown below is a listing of Accommodating strengths and struggles.

Accommodating Traits

Strengths	Struggles
Follow the set agenda	Can be unassertive
Process oriented	May be slow getting results
Good listeners	May delay hard decisions
Cooperative	May agree, then regret or resent it
Modest, share the credit	May lack confidence
Focus on the here and now	May lack strategic vision
Stay on task	May lack initiative
Good team player	May avoid taking charge
Speak tactfully	Often hesitate to speak up
Lead by consensus	May be indecisive

Prominent examples of this group might include TV personality Cokie Roberts; Generals Omar Bradley and Dwight Eisenhower; Presidents Thomas Jefferson, Abraham Lincoln, Gerald Ford, George H.W. Bush (George W's father); and sports baseball manager, Joe Torre.

ACCOMMODATING STRENGTHS

Team players, follow the set agenda. Rather than come out of the gate trying to project power, this group is much more into cooperation and collaboration. They are typically very loyal to their teammates and leaders and enjoy helping them be successful.

Because they are Accommodating, they can accept and operate from an already established agenda without having to put their own unique stamp on it. They are usually much more comfortable at maintaining or operating a program than in developing a new one.

Process oriented, like to focus on the practical, here and now. One of the key strengths of this group is their ability to see practical details that need to be executed. A good way to look at this talent is to compare it with their Right-Side teammates. The results-oriented and visionary Directing person may be touting, "We can double our revenues in three years." The process-oriented Accommodating person typically sees the world very differently and says, "That sounds great, but how are we going to make payroll at the end of this month?" Their realistic and practical insights are critical to success for any team.

Good listeners, nonconfrontational. Their combination of talents makes it natural for this group to be good listeners. Listening was the number-one rated leadership attribute in our poll of over three hundred first-line supervisors and mid-level managers. Accommodating people typically find it easy to apply the wisdom of Saint Francis of Assisi: "Grant that we may not so much seek to be understood as to understand." It has been institutionalized as Stephen Covey's habit number five.

This group generally interacts smoothly with others and prefers to cooperate, rather than cause a confrontation in order to get exactly what they want or to convince others of their opinion. Because they are not so personally (ego) invested in their own ideas, they find it easy to look for win-win alternatives. Their tendency to speak tactfully, using mild tones, can have a calming effect in what otherwise might be a hectic and stressful environment.

Team-oriented leaders. Accommodating personalities exhibit many excellent leadership characteristics. A good sense of humility enables them not to worry about who gets the credit; they just want to see things run smoothly and achieve success.

The value of these traits has been overlooked in many leadership discussions, until the recent appearance of the popular book, *Good to Great: Why Some Companies Make the Leap and Others Don't.*[2] In describing some of the characteristics of what his research team called the "Level 5" leader, author Jim Collins points out, "Those who worked with or wrote about the good to great leaders continually used words like *quiet, humble, modest, reserved, shy, gracious, mild-mannered, self-effacing, understated, did not believe his own clippings,* and so forth."

Remarkably, the leaders in all eleven good-to-great companies showed no interest in self-promotion. (I would hasten to point out that Collins and his team also identified key Directing traits in these "Level 5" leaders, such as "intense professional will," "fierce resolve," "fearless," "fanatically driven, infected with an incurable need to produce sustained results.")[3]

ACCOMMODATING STRUGGLES

May lack confidence, hesitant to speak out. I mentioned the "Awesome Traits Exercise" earlier as a way to see and experience strengths and struggles straight from the different personality traits. As part of the exercise, Accommodating people say that a consistent struggle they have is their "lack of confidence." In looking over the full list of their struggles, one could conclude that this is at the root of most of their issues.

It seems that no matter how prepared, how smart, or how skilled they are it's not unusual for them to second-guess their capability. Hence, they may feel uncomfortable taking risks or pushing their ideas—even when they know they have the right answer to a problem.

As part of our team sessions, we sometimes throw out a simple but tricky math puzzle for the group to solve. The Accommodating are often the first to get the right answer, yet they typically just say it once softly and then sit back. In the meantime, two Directing teammates (both with the wrong answer) may argue for ten minutes, while the Accommodating people just listen. Their soft-spoken nature can also add to the problem because, as we learned earlier, the Directing group tends to be poor listeners.

During the exercise debrief, we point out what happened and then show how it parallels reality on their team. The hesitancy of the Accommodating personalities to fight for their ideas is usually an ongoing issue on teams.

To overcome these struggles, they have to believe in themselves enough to risk speaking up. It will require getting out of their comfort zone, but by choosing their battles carefully they can gain success and further confidence for bigger challenges.

Slow to make decisions, initiate, or take action. Typically, this group is hesitant to step forward with a decision and prefers to get everyone's input first. Leadership by consensus has some good points, but it's not always appropriate and can delay action and preclude timely results. In working with some Accommodating leaders, we've seen them stagnate because of indecisiveness (usually accompanied by too much discussion in too many meetings). When this happens, people start to lose their enthusiasm for their projects/goals.

Overcoming this struggle also requires confidence and risk taking. An experienced mentor or coach who is a little more to the right on this scale—maybe Mid-Range—can provide insights and suggestions on how to handle specific situations. This type of coaching is ideal, because it reduces the "all alone" feeling and provides the Accommodating person an opportunity to gain knowledge, experience, and confidence.

May lack strategic vision. This group is typically so focused on the potholes and curves in the road ahead that they don't think about looking out over the horizon. Even if they did, it's usually not their talent or passion to keep up with all the trends and possibilities that could come together.

Accommodating people can overcome this struggle through several actions. To begin with, they likely need to become more aware of the trends in the current environment. Expanding their information sources and subjects to cover a broader perspective on events in business, technology, politics, medicine, and similar subjects can do this. Beyond that, there are usually plenty of visionaries in most organizations and industries. The challenge will be to pick which strategic horses they want to ride.

Ideal Work Environment. They work best when the goals are clearly defined and there is a consistent work process. They are usually more productive when their tasks focus on maintaining or operating, rather than on initiating or breaking new ground.

Managing the Accommodating personality. Encourage them to express their ideas by asking questions and then listening to their insights. Persist until you convince them that you really do want to know their true opinions. If they are in a leadership role, you can expect that they will be liked but may need your coaching to help them initiate action, take risks, and make some of the tough decisions.

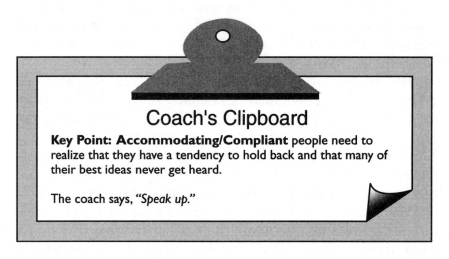

Coach's Clipboard

Key Point: Accommodating/Compliant people need to realize that they have a tendency to hold back and that many of their best ideas never get heard.

The coach says, *"Speak up."*

Left, Right, and Mid-Range—we need them all. From a leadership and management perspective, this first factor dealing with control and assertiveness seems to have a bias toward the right side, where we find the Directing traits. There is no denying that the characteristics that go with the Right Side—decisive, assertive, independent, and visionary—are strong leadership attributes for getting results. However, keep in mind that supervisors and managers identify the key attribute of their greatest leader as "a good listener." This is clearly a left-side behavioral talent.

Our research found an interesting balance between the left and right sides of this factor in terms of leadership attributes. We'll talk more about that later, but for now just realize that traits from both sides are required for success as a leader or follower.

Relationship Keys

Learn to recognize and encourage the unique talents of your opposite-side teammates. Understand their needs and expect their struggles. Let them know how much you value them because of who they are, and don't be offended or take it personally when they act like themselves instead of like you.

Revisiting your home on this range

Recall the information you read in Chapters 5 and 6 and reflect on the block you chose at the beginning of Chapter 5. Then **place a mark** on the continuum below where you most *naturally* fall. (The stronger you feel about your natural behavior, the farther toward the left or right your mark should go.)

FACTOR 1
Control and Agenda

Accommodating	Mid-Range	Directing

© 2002 RightPath Resources, Inc.
All rights reserved. Used with permission.

---

1. RightPath 4 Profile™ uses Accommodating–Directing.
   RightPath 6 Profile™ uses Compliant–Dominant.
2. James C. Collins, *Good to Great: Why Some Companies Make the Leap . . . and Others Don't* (NY: HarperCollins, 2001), 27.
3. Ibid., 22–35.

ENGAGING TRAITS

FACTOR 2
Interaction
Extroversion

Reserved	Mid-Range	**Engaging**
Introverted		*Extroverted*

© 2002 RightPath Resources, Inc.
All rights reserved. Used with permission.

Where's your home on this range?

To make the next two chapters covering this factor more relevant, look at the bullets below and choose the range (Left, Right, or Mid-Range) that you think might fit you best.

Think back over your entire life to consider your natural tendencies and decide which series of words is most like you. If you are sure that you have natural tendencies to act in both ways, depending on the situation, then place your mark in the Mid-Range.

☐ **RESERVED**   ☐ **MID-RANGE**   ☐ **ENGAGING**

• Reflect	• Express
• Avoid attention	• Gain attention
• Serious	• Humorous
• Realistic	• Optimistic

This continuum indicates how a person interacts with people. Of the two assessments that we use in our organization, the *RightPath 4 Profile* that I'm focusing on in this book uses the terms Engaging[1] for the Right Side and Reserved for the Left

Side. Our six-factor profile correlates fairly closely and uses the more common terms of Extroversion for the Right Side and Introversion for the Left Side. Since the factors are so closely correlated, I'll use the terms interchangeably in the discussion below. (However, to be technically accurate, Factor 2—Interaction—on the RightPath 4 Profile is very close but not quite a true measure of Extroversion.)

These concepts are quite obvious in relationships, so most people will have a general knowledge of these traits. You know that some people are Engaging/Extroverted and some are Reserved/Introverted. But we need to go much deeper, because this factor is rich with insights that can revolutionize your approach to work and team relationships.

Before launching into the traits, I need to clarify the most basic difference between Extroversion and Introversion. When exposed to strangers, extroverts are energized by the contact and introverts are de-energized. Thus, the extrovert will eagerly anticipate a large social event but the introvert will typically dread it. Like the previous factor, there is no good or bad side of this continuum; they are just different.

Right Side—Engaging/Extroverted

Interaction

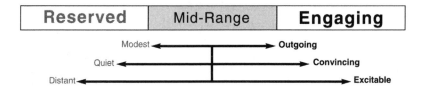

© 2002 RightPath Resources, Inc.
All rights reserved. Used with permission.

The expression "two are better than one" has special meaning for those who have Engaging behaviors, because for them being alone is no fun at all. They love to interact with others, regardless of where it is. They'll talk to strangers on the elevator, in the ticket line, even in cars while waiting for a green light at a traffic signal.

The Engaging/Extroverted folks are so outgoing that they are easy to recognize. If you observe someone who smiles often, laughs easily, and enjoys talking, then it's likely his or her natural "happy place" is on the Engaging side of this continuum. These bubbly, high-energy folks are hard to miss, because they naturally want to "go public" and usually maneuver their way into the limelight. Let's put them into the center of attention right now.

Strengths	Struggles
Outgoing, enjoy strangers	Working alone is difficult
Make a good impression	Need approval of others
Optimistic, upbeat, positive	Overly optimistic
Lighthearted, humorous	May be too uninhibited
Enthusiastic, energetic, passionate	May display strong emotions
Good at promotion, inspiring	May overstate, may be prideful
Comfortable in the spotlight	High need for attention
Good conversationalist, expressive	May talk too much
Like to develop people	May procrastinate on tasks
Open, flexible	Get distracted, forget promises

Engaging/Extroverted Traits

As you would expect, there are many well-known public figures who display characteristics from this group. In the entertainment industry, consider Goldie Hawn, Jim Carrey, Reba McEntyre, Oprah Winfrey, Kathie Lee Gifford, and Al Roker. Government leaders would include Prime Minister Tony Blair; Presidents John Adams, Ronald Reagan, Dwight Eisenhower, and Bill Clinton. Generals George Patton and Norman Schwarzkopf would fit in this group as well, but it's not their primary trait. Sports figures include golfer Lee Trevino; gold medal skaters Tara Lipinski and Sarah Hughes; gymnast Mary Lou Retton; and competitors-turned-broadcasters Deion Sanders, Joe Theisman, and Darrell Waltrip.

Understanding the core of the Engaging/Extrovert

Several strong underlying motivations relate to the Extroverts' drive to relate to others. First of all, their world is outwardly focused. Their attention is "out there," and they search for others with whom they can share their thoughts. This is a very important concept, because they do much of their best thinking and analyzing as they are talking. As strange as it might sound to a reserved Introvert, Extroverts often don't know what's coming out of their mouths until it "hits the street." In a sense, listeners are the midwives who assist the Extroverts in giving birth to many of their best thoughts and ideas.

Just as the Directing/Dominant personality needs power and control, the Extrovert has a strong need to be recognized, popular, and even admired. Their need to be acknowledged (even just speaking to them acknowledges their being) explains some of their dependence on relationships and why they want to engage at every opportunity. Social activity is important to them, because it meets so many of their needs. When they are alone for extended periods of time, they become like a fish out of water, searching for their survival environment.

There are two special considerations when you are evaluating someone's people needs. First, adolescents typically go through a socialization period that causes them to exhibit higher than normal Engaging traits, regardless of where they are on this continuum. During this period, even Introverts may place high importance on friends and fun. However, as they get past the teen years, their social needs begin to fade toward the Reserved side of the continuum. Also, as you would imagine, Extroverts who have extremely high public exposure may become saturated and withdraw somewhat, in order to have some private time.

ENGAGING STRENGTHS

Good at networking, make good first impressions, open to almost anything. If you want to know "whom" to call on for help or "who" knows something about such and such, then ask an Extrovert. If they don't know, then they know someone who does. They maintain an ever-expanding mental (and electronic) database of contacts with whom they touch base on a regular basis. Networking for them comes so naturally and is a powerful asset in many career fields. For an Extrovert, even discarding a business card of someone he or she met casually on a flight two years ago can be a painful process.

If you want someone to greet and welcome people at a social function or someone to host the international group that is coming to town, look first to this group. They smile easily, and they are genuine in their enthusiasm for strangers. All their talents collectively enable them to make good first impressions.

Openness is also an important asset for this group. They tend to be transparent and are willing to share their inner thoughts openly with others. They also have an openness to receive others into their circle of friends; and, they rarely encounter an idea that they are not open to trying. A closely related trait is optimism. Perhaps they can be open because they believe that everything is going to work out fine.

Good at promoting—enthusiastic, upbeat, positive, humorous. Extroverts are usually very good at promoting, because their natural traits are powerful tools to reach out and touch our feelings and emotions. I can think of no better person to represent this group than the likeable George Foreman. You may recall that George was twice the heavyweight boxing champion of the world. He converted from puncher to preacher and now has turned pitchman. After founding a church and youth ministry, he also preached on the sin of littering as a spokesperson for the "Don't Mess With Texas" campaign.

George has pushed corn chips, hamburgers, sneakers, hot dogs, mufflers, and now his own personal line of cooking devices. His natural personality exudes these Extrovert strengths that have enabled him to emerge as one of the most popular promoters on TV. And who but George, the personification of an Extrovert, would name four sons George, George, George, and George? This underscores the point that Extroverts can be pretty impressed with themselves.

Strong verbal skills. The Engaging group would love for

us to talk, and talk, and talk about their strengths. After all, they love the attention, and talk is their specialty. You may recall the comedienne Joan (Can we talk?) Rivers, and we'll probably always remember Deion Sanders and former President Clinton for their talking ability in front of the camera. Even though the outgoing president's nonstop sequence of farewell speeches seemed a little out of place, it was really in keeping with his extroverted verbal nature and the opportunities afforded by the press.

I think we've covered enough to give you a good first impression of Extroverts. It's time to bring things in balance and tell the rest of their story.

ENGAGING STRUGGLES

Too much talk (not enough action), overly optimistic, procrastination on tasks, have difficulty working alone. Not all work can be done through talk, so there comes a time when our fun-loving friends have to actually do some work. If it means shutting the door and performing a solitary mental task, expect them to procrastinate.

Of course, they don't see anything wrong with this, because their strong optimism is saying "No problem" right up until the last hour before the work is due. If you are in their network and you know they are up against the wall, be sure to check caller ID; and if it's one of them, you may not want to answer. They'll be calling on their friends for a little help on the pressing deadline.

All personality groups must learn to observe their interactions with others, using objective eyes and ears. For Extroverts, this feedback will alert them when their talking is out of control. Additionally, successful ones know that they must pay attention to schedules and develop plans that will allow them to meet deadlines. One of the best aids for these folks is to find appropriate role models who are good in these areas and then mimic their behaviors.

Unfocused, overcommitted, and overwhelmed. The downside of their openness is that they want to do everything. To

Extroverts most everything does look and sound like fun and seems like too good an opportunity to pass up. In addition, they crave approval; and one more commitment is another opportunity to look good. Extroverts can exhibit near manic behaviors when they suddenly discover they have ten balls in the air and can only catch six. In this overwhelmed, juggling state, quality/standards start to slip toward the "just get it done" level, and well-intended promises can be completely forgotten as the balls begin to drop.

The mantra of most Extroverts needs to be *focus, focus, focus, no, no, no,* and then *prioritize, prioritize, prioritize;* and, when that is finished, it needs to be repeated a few more times. The Extrovert will do well to prioritize and then lock on like a bulldog to stay on task. Constant self-coaching during the day can be a powerful tool for Extroverts (for all others as well) to help them deal with their struggles.

Emotional and uninhibited. Extroverts are not very good at hiding their emotions, and this can get them in trouble. Also, their personal/relational outlook makes it almost natural for them to interpret disagreement in very personal terms, which adds to the problem.

If you think about it, strong emotional expression would be a natural behavior from someone who tends to be verbal, open, uninhibited, and naturally expressive in other areas. Emotional expression is a good news/bad news situation. The good news is that Extroverts express their anger and get over it quickly; the bad news is that they express their anger and it sometimes gets them in trouble.

The tongue is one of the most dangerous weapons in the world. The Extrovert will do well to recall the wisdom of Proverbs and other writers in the Scriptures. *"There is one who speaks rashly like the thrusts of a sword, but the tongue of the wise brings healing."*[2] And another verse says, *"So also the tongue is a small part of the body, and yet it boasts of great things. See how great a forest is set aflame by such a small fire!"*[3]

Recently one of our clients, an extroverted and highly successful senior manager, whom I'll call Tom, called for advice.

Tom said he was thinking about leaving the company. As he shared the events that had begun his downward spiral, it really went back to a meeting in which he had made some emotional and cutting remarks to his boss in front of others. This event soured his boss and began the decline in their relationship.

Jerry, my associate, reviewed the facts and helped Tom see that his emotional remarks had really been the cause of the problem. Jerry suggested that Tom sit down, write a letter to his boss, apologize, and ask for his forgiveness. Tom wrote the letter and dropped it off at the boss's office in the morning. By that afternoon, the boss had called with a totally different tone and asked Tom to come over for a meeting.

It's very important for Extroverts to learn to depersonalize conflict and view it more objectively—as a different viewpoint or the other person's problem—but not necessarily as a personal affront. Still, Extroverts will need to express their emotions, so they need a plan that allows them to do it without damage. A good technique is for them to have a friend or mentor who can serve as a sponge or a punching bag—someone to absorb their emotions without damage to anyone.

The bottom line for Extroverts (and others also) is that emotions are like dynamite. In the right amount and at the right time, dynamite can be used to make a tunnel through the mountains. But an out-of-control blast can destroy the entire mountain and injure many people in the process.

Ideal Work Environment. Extroverts are best suited for a fast-paced, fun-oriented, environment, in which their primary work centers on relating to people. They need variety, mobility, and the opportunity to influence, impact, train, or encourage others, using their enthusiasm and strong verbal skills.

Managing Extroverts. Remember, their strengths are in relating to people, so try to match their work accordingly. Give them a lot of encouraging feedback. Plan time to go by their offices (that way you can escape when needed) and just listen. This gives them time to talk, and you may hear some good ideas. Keep in mind that they use talking as their method of thinking and analyzing, so try to avoid putting value judgments on everything they say.

Expect them to have difficulty staying focused on solitary and thinking tasks. Since they know this can be a problem, they usually appreciate help. Schedule meetings regularly—to track progress, review priorities, and ensure that they are not procrastinating or getting overcommitted.

Remember, these struggles do not mean that they have character flaws. It may seem that way to you, but it's not so. Their struggles are just the shadows of their strengths. Get them to develop a list of their struggles, and then you can review them occasionally and, when you see them happening, use humor to point it out. That really serves to help them depersonalize it. If the two of you can laugh about it but also know that it's serious, then it can be a growth experience for you both.

Coach's Clipboard

Key Point: Engaging/Extroverted people should remember that an effusive nature could be offensive to introverted friends.

The coach says, "*Button up, tone it down, and share the limelight with others.*"

---

1. RightPath 4 Profile™ uses Reserved–Engaging.
   RightPath 6 Profile™ uses Introverted–Extroverted.
2. Proverbs 12:18, NASB.
3. James 3:5, NASB.

RESERVED TRAITS

Interaction

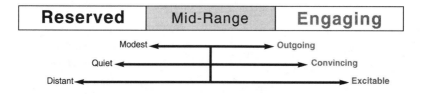

© 2002 RightPath Resources, Inc.
All rights reserved. Used with permission.

In a society that is fed by television and the entertainment industry, it often appears that the important people are all highly Engaging/Extroverted.[1] That's misleading, because underneath the hype the Reserved/Introverted are often the ones calling the shots and reaping the cash. There's a saying that "still waters run deep," and this is usually true of those who roost on the quiet, reserved, almost nonpublic end of the people continuum.

From experience, we can predict that the Introverts who are reading this are starting to feel uncomfortable with this exposé of their nature. If they were here, they would say, "Let's just skip over this section and move on to the next chapter."

You see, Reserved people much prefer to keep personal information private. If that's you, then I ask your indulgence for two reasons. First of all, Extroverts need to know you better so they can understand you, quit trying to change you, and learn to value your reserved nature. Second, by understanding yourself better, you will be able to better coach others and manage yourself. Let's put the spotlight (or if that makes you uncomfortable think of it as a candle) on Reserved Introverts and learn more about them.

Reserved/Introverted Traits

Strengths	Struggles
Work well alone	Drained by social contact
Reflective, think before speaking	May be slow to respond
Stay on task, limit projects, prioritize	May lack flexibility
Modest, quiet (let actions speak)	May fear public speaking
Deliberate, serious	May appear shy or distant
Focused, not easily distracted	May be curt, unfriendly
Dry sense of humor	May reject fun-loving people
Take a realistic approach	Skeptical, tend toward pessimism
Unemotional, matter of fact	May appear unenthusiastic
Like closure, finish what they start	May seem quietly self-righteous

Although they usually don't seek public attention and fame, many famous people are Introverts. They just learn to adapt their behaviors to accomplish their up-front or "on-camera" responsibilities. To readily recognize Introverts, it can be helpful to think of them alongside an extroverted contemporary.

For example, compare the following Reserved individuals with the Extrovert in parenthesis. Consider these examples from television news and talk shows: Cokie Roberts (Kathie Lee Gifford), Barbara Walters (Oprah Winfrey), and George Will (George Stephanopoulos). In politics, Presidents Jimmy Carter (President Bill Clinton), Thomas Jefferson (John Adams), and Senator Bob Dole (Elizabeth Dole). In sports, skaters Dorothy Hamill (Tara Lipinski); basketball stars Larry Bird (Magic Johnson); NASCAR drivers, the late Dale Earnhardt (Darrell Waltrip); broadcasters Frank Gifford (Terry Bradshaw); baseball pitchers Greg Maddux (John Smoltz).

RESERVED/INTROVERT STRENGTHS

Their greatest strength is that they are task focused. They are not distracted with concerns about who else is involved or what other people are saying. They're busy getting their own work done.

We have seen some unique and creative illustrations of this personality style as part of the "Awesome Traits Exercise" during team-building sessions, and one group stands out above all the rest. When it was time for them to present, the Reserved/Introverted group stood beside their flip chart and lifted the cover sheet to reveal what they had written during the ten-minute prep time. The spokesperson said nothing but used a pointer to deliver the brief message that said, "We don't talk it; we walk it." Then, they all sat down without saying a word. The audience was initially stunned; then they cheered at this powerful illustration of introverted traits.

Work well alone, focused, stay on task, finish what they start. Reserved people are usually quite comfortable alone and even prefer their own inner world to constant interaction with others. This more solitary approach complements their desire to avoid the interruptions and distractions that come from having others around. In fact, one of the most common complaints of this group is that other people come into their offices and talk when they've got work to do. They prefer to stay focused on their tasks in order to finish what they start.

Quiet, reflective, deliberate. Since they typically process internally, Introverts find it quite normal not to express everything that's on their minds. Rather than talk, they prefer to reflect, play out, or mull over their thoughts and ideas. This explains why they often respond to a question with, "Let me think about it." When they do give their answers, you know there will be a well-thought-out, reasoned approach.

I remember the day I asked my associate Bob a question about marketing. He had been in the business world many years and had had lots of exposure to marketing and advertising, so when he responded, "Let me think about it," it got my attention. Since we both knew that he had ten times the knowledge I did, it was difficult for me to comprehend why he needed to think about it.

Bob came back later in the day and provided a brilliant answer that was exactly what I needed to hear. In many settings since then, I've watched other Introverts respond similarly. They resist giving an off-the-cuff answer in order to take time to reflect and provide a very deliberately thought-out response.

Unemotional, matter of fact, realistic. This group tends to be low key, so it's rare to see them respond emotionally—either to problems or to successes. And to their credit, they are much less likely than Extroverts to get in trouble by overreacting with harsh words. In part, this may be because they just don't express their feelings as much and in part because they don't take things as personally.

I'm not a gambler, but if I were I'd bet that the best card players are Introverts. In a crowd of people, you can usually identify them because of their poker-faced expressions. In addition, Introverts typically communicate in a straightforward, matter-of-fact style. Whether asking or responding, they like to use a minimum of words and little emotion. Sergeant Joe Friday from *Dragnet* would be the poster boy for this group. His "Just the facts, ma'a'm" approach stands out as a classic example of the Introverts' communication efficiency.

Introverts also like to be realistic in giving appraisals and making commitments. Their tendency is to be conservative in their appraisals and estimates in order not to overstate. They much prefer to say no than to overcommit what they think they can do. And they often will downplay their capabilities (sandbagging) in order to under-promise and over-deliver on their obligations.

RESERVED/INTROVERT STRUGGLES

Drained by social contact, can come across as shy or unfriendly and closed to others. During a session with a leadership group, we were discussing individual traits and sharing strengths and struggles. One senior engineer underscored this struggle: "I'd rather have a root canal than go to a party where there are a bunch of people I don't know." Those who have a reserved nature echo this basic sentiment in virtually every session.

In most lines of work, some degree of socializing is necessary, so people do learn to adapt—some even become very good at it. When reviewing his profile report, one entrepreneur friend was relieved to see that he came out on the introverted side of this factor. He said that because he had worked in sales and learned to socialize, most people thought he was an Extrovert. His relief came in knowing that he was not being a phony but, rather, an Introvert who had adapted to meet the needs of the situation.

Gary, an associate at RightPath, is a consummate facilitator, having trained more than 100,000 people in corporate America. When he's up front, his enthusiasm and verbal energy give the impression that he might be an Extrovert. But when the day is over he prefers to retreat straight to his hotel room, order dinner from room service, and sequester himself in order to recharge his batteries for the next day.

I recall a young lady who was about to lose her job as the front desk receptionist. When she was hired, no one considered that as an Introvert she would be severely stressed by having to interact constantly with strangers. She called in sick almost every week until finally someone realized it might be a bad job match for her. She was moved to another job where her attendance and performance improved dramatically.

At times, Introverts do need to push themselves to meet the social needs of work and their families. However, they need to be realistic about their need for time alone in their job choices and plan for extra rest when they have extensive people exposure.

Pessimistic, negative, skeptical, closed, unenthusiastic. If Introverts are not careful, their strength of being very realistic can easily slide into pessimism. As one highly reserved person put it, "We sometimes tend to see the roadblocks, rather than the finish line." Also, at times I've watched them take a wet-blanket approach just to counteract some of the optimism and hype of their extroverted teammates. Introverts can get uncomfortable and turn negative when the environment gets to be what they consider too out of control with enthusiasm.

Introverts should keep in mind that they can play a very important role by using their natural skepticism to bring reality to the dialogue. At the same time, they need to remember that optimism and a positive attitude are essential for progress.

Tend to isolate, may not communicate, and slow to respond.

By their nature, Introverts drift toward isolation from the group. Additionally, their words and body language can send a message that says, "Leave me alone." When a "team matrix"[2] shows most of the people as Introverts, we can predict with a high degree of accuracy that they have poor communications. Getting them to talk and share needed information can be like herding cats. They may say, "Yes, we need to talk more," but usually they go right back to their old ways, which is to keep things to themselves.

The best solution to this struggle is about the same as with most other struggles: adapt your behaviors to the point that you feel out of your comfort zone. At that point, you are probably starting to make progress in overcoming the struggle, at least to an acceptable level. Remember, even a little change can pay big dividends.

Ideal Work Environment. Introverts work best in a quiet environment where they have time and space to work alone for extended periods. They are usually more productive and less stressed by working task assignments with data and things, rather than engaging people and people problems.

Managing Introverts. Give them protection from too much people interaction. Allow them to stay focused on a project until they can achieve completion and closure. Don't mistake their lack of response for inattention. Allow them time to process and reflect before they respond. Draw them into the discussions, ask questions, and then prove to them that you really want to hear what they have to say. Over a period of time, build their trust by learning to see the world from their viewpoints and communicate your respect for them, even if you don't agree. They must be convinced their opinions are valuable to you.

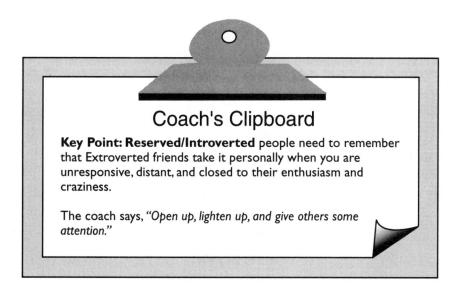

Coach's Clipboard

Key Point: Reserved/Introverted people need to remember that Extroverted friends take it personally when you are unresponsive, distant, and closed to their enthusiasm and craziness.

The coach says, *"Open up, lighten up, and give others some attention."*

Left, Right, and Mid-Range—we need them all

After observing and participating in many discussions with Extrovert/Introvert groups, I'm convinced that it's almost impossible for either side of this continuum to ever fully understand the other. They are wired so differently that they can irritate each other by just being who they are. If each side can just make a little effort to adapt to the other, it will draw everyone sufficiently closer together to make a huge difference.

Relationship Keys

Learn to recognize and encourage the unique talents of your opposite-side teammates. Understand their needs and expect their struggles. Let them know how much you value them because of who they are, and don't be offended when they act like themselves instead of like you.

- ■ - ■ - ■ - ■ - ■ - ■ - ■ - ■ - ■ - ■ - ■ -

Revisiting your home on this range

Recall the information you read in Chapters 7 and 8, reflect on the block you chose at the beginning of Chapter 7, and **place a mark** on the continuum below where you most *naturally* fall. (The stronger you feel about your natural behavior, the further toward the left or right your mark should go.)

FACTOR 2

Interaction

Reserved	Mid-Range	Engaging

© 2002 RightPath Resources, Inc.
All rights reserved. Used with permission.

---

1. RightPath 4 Profile™ uses Reserved–Engaging.

   RightPath 6 Profile™ uses Introverted–Extroverted.

2. A graphic depiction of the team that shows where each person falls in the four factors. Chapter 17 has examples.

```
C H A P T E R     9
```

HARMONIOUS TRAITS

FACTOR 3
Conflict and Pace
Compassion

Objective	Mid-Range	**Harmonious**
Detached		*Compassionate*

© 2002 RightPath Resources, Inc.
All rights reserved. Used with permission.

Where's your home on this range?

To make the next two chapters covering this factor more relevant, look at the bullets below and choose the range (Left, Right, or Mid-Range) that you think might fit you best.

☐ **OBJECTIVE**   ☐ **MID-RANGE**   ☐ **HARMONIOUS**

- Value logic
- Confront
- Like change
- Impatient

- Value feelings
- Support
- Like stability
- Patient

Think back over your entire life to consider your natural tendencies and decide which series of words is most like you. If you are sure that you have natural tendencies to act in both ways, depending on the situation, then place your mark in the Mid-Range.

We call this factor Conflict and Pace, because it predicts a person's need for harmony and a steady pace. In the discussions that follow, Right-Side people are considered Harmonious (Compassionate) [1] and Left-Side people are considered Objective (Detached). Please note that in Chapter 3 we used the word *Objective* to mean *impartial, not biased and able to see things as they really are*. In using it here for the Left-Side trait, the word Objective/Detached means *a nature that values logic over feelings*. In this sense, it does not mean that bias and filters do not affect Objective people.

A person's nesting place on this factor is partly determined by his or her priority between feelings and logic. Those who score on the Harmonious (right) side are very compassionate and have a radar-like sensitivity to the feelings and needs of others. The Objective, those who score on the left side, are detached and naturally focus on logic and may not pick up on feelings.

Obviously, both the feelings of others and the logic of the situation are important, so this is a good time to reiterate an important point on the nature of the personality factors. There are significant advantages (and disadvantages) of being on either side (or any point) of the continuum for any of the four factors we are discussing.

An underlying issue for this factor is how the two sides handle conflict. The Right Side has a strong need to promote harmony and avoid conflict (strength) but may not confront appropriately (struggle). As you would expect, the Left Side can be comfortable with confrontation (strength) but may be too confrontational and critical (struggle).

Another overall characteristic of this factor relates to pace and patience. The Right Side typically prefers a more patient and consistent pace.[2] The Left Side likes a fast pace and quick action. Closely tied to these opposite characteristics is the way that each group deals with stability and change. The Right Side promotes stability and does not change easily. The Left Side enjoys change and becomes quickly bored if things stay the same.

Speaking of change, right now you may be thinking of how you would like to change those irritating (different) people in your life so that they would be more like you. Let me encourage you to give up that idea. One of the best things you can do for your own success, as well as to be a better teammate, is to quit trying to change people who are different and learn to value what they bring to the table. They are the ones on the team who can cover some of your areas of struggle and model the way for your growth. We will explore in later chapters the challenge we all face in modifying our own behaviors to change and grow.

Right Side–Harmonious/Compassionate

FACTOR 3
Conflict and Pace

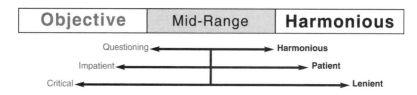

© 2002 RightPath Resources, Inc.
All rights reserved. Used with permission.

As we have already seen, those who roost on the Harmonious side of this continuum naturally exhibit many of the behaviors that we commonly think of as being kind, peaceful, patient, and supportive. Their strong drive for harmony usually translates into a go-along demeanor that enables them to interact well with others. Like the Extroverts, this group is typically very relational—but for different reasons. The Extrovert tends to relate out of a need for interaction and attention, but the Harmonious/Compassionate person is relational out of a strong need to support and care for others. Let's examine a snapshot of their typical strengths and struggles.

Harmonious/Compassionate Traits

Strengths	Struggles
Sense feelings, favor empathy	Sensitive, easily hurt
Compassionate and kind	May be naïve and too trusting
Agreeable, promote harmony	May be slow to confront
Patient, willing to wait	May put off making decisions
Supportive, helpful	May not set boundaries or say no, tolerant
Understanding	
Loyal and consistent	May compromise too much
Dependable, work at a steady pace	May be complacent, get in a rut
	May resist change or innovation
Persistent, able to stick to it	May be stubborn
Natural team players	May not verbalize true feelings

Examples from this group include former Presidents Thomas Jefferson, George H.W. Bush, Gerald Ford, and Abraham Lincoln (who was recently voted as the most admired president of all time). Sports figures include former NFL Cowboys coach, Tom Landry; former North Carolina basketball coach, Dean Smith; and Yankee baseball manager, Joe Torre.

HARMONIOUS STRENGTHS

Compassionate, understanding, supportive. Those on the Right Side of the continuum seem to have a natural ability to be *nice*. Unlike the Directing/Dominant group, they are not personally driven to be number one, and they don't have a great need to be in the limelight like the Extroverts. No, what the Harmonious want most is to be caring friends and just have everyone "get along." In many ways they are the antidote to today's fast-paced, highly stressful, and in-your-face lifestyle.

The Harmonious/Compassionate person truly has both a natural desire and ability to support others. Unlike any of the other profiles, they can actually be more concerned about making others look good than doing the same for themselves. Consequently, they often are very content to remain in the background, doing the quiet but necessary things that make the gears in an organization run smoothly. This low concern about attention often means that they get little recognition for the important work they do.

Harmonious traits are very powerful in any situation in which building relationships and giving support and encouragement are involved. Counselors and therapists typically score in the Harmonious/Compassionate range of this continuum, as do many pediatricians, teachers, and successful coaches. Harmonious people are usually very versatile and can excel in many roles with either people or data, as long as it's in a consistent and pleasant environment. They excel at being able to build and create consensus.

As businesses try to regain a focus on customer service, Harmonious traits are in high demand. A recent nationally syndicated newspaper article on using personalities to match people to their work highlighted the importance of some of these Right-Side characteristics. This article quoted a manager from one of the Ritz Carlton hotels: "Almost everyone was hired here based on personality, not on experience. We made a real effort to hire people who had consideration for guests' concerns. When people come to a hotel, they bring more baggage than what's under their arm."[3]

Harmonious, peacemakers, tolerant, team players. One of the best things about the Harmonious people is that they tend to say nice things or nothing at all. Their sensitivity seems to help them avoid being critical or harsh in their comments about others. They seem to be much more interested in promoting peace and harmony than in arguing with other viewpoints. They also tend to ignore or downplay negative and inflammatory comments.

Because so much of my work relates to understanding behaviors, I carefully observe people on television, to look for indications of their personality styles. Once, when I had taped *JAG*, the tape kept rolling into the CBS program *60 Minutes II*, which featured Yankee baseball manager, Joe Torre. The segment turned out to be an excellent presentation of the characteristics of a Harmonious/Compassionate leader.

Charlie Rose, the *60 Minutes II* commentator, described Torre as "understanding" and "like a loyal father" and said "he treats them [his players] like his own kids." (In a different article, former Braves outfielder Brian Jordan referred to Torre as "my father figure.")[4]

In talking about his own leadership style, Torre used a number of key words that are also indicative of his Harmonious talents. He said, "I hate that confrontational stuff . . . I try to see it from their side . . . I feel for them. . . . You blame yourself. . . . The subway series was war—[indicating painful conflict]."[5]

Joe Torre's ability to promote harmony among his highly paid players has certainly contributed to the Yankees' tremendous success in recent years. Likewise, his ability to work for an owner that few have been able to tolerate has given the team continuity in leadership, and it contributed to four World Series championships in five years.

Before we leave this scene, it's a good opportunity to bring out two other interesting traits that are related to the Harmonious/Compassionate group. Family seems to take a higher priority for them than any other group. They seem to have a natural ability to nurture and care for others. (It's very consistent that a Harmonious person like Joe Torre would be referred to as a father figure.)

Author and counselor Dr. John Trent calls this group the "Golden Retrievers," because they are so loyal about staying close to home and protecting the family. Over the years, I've also noted that this group has the greatest need for stability at work. They like to go to work in the same office every day and go home to sleep in their own beds at night. Typically, they are not comfortable as road warriors.

Persistent, dependable, steady. Probably one of the best analogies of these important talents is the potter's wheel. The function of the heavy wheel is to provide inertia and keep the turning process going at a constant speed. It doesn't slow down or speed up but just keeps on turning. Harmonious people tend to operate similarly. They don't change speeds easily; they just keep on producing at a dependable, steady pace.

It should not be a surprise that these folks have the sticking power of strong glue. When they commit, they are in for the duration. Given a stable situation, they are not likely to miss school or work and often are the ones who set attendance records. These natural traits give them an advantage in projects that require long-term commitment. And interestingly, they also have the least need for mobility and, therefore, are among the best at working in one place for extended periods.

HARMONIOUS STRUGGLES

Sensitive, naïve, may compromise too much. Underneath their genuine concern and sensitivity for others, there is often an ego that tends to struggle with its own self-worth. In this situation, it doesn't take much criticism to injure the feelings of those who have a Harmonious bent. Their sensors are so acute that even someone's unspoken anger can cause them significant stress or discouragement. Of course, at its extreme this sensitivity can make it difficult for others who are not so Harmonious, because they end up having to walk on eggshells to avoid hurting the Harmonious person's feelings.

The Harmonious naturally perceive the best and want to believe the best in others, so they tend to trust when trust might not be warranted. Because they do not naturally take a critical and skeptical approach, they are more likely than other groups to be deceived. The same person who cares deeply and goes above and beyond to understand and support others is also the one who is likely to be manipulated, controlled, and unscrupulously treated. Balancing sensitivity and kindness with a good dose of doubt and discernment will help Harmonious people avoid some of the pains and problems that come when trust is betrayed.

The Harmonious also have a tendency to compromise too much. They often give away too much of themselves, their power, and especially their time in an attempt to please others. They need to be honest about what is reasonable and then set boundaries on what is appropriate.

The easiest cure for these boundary struggles is to "Just say 'No.'" Of course, this can be very difficult to do, because if people have been accustomed to a "yes," they may become angry when they hear "no." But it must be done, because in the long run it's the right thing to do for others and it's the only way for the individual to preserve his or her dignity.

To say no requires personal courage and confidence that what you are doing is right—and even then it takes practice. Others can be a big help also. Good leaders, coaches, and teammates are able to discern when the Harmonious person is becoming overwhelmed from saying yes. They can help them understand why *no* is sometimes the best, most loyal, and most caring answer.

Slow to confront, avoid conflict, don't verbalize true feelings. As a young lieutenant in flight school, our academic instructors used an instructional technique that has stayed with me over the years. During class, it was common practice for the instructors to put us on notice of important topics that we likely would see on the exam by stomping their feet; hence, the term "foot-stomper." Well, here's a foot-stomper: The biggest issue for the Harmonious is that they are hesitant to confront when confrontation is needed and appropriate.

One of my favorite Air Force leaders once counseled, "Problems never get better when they are ignored. They just fester and get worse. Address them head on at the earliest appropriate time." This was one of the most important pieces of advice I ever received; and, in many years of supervising and training leaders, this probably has been the counsel I've most frequently passed along. That great philosopher, Barney Fife, offered the same sage counsel when he told Andy Griffith to "Nip it. Nip it in the bud!" That's a foot-stomper that you can remember and use to coach yourself.

The Harmonious usually delay or avoid confrontation, and that's not always good. It shouldn't be a normal thing to enjoy conflict, but conflict is normal, so they would do well to learn how to operate in it with some effectiveness. For example, it may be necessary to risk conflict in order to correct or discipline someone or show that person the path to integrity. Or it may take some degree of conflict just to be heard by some people, because they don't even listen unless they are challenged. Entering conflict is somewhat like war: It should only be pursued when it is the best alternative—and then with a cool head, good counsel, and a commitment to see it through to a successful conclusion.

Many times I've watched meetings in which Harmonious people sit quietly and let a decision be made without expressing their true feelings. This was especially puzzling when I knew they didn't agree with the direction that the decision was heading. It apparently goes back to those same issues of needing harmony and not having a strong enough feeling of self-worth to take a stand against someone in power.

For teams to function with their full complement of talents, everyone must be willing to take the risk of speaking out with their ideas. Since Harmonious people typically have a reputation for being prudent, reasonable, and considerate, they should expect to be heard and respected. Accordingly, they should not hesitate to express their ideas and beliefs. Anything less is holding back, which is in itself a kind of disloyalty.

Ideal Work Environment. The Harmonious are typically very versatile and can work in most any field in which they have an interest, as long as there is harmony and stability. They will be the most satisfied when they can see their efforts directly contribute to the overall growth, development, and success of others.

Managing the Harmonious. Remember their need for stability, harmony, and a steady pace. When change is required, give them appropriate training and time to adapt through a step-by-step process. Help them realize the value of confronting problems sooner rather than later. If you are a fast-paced, intense person, turn down your rheostat so that you can slow the pace, reduce your intensity, and lower your vocal volume. This frees them to relax and interact in a more productive way. Remember they operate like a potter's wheel—not like a tachometer in stop-and-go traffic.

Coach's Clipboard

Key Point: Harmonious/Compassionate people must remember that a sensitive nature and patient style do not always yield the best results.

The coach says, *"Toughen up, speed up, and speak up."*

1. RightPath 4 Profile™ uses Objective–Harmonious.
   RightPath 6 Profile™ uses Detached–Compassionate.
2. This need for patience and stability may be offset or modified when other fast-paced traits are present. For example, someone who also has Engaging/Extroverted traits will enjoy a faster pace and more change than a Harmonious person who is also Reserved.
3. "When Something Is Wrong, Those Who Care Make It Right," *USA Today* September 12, 2000, 11E.
4. "Joe Torre's Secret for Success" (NY: CBSNEWS.com, December 13, 1999).
5. "Heading for Home" (*60 Minutes II*, May 8, 2001 and NY: CBSNEWS.com. May 8, 2001).

CHAPTER 10

OBJECTIVE TRAITS

FACTOR 3
Conflict and Pace

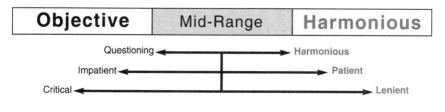

© 2002 RightPath Resources, Inc.

I can still remember the many discussions our development team had on what to name the Left-Side traits of this factor. The Right-Side Harmonious/Compassionate[1] people were somewhat sensitive to some of the cold and calculating words that were suggested for their opposites. On the other hand, the Left-Side folks thought those labels were just fine, because to them words like *objective* and *detached* sounded logical and definitely not too sensitive. And that little insight tells a lot about the nature of the Left-Side people.

Objective/Detached Traits

Strengths	Struggles
Favor logic over feelings	Afraid of having/showing feelings
Objective and cool	May appear coldhearted
Operate well in conflict	May be combative, in your face
Confront easily, questions	May be judgmental, critical
Make the difficult calls	Not easy to please
Thick skinned	May be insensitive to others
Tough minded	May be contentious
Fast paced, respond quickly	Restless, need to be on the move
Action oriented—now!	Impatient, tend toward hyperactivity
Like and promote change	May stir the pot when it's not needed

Objective people are usually easy to spot, because they don't hesitate to tell it like it is. And in today's culture it's easy to find public figures that seem to be perfectly comfortable and even achieve some of their fame from working in conflict. Just consider what's similar about CBS anchor Dan Rather, Rev. Jesse Jackson, former Prime Minister Margaret Thatcher, Ted Turner, Dr. Phil McGraw, Dr. James Dobson, and Senator Maxine Waters. They all have strongly held views and don't hesitate to confront those with whom they disagree.

Presidents John Adams, Teddy Roosevelt, and Harry Truman; generals George Patton and Norman Schwarzkopf; basketball player Charles Barkley; golfer Jack Nicklaus; and coaches Bobby Bowden and Steve Spurrier also are good examples for the Objective group.

News and talk show host personalities are often from this Objective group. Consider Rush Limbaugh, Dr. Laura Schlessinger, Wolf Blitzer, Sam Donaldson, and Bill O'Reilly. Most of the cable news networks have programs that typically feature highly Objective (and Directing) personalities who argue opposing political views. For example, CNN has *Crossfire*, FOX has *Hannity and Combs*, and MSNBC has *Hardball*. There is certainly more than enough exposure of this group's strengths and struggles, but let's analyze them more closely.

OBJECTIVE STRENGTHS

Logical, detached, make the difficult calls, tough minded. This Left-Side group typically has the ability to detach themselves from emotions and feelings. This enables them to make decisions on what they see as the most logical basis, regardless of how others feel about it.[2] This can be an important talent in many situations, because sometimes the best long-term course of action may be painful and unpopular at the time.

In my days as an instructor pilot and flight school manager, I often sat on faculty boards to determine if a deficient student pilot should be given additional training or eliminated from the program. Although the guidelines for these situations were clear-cut, the human factor always entered into the deliberation, as well it should. The decision usually hinged on whether the individual had been given a reasonable opportunity to learn and progress. After determining that he or she had received good instruction, we examined the record to see if there were any extenuating circumstances. In other words, if the person really had been given a fair attempt to progress in the time allotted or if there were other issues beyond his or her control.

These decisions were difficult because they were thumbs-up or thumbs-down on the flying career of some very fine young people. It became clear that these tough decisions were much more difficult for some people than for others. I didn't know anything about personality factors then, but looking back I can see that some board members were Objective and some were more Harmonious. The Objective found it much easier to ignore the short-term disappointment (feelings) that the students might suffer and focus on what was in the best interest of the Air Force and the safety of the individual.

Leaders, teammates, coaches, and parents face similar difficult, and sometimes unpopular, decisions every day. Whether it's initiating a corporate layoff, telling someone you can't do what he or she wants you to do, or employing tough love with a teen, the Objective person has the edge in natural talents for handling these decisions. Although, I should hasten to add that feelings should always be considered, because leaders (and parents) are dealing with people's feelings.

Confront easily, comfortable in conflict, thick skinned. Objective people are naturally wired to confront wrongs, to correct them before they get very far off track. The story of my friend's young daughter illustrates this very well. Gary is a Harmonious person who can just ignore many of the little irritants of everyday life. But his daughter is very different in this factor, and this was evident at an early age.

Gary's family had stopped at a fast-food restaurant to pick up some burgers. As they were discussing the order, his daughter said, "Dad, I don't want any mustard."

In an effort to teach her how to order, he suggested that she tell the person taking the order, so she turned and looked the employee straight in the eye and said, "No mustard."

They took their burgers and went back to the car. As Gary was about to drive off, he heard the back car door open and saw his daughter walking back into the restaurant. When he caught up with her, she was in someone's face for putting mustard on her burger. As Gary extracted his four-year-old daughter from the store he asked, "What were you doing?"

She replied, "Dad, they have to learn!"

Now fast-forward twenty-two years. Gary was visiting at his daughter's home and she had just come home with the groceries, which included a box of doughnuts. Opening them, she expressed her disappointment at their size and freshness. Using the toll-free number on the box, she immediately called the headquarters of this nationally known brand to register her strong complaints. When she hung up and looked over at Gary, she said, "Dad, they have to learn." The light clicked in Gary's head, and he flashed back to the no-mustard incident of her childhood. His daughter, of course, didn't remember that event, but it was clear that her personality had not changed; she still had to *confront* an obvious wrong.

Now that you are getting the picture of these Objective traits, let's go a bit further to find how they can be comfortable in conflict. Several years ago, I was conducting a team session for an auditing firm. During the discussions, two people who had scored in the Objective range (one male and one female) got in a heavy discussion about how the work was scheduled. Their voices got louder, and their jaws tightened, but it was obvious to me that this was normal behavior for them. In fact, they seemed to be enjoying it so much that they didn't notice how uncomfortable their Harmonious teammates were with their game of conflict. But this exchange evidently was beneficial to them, because one of those in the conflict recently told me that their relationship had improved steadily since that day.

Fast paced, action oriented, promote change. Objective people thrive on a fast pace and quick action. They walk fast, they usually talk fast, they think and respond fast, and they definitely want fast action. When they have to sit still, they are like coiled springs just waiting for the opportunity to uncoil and start moving again. I've even timed their body language. In one-on-one situations, about seven minutes seems to be the threshold; that's when they start to get noticeably restless. So, if you are presenting to them, keep it moving and keep it short.

This group also excels in rapidly changing situations. They can quickly shift their focus from one priority to another; a talent that helps them excel in a multitasking environment. If you want someone who is fast paced and can juggle responsibilities at work, look for someone who is Objective.

The Objectives are energized by change. Their comfort with and even preference for change is likely rooted in their love of a challenge, their penchant for action, and a low threshold for the routine. They adopt new systems and situations and move on as though the old never existed. Their drive for change is so strong that it can be difficult for them to do something the same way twice. When driving regularly to the same places, they may take different routes. If speaking, they will usually change their presentations each time they give them.

These talents make Objective people ideally suited for environments that are unpredictable. The unexpected does not throw them off, and surprises only seem to inspire them to action. It seems natural that these folks are able not only to respond but also to thrive in crises.

OBJECTIVE STRUGGLES

Insensitive, can seem coldhearted, deny feelings. As you probably have guessed by now, the Objectives don't hide their struggles very well and, unfortunately, they often don't care. Because they are so keen on following logic, this group can be insensitive to others and never know it. Also, most Objective people have Directing traits, and when you put these two traits together their struggles compound.

When Objective/Directing individuals are really focused on their results, they may unknowingly work people until they drop. I've often remarked that this personality combination unintentionally can be so insensitive that they could be emotionally crushing others and never realize it. It was said that General "MacArthur seemed unaware of the fact that he caused inconvenience to others."[3] Eisenhower said of him, "MacArthur could never see another sun, or even a moon for that matter, in the heavens as long as he was the sun."[4] This speaks to the struggles from his Directing (high ego) and Objective (insensitive) nature.

These struggles have been associated with many senior leaders in the military and corporate world (which often models leadership from the boot-camp experience of the military). After graduating from staff college, I almost was assigned to a four-star general who was known behind his back as "The Alligator." He was a talented individual, but he thrived on berating people, regardless of rank. When I learned of his reputation, I quickly found another position.

One of my peers observed The Alligator pinning a medal on one of the squadron pilots and saying, "I'm pinning this medal on you because you did something good. Keep it up or I'll personally come back to this base and rip it off." With that, the general turned and stormed out of the building.

Because they don't naturally think about feelings, Objective people sometimes treat people in a coldhearted fashion, as though they were inanimate objects. Corporate America is rife with horror stories of senior leaders and CEOs who treat people like sticks of wood; they grind them into sawdust and toss them on the heap without thinking.

Whether they are alligators or chain saws, Objective people who disregard the dignity and feelings of others need to be nipped in the bud early in their careers. If they don't shape up, they must be shipped out—and the sooner the better. Jack Welch, legendary CEO at GE, realized that and, to his credit, he had the courage to ship them out of his organization, regardless of the results they produced.[5]

Judgmental and critical. This group seems to have radar for identifying the struggles of other people, and they can easily fall into the trap of "just being honest." Their impatience and low tolerance for being irritated, along with their confronting nature, make it easy for them to bring out the "truth" by judging and criticizing.

In working with teams, I've noticed that when most of the people are Harmonious and one or two are highly Objective, this tendency can cause strong tensions. The Objective folks think they are just being honest and telling it like it is, but their candor can be discouraging and even painful to their teammates.

Not only does this critical nature affect teams at work, but it also can lead to serious problems at home. We all need encouragement at a much greater ratio than we do criticism, and home should be a place where everyone gets much more positive than negative feedback. Unfortunately, the self-confidence of many children is undermined by too much criticism from highly Objective (and Controlling/Dominant) parents. This same problem can be the cause of strife between spouses who actually care for each other very much.

As with all of the struggles, it's not that we don't know better; it's just hard to do better. Natural personality wiring, combined with the experiences of our past, gives all of us strong undercurrents of behaviors that are difficult to overcome. When Objective people (who usually pride themselves on being objective) take an honest look, they will see the consequences of their behaviors. But it takes more than knowledge; it takes a change in viewpoint and viewing point—from the throne of judgment to the seat of mercy and grace.

Impatient, restless, too many changes. We've already touched on these to some degree because they relate so closely to the other struggles, but they deserve a word or two on their own. We have acknowledged that there are many benefits from these same traits. In fact, without the positive side of these traits, we likely would still be living in caves.

However, at some point, impatience with others also can send a strong message that "I'm more important than you." If you think about it, showing patience is, in effect, giving up some control. The Objective and Directing person is likely to exhibit behaviors that say, "By being patient, I'm allowing you to control me and I don't like that. I've got to get back on my own agenda, so your time is up." The solution to impatience usually comes from a willingness to *give* to the other person rather than *take* for yourself. It's as simple as that. But to actually *give* patience can be about as difficult as redirecting a river.

The struggle of being restless and wanting to always change things can put enormous stress on others. As we have already seen, people with Right-Side, Harmonious traits do not adapt to change easily. Beyond that, change generates extra work and additional problems that can lead to chaos. Objective people can actually enjoy a crisis, because that's when they are at their best. Unconsciously, this may be part of their desire to make changes, but change does not come without a price. And so the solution really is to step back and count the cost. Are the real costs of the changes worth the expected benefits? If not, maybe it's a good time just to let the urge to change pass.

Ideal Work Environment. Give them problems to solve and a fast pace. They thrive on change and usually do well in crises. Since they are naturally confrontive, make sure they have significant challenges to absorb their combative energy.

Managing the Objective. Don't tiptoe around what you want to say. Just talk straight to these people, and do it fast, before they quit listening. Give them opportunities for mobility, and challenge them with problems to solve. Short-term projects work best, since they may have difficulty staying with one thing for extended periods. Use their talents for change and quick action, but coach them on how to tone it down for others, depending on the situation.

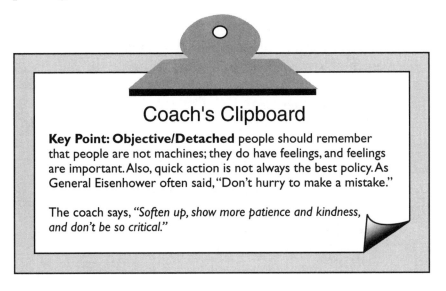

Coach's Clipboard

Key Point: Objective/Detached people should remember that people are not machines; they do have feelings, and feelings are important. Also, quick action is not always the best policy. As General Eisenhower often said, "Don't hurry to make a mistake."

The coach says, *"Soften up, show more patience and kindness, and don't be so critical."*

Left, Right, and Mid-Range—we need them all.

Both Harmonious and Objective people should learn to honor those who are different, even when their ways seem irritating. Each side needs to value the unique attributes of the other and try to adapt their own behaviors, rather than trying to change someone else's.

Relationship Keys

Learn to recognize and encourage the unique talents of your opposite-side teammates. Understand their needs and expect their struggles. Let them know how much you value them because of who they are, and don't be offended when they act like themselves instead of like you.

Revisiting your home on this range

Recall the information you read in Chapters 9 and 10 and reflect on the block you chose at the beginning of Chapter 9. **Place a mark** on the continuum below where you most *naturally* fall. (The stronger you feel about your natural behavior, the further toward the left or right your mark should go.)

FACTOR 3
Conflict and Pace

Objective	Mid-Range	Harmonious

© 2002 RightPath Resources, Inc.
All rights reserved. Used with permission.

1. RightPath 4 Profile™ uses Objective–Harmonious.
   RightPath 6 Profile™ uses Detached–Compassionate.

2. Recalling Chapter 3, remember that they may not always be objective about themselves, family members, and certain others with whom they have special relationships.

3. Merle Miller, *Ike the Soldier: As They Knew Him* (NY: Perigee Books, The Putnam Publishing Group, 1987), 26.

4. Ibid.

5. Jack Welch and John A. Byrne, *Jack Straight from the Gut* (NY: Warner Books), 188–189.

METHODICAL TRAITS

FACTOR 4
Order and Detail
Conscientiousness

Spontaneous	Mid-Range	Methodical
Unstructured		*Structured*

© 2002 RightPath Resources, Inc.
All rights reserved. Used with permission.

Where's your home on this range?

To make the next two chapters covering this factor more relevant, look at the bullets below and choose the range (Left, Right, or Mid-Range) that you think might fit you best.

Think back over your entire life to consider your natural tendencies and decide which series of words is most like you. If you are sure that you have natural tendencies to act in both ways, depending on the situation, then place your mark in the Mid-Range.

☐ **SPONTANEOUS**   ☐ **MID-RANGE**   ☐ **METHODICAL**

• Free	• Accurate
• Flexible	• Scheduled
• Impromptu	• Prepared
• Instinctive	• Systematic

This factor provides insights into how a person handles details, accuracy, structure, and preparation for upcoming events. The Methodical/Structured (Right Side)[1] of the continuum is naturally motivated to organize, plan, schedule, and manage details in order to "get it right." The Spontaneous/Unstructured (Left Side) can be conscientious also, but they prefer to operate with ballpark accuracy and move along to something else. They are naturally motivated to seek freedom and flexibility and will typically resist the confining nature of structure.

Obviously, there are significant advantages for each side, depending on the job, so try to avoid value judgments on what is good or bad. As we'll see, they both have their strengths and struggles.

Of the factors covered thus far, most people generally are able to see themselves correctly as leaning toward or even being clearly positioned on one side or the other of the continuum. However, some Spontaneous (Left-Side) people have difficulty initially seeing themselves accurately on this factor, because they have developed Right-Side, Methodical behaviors sufficient to reach their goals. We'll talk more about that when we get to the Spontaneous side, but for now remember that we are talking about natural behaviors, not what a person does out of a need to achieve.

Right Side—Methodical/Structured

FACTOR 4

Order and Detail

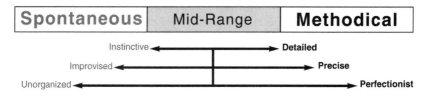

© 2002 RightPath Resources, Inc.
All rights reserved. Used with permission.

To be organized, prepared, and accurate, Methodical people naturally operate from a Structured approach. Of course, almost everyone likes to think of himself or herself as having those traits. But consider whether you are a true Methodical, who is naturally compelled toward the strengths and struggles below, or are you a wanna-be who has overcome your Spontaneous nature in order to perform in an ordered and detailed fashion.

Methodical/Structured Traits

Strengths	Struggles
Organized and scheduled	Tend to be inflexible
Accurate, good with details	Perfectionistic to avoid mistakes
Plan ahead, establish systems	May over-rely on procedures, rules
Prepared, rehearse carefully	Over-prepare but lack confidence
Analyze before deciding	Paralysis by analysis syndrome
Conduct research, determine facts	May be too slow
Respond diplomatically	May be too formal, rigid
Disciplined to follow procedures	May be too critical of self
Focused on one thing at a time	May forget big picture
Thorough	May be too picky

Some examples of people who exhibit these traits include television personalities George Will, Cokie Roberts, and Barbara Walters. Government leaders include Presidents Thomas Jefferson, Abraham Lincoln, and Jimmy Carter; former Secretaries of State Henry Kissinger and George Schultz; Treasury Secretaries William Simon and Paul O'Neill; Former Ambassador Anne Armstrong; National Security Advisor Condoleezza Rice; and longtime Federal Reserve Board Chairman Alan Greenspan. Other examples are military leaders: Generals Omar Bradley and George C. Marshall; sports figures are skater Dorothy Hamill, basketball star David Robinson, golfer Jack Nicklaus, Braves pitcher Greg Maddux, and Duke's coach Mike Krzyzewski.

METHODICAL STRENGTHS

Accurate, good with details, focused, thorough. A key motif that runs through all the Methodical strengths is the desire, even compulsion, to "get it right." Perhaps you will recall that the Directing group typically assumes they are "right" and all the different traits like to be right, but this group will work like beavers to get it right. Not only do they want to get it right, these Methodical people find it very important to get it right the first time; none of this trial and error stuff for them.

The Methodical group's standards of perfection do not go unnoticed, for they extend to nearly every area of their work and lives. Even when they suspect something is probably true, they want to prove it before they believe it. Realistically, some of you reading this are probably thinking, "How does the author know this is true? I wonder if he can prove it?"

Methodical people know that the devil is in the details, so they naturally dig into the nitty-gritty to check things out and understand why things are the way they are. This need to "know that they know," and to ask "why" is fundamental to career fields that require extensive analysis and research. In my previous work in the field of career assessment, we saw a high correlation between Methodical personality types and those who scored highest on the investigative career fields in the "Strong Interest Inventory."

Typically, this group is not interested in or impressed by general statements; rather, they want specifics. In an off-site team session I facilitated, there were two Methodical individuals who provided staff support to about a dozen regional sales managers (only one of eleven sales managers was Methodical). In describing how he liked to be communicated with, one of the Methodical people gave his first item as "Be specific. I can't work with a lot of general pie-in-the-sky stuff. I need specifics if I'm going to do my job."

As you would suspect, Methodical people also like discipline, and they enjoy having rules and procedures for themselves and for others. A systematic environment allows them to focus their attention on one thing at a time. They are proficient at resisting distractions or attempts by others to pull them away from the tasks at hand. They value thoroughness and, to make sure projects are done right, they will seek to tie up every loose end and account for every detail. These people are good at persisting—to get closure before they close the book on any undertaking.

Sometimes Methodicals may exhibit behaviors that are similar to those of the Directing group.[2] They can be aggressive and even controlling when it comes to getting results. They may even walk right over someone who is blocking them from achieving their goals. The difference is that afterward they will give you back the "keys to the shop." Their motivation is not to dominate or even to run the show; they are just highly focused and insistent when it comes to getting results and achieving their goals.

Organized, planned, scheduled, systematic, prepared. I recently asked participants in a team session to think of an animal that represented their personality. One of the Methodical people said that his animal icon would be a kangaroo. Of course, the team wanted to know why, and he answered, "I like the idea of having a pouch to keep all my stuff organized." That says a lot about this group, because they get uneasy with disorder. In fact, a key strength of Methodical people is that they take the time to put things back in place immediately, knowing they are saving time later. Our friend John, husband to our star teammate Sue, is so highly structured that not only does he always keep things straight, but when he gets bored he goes out to his workshop just to sort bolts and nuts.

Methodical people also like to prepare ahead of time for any upcoming events or responsibilities. This makes sense, because if they wait until the last minute they might not have enough time to get it right. Everyone likes to be prepared, but this group takes it very seriously and will start early to be sure they are ready.

Jerry and Gary, two associates at RightPath, are both highly Methodical: they thrive on preparation, and if they can't prepare they prefer not to take on the task. When they accept an assignment, they begin immediately to schedule tasks, do the research, and plan every detail to make sure they are thoroughly prepared. In a similar manner, John and Sue began planning a year in advance for a trip to Europe with their adult children and spouses. To maximize their preparation, they chose their highly structured daughter-in-law as the lead researcher for the planning and preparation process.

While leading a workshop at the SHRM (Society of Human Resource Managers) Southeast convention on the subject of managing differences, I asked for a volunteer from each end of this personality continuum to share some insights. A young lady who said she was on the Spontaneous and highly unstructured side related her experience of traveling to Europe with her best friend, who was her opposite in this factor.

The speaker (Spontaneous) said that her idea of a good vacation trip was to have a general plan but no firm schedules. She preferred the spur-of-the-moment lifestyle that offered the adventure and flexibility of just going with the flow as the day developed. Her Structured friend, of course, was just the opposite and wanted definite plans for each day. They agreed to compromise and do two days of scheduled and planned activities followed by two days of just winging it. She said it was a great trip, and they both benefited by seeing, from a new and more positive viewpoint, how the other side lived.

When teaching college students as part of the Air Force ROTC program, I noticed that some students always kept a spiral-bound student calendar with them to keep up with their assignments and schedule their upcoming meetings. (This was in the 80s when time management systems were just becoming popular and well before electronic personal organizers became available.) These students were usually the ones who turned in quality work on time and also the ones who remembered cadet corps meetings.

Methodical people have an advantage in academic institutions because of these traits. Research at the Johnson-O'Conner Institute shows that people who have high graphoria (the ability to keep neat notes, homework, and records) also do better than their personality opposites in large university classes. Their natural organizational skills and drive to prepare give them an edge in these impersonal, self-directed environments. Spontaneous people (typically low in graphoria) tend to achieve better in smaller classes where there is more instructor interaction and fewer requirements for student-initiated organization and preparation.

Methodical people have a strong natural gift for systems. More than any other group, they are willing to invest the time and effort up front to develop plans, procedures, and processes that can be used over and over again. They hate to reinvent the wheel, so as soon as they experience that something is going to be repetitive they develop a system. As you would expect, this talent for structure is usually present in those who make their living in engineering, architecture, accounting, and similar fields, where structure and systems are so important.

Analytical, conduct research, good with facts and data. These folks are most comfortable when they can follow their own natural process (system) to research and collect facts and then analyze them before reaching conclusions. I've found a good word picture is to imagine someone taking a gadget apart, examining each piece, and then carefully reassembling it. When they have finished, they understand it; they know it's put together well and that it is accurate, solid, and well thought out. Only when they have been through these steps are they comfortable putting their stamp of approval on decisions or finished products.

Careful, disciplined, neat, diplomatic. The need to do things right carries over into every area of their lives. They are especially exacting with their things; they keep their desk drawers neat, and they are particular with equipment. This accounts for some of their territorial nature and explains why they don't like to loan things or have others "messing with their stuff."

They typically lead disciplined lifestyles. They have established routines for everything, even the way they take care of their teeth and their clothing. If a picture is crooked, they notice it and straighten it immediately. They ensure that the yard is mowed perfectly and that the oil is changed on schedule. If you looked in their cupboards, you would likely find that all the packages are arranged by type and all the labels are in the same direction so they can be read easily. If they offer you grapes, don't just pull some off the branch; you are *supposed to* carefully break off a small stem of grapes. For truly Methodical people, there is a right way to do everything.

METHODICAL STRUGGLES

Perfectionism, too picky, unrealistic standards, self-critical. As mentioned earlier, struggles are often the overextension of strengths, and this problem is very evident here. With standards and expectations so high, these folks can easily get tied up in trying to reach a level of accuracy and detail that is past the point of diminishing returns. They need to distinguish between areas in which 100 percent accuracy can be life or death (like nuclear materials and brain surgery) and the part of everyday life that just needs to get done.

Interestingly, these folks can be the hardest on themselves of any of the groups. Their standards are so high that even they can't reach them, and this can undermine self-confidence. In observing the "Awesome Traits Exercise" that we use in corporate team sessions, I've noticed that the Methodicals often develop their list of struggles before addressing their strengths. Although there is conflicting research on this subject, my observations have been that those who are highly structured and Methodical seem to be more likely to suffer from headaches, migraines, digestive disorders, and depression.

There is much to be admired about this group's conscientious approach to life, but a more balanced approach in some areas probably would be healthier. Most Methodical people could improve their performance, relationships, and health by learning to live at peace amidst the tension between striving for personal perfection and realizing that it is an unattainable goal.

Rigid, over-prepare but lack confidence, overrely on procedures. The downside of being highly organized is often a lack of flexibility. Systems and schedules are like fences: they are both helpful and problematic. They provide security but they also can limit those who are inside if the gates are not open. Typically, highly organized and scheduled people do not like to open the gates and venture from the secure boundaries of their schedules, plans, habit patterns, rules, and procedures. It's not unusual for their confidence to fade when they encounter unfamiliar or unpredictable situations.

Many in this group tend to trust their fortress of plans and preparation more than themselves when it comes to execution.[3] Though we all know that *prior preparation and planning precludes poor performance*, there comes a time to step away from that preparation and act with confidence.

As a flight instructor, I found that the successful student pilots were those who could prepare on the ground and then execute their plans in the air with confidence and flexibility. Their preparation, plus their confidence, gave them the ability to deal with the unexpected changes that arise in any situation. Those who trusted their plans more than their own ingenuity did have problems. Methodical people can improve their successes by developing the ability to adjust to changing situations.

Paralysis by analysis, slow to decide. This group often operates by the process of "ready, ready, ready . . . aim, aim, aim." To make sure they fire perfectly the first time, they want every possible piece of information. Thus, more facts and data with more analysis can seem as important as actually doing something. For this group, it's often more comfortable and less risky.

Unfortunately, there is another component that we all have to deal with, and that is time. A key to success is learning that a good solution timely executed is far superior to a perfect solution executed too late. Thus, the challenge for the Methodical person is to realize when enough preparation is enough. Self-awareness is helpful and the perspective of an opposite-side teammate can be extremely valuable in bringing a balanced viewpoint.

Ideal Work Environment. Highly Methodical people operate at their best in situations that are neat, orderly, and systematic. They thrive where accuracy and details are important to success and are valued accordingly.

Managing Methodical people. Value and encourage their systematic approach and their commitment to accuracy and details. Respect their need for organization and planning, and protect them from chaotic or crisis management. Try to avoid putting them on the spot with unexpected questions, especially in public settings. Give them time to check the facts, analyze details, and thoroughly prepare their responses.

Coach's Clipboard

Key Point: Methodical/Structured people should remember that perfection is not always needed and that rules and schedules are to enhance success—not preclude it. Analyze, but don't get paralyzed in the process.

The coach says, *"Loosen up."*

---

1. RightPath 4 Profile™ uses Spontaneous–Methodical.
   RightPath 6 Profile™ uses Structured–Unstructured.
2. Blends of factors are common so a person could be both Directing and Methodical. As shown in Appendix C, this combination is highly results oriented. (See Analyzer and Strategic Thinker blended profiles.)
3. This is typically not true for Methodical/Structured people who also score on the Directing/Dominant side of Factor 1. Their confidence can override these concerns.

CHAPTER 12

SPONTANEOUS TRAITS

FACTOR 4
Order and Detail

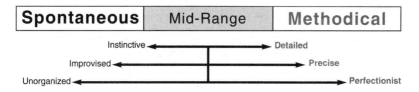

© 2002 RightPath Resources, Inc.
All rights reserved. Used with permission.

Spontaneous is the key word that best describes the naturally motivated behaviors of this group.[1] These folks do their best work when they are operating from a generalist perspective and using their gut instincts. When you put them in systematic details, their effectiveness and efficiency slows down like molasses on a cold day. With that general understanding, let's look at their strengths and struggles.

Spontaneous/Unstructured Traits

Strengths	Struggles
Spontaneous, operate instinctively	May wing it too much
Flexible and versatile	Not naturally organized
Generalist, work with broad concepts	May struggle with focus
Improvise as they go along	May ignore rules
Make on-the-spot decisions	May be impulsive
Synthesize, give a quick appraisal	May overlook key details
Respond openly and quickly	Too informal at times
Speak extemporaneously	May be unprepared
Start quickly	May not finish or tie up loose ends
Unconventional	May be rebellious

Famous people who exhibit the spontaneous traits include media personalities Oprah Winfrey, Goldie Hawn, Billy Crystal, Bette Midler, Will Smith, Kathie Lee Gifford, and Shawn Hannity. Political leaders in this group include Presidents John Adams, Teddy Roosevelt, Dwight Eisenhower, and Prime Minister Tony Blair. Military leaders, Generals Norman Schwarzkopf and George Patton, are also clearly at home in this group, as are sports personalities Terry Bradshaw, John Madden, Deion Sanders, and NASCAR's Darrell and Michael Waltrip.

You may have noticed that there are some of the same people in this list that were used as examples of the Extroverted/ Engaging personality group. Statistically there is a positive correlation between the Engaging and Spontaneous, and these two groups and their traits do tend to overlap in some areas.[2]

A Unique Feature: Their preferred action is synthesis, not analysis. If you want them to analyze, give them an audience. Before jumping (Spontaneous word) into their strengths and struggles, let's look at one unique difference in the way the Methodical and Spontaneous groups process. Methodicals like to analyze, but the Spontaneous like to synthesize. We'll look at how they synthesize later on, but first consider how this Spontaneous group operates when they have to analyze.

As you will recall, Engaging/Extroverted people do much of their best thinking when they are verbalizing their thoughts. When they are also Unstructured and highly Spontaneous, they do their best analysis the same way. Quiet, reflective, analytical thinking is not a comfortable experience for this group, because it's next to impossible. When they go internal, their thoughts tend to jump from one area to another, making it difficult to maintain focus.

They do their best analytical thinking when they can talk things out while making it visual with some sort of sketch, outline, or writings. When you go into offices where one-third of the wall space is covered with whiteboard, the odds are good that the occupants are Spontaneous. As you read about their strengths, you'll get more insights into their thought processing system and see why they are so different from their Methodical teammates.

SPONTANEOUS STRENGTHS

Spontaneous, instinctive, on-the-spot appraisals/decisions, start quickly. This group seems to have unique brain skills that support most of the talents associated with their traits. They operate somewhat like a video camera connected to a computer hard drive; their opposite-side counterparts operate more like a card catalog in a library. Before going any further with this analogy, I should clarify that to my knowledge this has never been researched or documented in any scientific or medical journal. I'm just sharing the best word picture I can think of to communicate the process that I've observed with this group over the last twelve years.

Remember that most who are Spontaneous are also going to be Engaging, so they are focused outward. Their scanner instantly collects massive data inputs from their environment through visual, audio, and other stimuli. This information is not just put away in some filing cabinet in the basement of the brain. Instead, it is somehow pictured and experienced in a way that leaves a marker on it, as it is written (randomly) to the brain's hard drive. This memory marker provides a hook for what seems to be a quick retrieval system—a system that works similar to the way a computer learns your most used programs and prepositions them for a quick start.

The effect of this process is that Spontaneous people are able to access their mental files and almost instantaneously synthesize relevant information for a quick response. Granted, their answers may not be perfect, but they are usually in the ballpark. So, if you ask questions, you usually are going to get reasonable answers immediately. Their off-the-cuff appraisals can be amazingly close, because they have the appropriate data stored for ready access.

This Spontaneous retrieval system seems to work well for this group because, as we'll see later, they dislike and struggle significantly with organizing and retrieving pieces of paper, files, and such. Carrying the previous analogy further, their minds seem to work better with a random storage system in the brain than a linear physical one—like a filing cabinet.

This ability to extract stored data and synthesize it on the fly into a plan or decision or an immediate action is an especially important trait for those who work in highly dynamic fields, such as sales, customer support, or crisis management activities. The expression "on the fly" gives a good word picture of the way these people operate. Their conscious thinking doesn't stay long in one place; it's on the move, and this enables them to cover a lot of ground in a hurry.

Another similar expression often used to describe this group is, "They like to wing it," and this can be the way they do some of their best work. It's as if the excitement, challenge, adventure, and danger of the moment gets their brains to work in a high-efficiency mode, which helps them bring their thoughts into a clear focus.

For this reason, Spontaneous people are usually at their best when there is some outside stress or pressing deadlines. More than likely, those people were the ones you knew at school who did most of their work at the last minute. For them, it just would not come together until there was a crisis, but then the mental electrons flowed and the work got done.

Generalists, impromptu, flexible, versatile. Spontaneous people typically see and think in general terms, rather than in specifics. Like a wide-angle photograph taken at high altitude, they see the breadth of the landscape, rather than the details. Their receptors capture the prominent features and quickly assimilate them into broad pictures and concepts. This enables them to catch on quickly to the general concepts without knowing all the details.

In training sessions, I often use Oprah Winfrey as an example to explain the strengths of the Spontaneous personality group. If you've watched her program, you know that her talents for spontaneity and flexibility really help make the show. She can be in the middle of a discussion, but when her radar picks up someone in the audience who is a good target of opportunity, in a flash, she engages that person. Oprah also did not hesitate to interrupt her frequent guest and friend, psychologist Dr. Phil McGraw, with an impromptu but usually very meaningful question or comment.

It's obvious that her energy and excitement flow to the audience as she wings her way through the show. Without question, someone has done a lot of planning to make each program successful, and no doubt Oprah does some preparation. But when the spotlights come on, it's clear that she's at her best when she takes the general plan and implements it through her natural Spontaneous talents.

Oprah's natural penchant to operate on instinct is prominent in her business endeavors as well, and the April 1, 2002 edition of *Fortune* magazine cover story details her financial success. One of the highlights of the article is that Oprah isn't bothered by the fact that she doesn't know how to read a balance sheet. She seems quite happy to delegate the details and manage her reported $1 billion fortune from a big picture perspective. The article also reported that her idea of due diligence is to ask one question: "Can I trust you?"[3] Doesn't that sound like someone who trusts herself and her own instincts?

As you may have guessed by now, I enjoy watching, listening to, and reading biographies—especially about military and political leaders. (Since I didn't get to profile them, I like to look for evidence of their personality traits.) As allied commander and later as president of the United States, General Dwight Eisenhower demonstrated the talent for impromptu speaking that is typical of this group.

According to historian Merle Miller, Ike's performance with the reporters after the Yalta conference prompted President Roosevelt's Press Secretary Steve Early to comment that Eisenhower's was "the most magnificent performance of any man at a press conference that I've ever seen. He knows the facts, he speaks freely and frankly, and he has a sense of humor, he has poise, and he has command."[4] Speaking of that same press conference, Ike's aid Colonel Butcher said, "I marveled the way he turned possibilities for error into diplomatic but honest answers."[5]

Unconventional, respond candidly and openly. Watching Spontaneous people like Oprah, Terry Bradshaw, and Deion Sanders, you notice that each one is his or her own person. They say what they think, and they don't take themselves seriously.

These characteristics often are singled out in the "Awesome Traits Exercise" during team sessions.

I remember one example in particular when four ladies made up the Spontaneous/Unstructured group. In telling about their strengths and struggles, they said, "We like to fly by the seat of the pants." (This old aviation expression originally meant flying by instinct and the feel of g-forces in your seat, rather than by precise reference to gauges.) They went on to tell the story of how they had attended an office costume party wearing a set of homemade wings strapped to their bottoms. Their story was a riot, and it really gave us great insights into the awesome traits of the Spontaneous personality style.

Out-of-the-box thinking and expression is often the norm for Spontaneous people, because they rarely allow themselves to get totally into a box. Rules, lines, procedures, and protocol are not the final word for these folks. They use them when there is a purpose, but when they limit their instincts they are likely to ignore them entirely. General Patton was a stickler for discipline and strictly followed orders and enforced regulations most of the time. However, when they conflicted with his battlefield judgment, he didn't hesitate to ignore orders and rules, if he was willing to take responsibility for the outcome.[6]

SPONTANEOUS STRUGGLES

Disorganized, skimp on preparation, and then wing it too much. As mentioned earlier, the Spontaneous mind tends to work randomly and at warp-8 speed. These characteristics make organization an unnatural act for this group. Trying to keep up with papers, schedules, and assignments, as well as keys, glasses, organizers, and countless other things can be an almost debilitating experience for them.

Generally, the Spontaneous have good intentions of storing or situating their things in some logical order so they can find them later. Unfortunately, they often neglect the tedious work of really organizing them, because they are in too much of a hurry to stop and do it right the first time. And, many times, something else attracts their attention and their minds launch into different directions. Even when they do organize, they may not be able to remember which folder something is in or which organizational scheme they used.

In today's fast-paced environment, there is some good news and bad news for this group. The good news is that there are a lot of good tools and there is training available to help with organization. The bad news is that there is a lot more to organize—more information, more meetings, more phone calls, and more e-mail—and it's coming at an increasing rate. The best advice for these folks is to get training, work at it, and enlist highly organized teammates and associates to assist. Also, have enough self-doubt and fear of failure to check and double-check yourself.

Detail preparation is also a challenge for this group. Although they may be well aware of the five "Ps" of prior preparation mentioned in the previous chapter, it's still very difficult for them to sit down and do the work. They procrastinate because it requires detailed, linear, internal processing that is difficult—even painful—for them. Their overly optimistic appraisal of how much work it's going to take also causes problems. And even though they may do their best work when they are in the crisis mode, they may neglect important preparation until it's too late. The results are predictable: They are more susceptible to incomplete assignments, missed deadlines, and often just leaving some things unfinished.

To overcome this struggle, there are two antidotes. First, they should step back and look at managing themselves, as if they were their own bosses (which of course they are). If that doesn't work, then they need someone else to help—perhaps coaches. Coaches (could be associates, supervisors, or managers) hold them accountable to accomplish the tasks and events in a timely manner.

Overlook details, impulsive, get distracted, lose focus, and don't finish. As you probably know, a growing number in our population have now been diagnosed with Attention Deficit Disorder (ADD), but an even larger number have Attention to Detail Disorder, and many in the Spontaneous group often fall into this category.

To the Methodical person, this lack of attention to detail can seem like a character flaw. But in reality it's just the by-product of the natural talents of the Spontaneous group. Stop for a moment and recall that we have been very up front in listing some difficult struggles for all the personality groups. Rather than judge struggles as wrong or bad, we just need to perceive them as part of the package and accept people for who they are.

If you really want to understand why Spontaneous people avoid details, just watch their body language when they are trying to absorb them. Their random access memory systems are not very well equipped to absorb and file those little pieces of data. When the minutia is streaming toward them, you can almost see a dark cloud descend over their countenances. Very quickly, the details start deflecting off their heads like hail hitting a Texas pickup.

The best thing they can do is just say, "Whoa, buddy, this dog won't hunt. Your details are not sticking right now, so let's start with the main points and see if I can connect the dots. Then I'll fill in the details as I need them."

Distractibility and lack of focus are struggles that also hound this group. Their natural radar works best in the search mode; so, even when they do lock on to something, it's easy for them to get distracted by something else and lose focus on their primary assignments. The result is that they may start projects only to lose interest and move on to the latest, newest, and most exciting opportunities.

The struggle to gain focus and avoid distractions will always be a challenge for most Spontaneous people. At the same time, it offers them an area of great potential for personal and professional growth. Developing mental discipline and learning to live by the mantra of "focus, focus, focus" can be a big help. Likewise, learning to prioritize tasks in order to bring projects to closure will be important.

Ideal Work Environment. Spontaneous people do best in environments that require flexibility and on-the-spot responses. They need situations that allow them to work with broad con-

cepts in impromptu settings. Most importantly, their work should involve a minimum of detailed and structured assignments.

Managing Spontaneous. Let them know that as their teammate and coach you will help them reach their highest potential by giving them maximum opportunities with their talents. Likewise, in a lighthearted way tell them that you anticipate their struggles and will use the stick-and-carrot method to help them in those areas. Use strong accountability to keep them on task and then, when they make it to the finish line, celebrate to reward and reinforce their efforts. Remember they thrive (and learn best) in the heat of battle. If you think they are reasonably prepared, throw them in the fire and watch them excel.

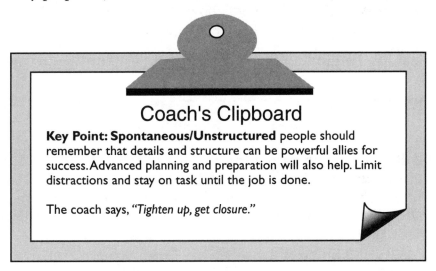

Coach's Clipboard

Key Point: Spontaneous/Unstructured people should remember that details and structure can be powerful allies for success. Advanced planning and preparation will also help. Limit distractions and stay on task until the job is done.

The coach says, *"Tighten up, get closure."*

Left, Right, and Mid-Range—all needed

In military operations, these two seemingly opposing philosophies have shown that success comes from the best of both the Left Side and the Right Side of this personality continuum. Staff officers comb through intelligence, weather reports, logistical data, and a hundred other sources in order to analyze all the data to plan and prepare in detail for an operation. But once the shooting starts, we expect commanders to synthesize the dynamics of the real battlefield and make on-the-spot decisions and execute the best course of action.

This combination of structure and flexibility (tight and loose) analysis and synthesis planning and execution is also essential in business or any complex operation. Teamwork between the Methodical and Spontaneous personalities is always going to be critical to success.

Relationship Keys

Learn to recognize and encourage the unique talents of your opposite-side teammates. Understand their needs and expect their struggles. Let them know how much you value them because of who they are, and don't be offended when they act like themselves instead of like you.

Revisiting your home on this range

Recall the information you read in Chapters 11 and 12 and reflect on the block you chose at the beginning of Chapter 11. **Place a mark** on the continuum below where you most *naturally* fall. (The stronger you feel about your natural behavior, the farther toward the left or right your mark should go.)

FACTOR 4
Order and Detail
Conscientiousness

Spontaneous	Mid-Range	Methodical
Unstructured		*Structured*

© 2002 RightPath Resources, Inc.
All rights reserved. Used with permission.

Put all four together to determine your profile.

Look back at the end of Chapters 6, 8, 10, and the graphic on page 136 to capture your marks from each range. Plot them here and then compare your graph to those in Appendix C to discover your most likely blended profile.

RightPATH 4 Graph

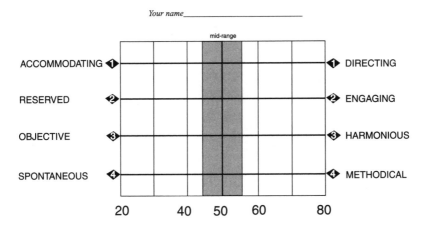

© 2002 RightPath Resources, Inc.
All rights reserved. Used with permission.

---

1. RightPath 4 Profile™ uses Spontaneous–Methodical. RightPath 6 Profile™ uses Structured–Unstructured.

2 For more on factor relationships, see Appendix B.

3. "Oprah," *Fortune* (April 1, 2002), 60.

4. Merle Miller, *Ike the Soldier: As They Knew Him* (NY: Perigee Books, The Putnam Publishing Group, 1987), 751.

5. Ibid., 752.

6. Alan Axelrod, *Patton on Leadership: Strategic Lessons for Corporate Warfare* (NY: Simon & Schuster, 1999).

CHAPTER 13

MATCHING TALENTS/TRAITS TO TASKS

Great leadership can come from any behavioral profile. When you were reading through the eight traits discussed in Chapters 5 to 12, you may have automatically (and incorrectly) assumed that certain traits were superior for the leadership role.

I can think of no better way of illustrating that leadership can come from any trait or profile than by comparing James Adams and Thomas Jefferson. Note the achievements of these two patriots.

John Adams

- Massachusetts delegate and leading member of the Continental Congress
- Leading advocate and signer of the Declaration of Independence
- Author, Massachusetts Constitution
- Diplomat to France
- Negotiator and signer of the Paris Peace Accord, ending the war with England
- Minister to England
- First vice president of U.S.
- Second president of U.S.
- President of the Massachusetts Society of Arts and Sciences

Thomas Jefferson

- Delegate to the Virginia House of Burgesses and the Continental Congress
- Author of the Declaration of Independence
- Governor of Virginia
- Diplomat to France
- Negotiator and signer of the Paris Peace Accord, ending the war with England
- Secretary of State U.S.
- Vice president of U.S.
- President of U.S. (2 terms)
- Founder of the University of Virginia

Aside from George Washington, Adams and Jefferson were the two most influential leaders of the American Revolution, and they were virtually opposite in every way except for their common love of knowledge and their dedication to their country.

In the exceptionally documented and highly moving biography, *John Adams*, Pulitzer-prize-winning author David McCullough offers detailed insights into the very different personalities of Adams and Jefferson. The following chart outlines their traits as related by McCullough and other authors. I have classified them according to the eight traits discussed earlier and encourage you to look back and compare them to the descriptions in the earlier chapters. (Also, you may want to compare Adams to the Directing and Motivator profiles and Jefferson to the Deep Thinker and Cautious Thinker profiles in Appendix C.)

MATCHING TALENTS/TRAITS TO TASKS ❖ 141

Accommodating	Directing
Thomas Jefferson	**John Adams**
• Never blunt or assertive • Subtle, soft-spoken • Could be ambivalent • Moved slowly, cautious	• Assertive, self-assured, got results • Candid, boldly asserted his opinion • Intolerant of indifference • Ambitious, wanted to "seize hold"

Reserved	Engaging
Thomas Jefferson	**John Adams**
• In Congress, scarcely said a word • Serene, somewhat remote • Rarely revealed his inner feelings • Little sense of humor • Refused to be drawn out or explain himself	• A talker, entertaining, thrived on company • Generous, affectionate, cared deeply for his friends • Responsive to praise, good sense of humor • Passionate, quick to anger, but forgiving • Regretted being proud and conceited

Objective	Harmonious
John Adams	**Thomas Jefferson**
• Let others know where he stood • Confronting, never learned to flatter • Impetuous, tactless • Cranky, impulsive	• Gracious, rarely disagreed with anyone to his face • Shrank from the contentiousness of politics • Avoided confrontation • Abhorred dispute

Spontaneous	Methodical
John Adams	**Thomas Jefferson**
• Extemporaneous • Struggled with bringing order to his life • Always had a clutter of books and papers • Couldn't stay focused with just one book or subject	• Always polite, diplomatic • Could be intentionally ambiguous • A man of science • Neat, kept letter perfect records, detailed

Adapted from *John Adams*, by David McCullough, (NY: Simon & Schuster, 2002).

Clearly these two giants of the Revolutionary period were great leaders, yet they were opposite in their natural talents.

So if you have wondered what the best traits for a leader are, the answer for each person is that it's his or her own traits. You will be your best when you know your strengths and struggles and you manage them appropriately and then act with the courage and commitment to do what you know to be the right thing.

Matching Talents to Tasks

Now that we've seen that leadership can come from any profile, I want to turn to another powerful principle related to talents that at first may seem to be a contradiction to what we just said. Many positions require special talents for success, so there can be a significant advantage to matching the person to the job. Without this match or job fit, we are back to the square peg in the round hole, and high performance is unlikely. With a good talent-to-task fit, the chances of success are much greater.

During my days as a career consultant, I saw the pain in people's lives—the result of not using good criteria for making career decisions. I can remember one man in his early forties who came to talk with me at the conclusion of a career workshop. He had enjoyed an excellent career in high-tech engineering but had left to go to seminary and then into evangelical preaching. He explained that he was recovering from a deep bout of depression and was thinking about going back into his technical career field. When I asked why he had left it, he explained that it was to honor his parents, who had been in the ministry and had always wanted him to do the same.

I explained that his parents' hopes were obviously well meaning, but they did not fully understand that his talents were not suited for that occupation. (His Accommodating, extremely Introverted, Harmonious, and highly Methodical talents were not a good fit for that role.) I told him that he could be a godly servant by fulfilling his calling to be an excellent engineer. It seemed to me that if he and his parents had followed conventional wisdom—or biblical wisdom for that matter—he could have avoided much suffering.

Another friend who is a career counselor told me of seeing a middle-aged man weep as he read his career assessment, saw his true shape, and realized that he had spent most of his adult life struggling to succeed as a round peg in a square hole.

A few years ago, after doing a live radio interview broadcast from the floor of a convention, a man came up to tell me that he had taken our behavioral profile and had shown the results to his boss. Based on this information, he was given a different role in the company. Within two years, he had three promotions and was at that time a national sales manager. The profile had helped him and his boss see the shape of his talents, and they had used that information to find his best match to the benefit of everyone and bottom-line profits.

Though our society has made great progress in many fields, such as science and technology, conventional wisdom (putting the square peg in the square hole) is still not commonly used. A friend working in human resources in a Fortune 500 company further confirmed that assertion. He said that he had recently attended a meeting on retention, and the idea of matching people to their jobs was not even on the agenda as a solution to the talent losses they were experiencing. Yet all the data suggests that this is one of the major reasons why people change jobs and even careers.

One of my goals (and I trust that it's one of yours also) is to make this conventional wisdom about job-fit the standard for individuals and companies. To that end, let's take a closer look at how to match the person to the task.

Reflect for a moment on Chapter 4, when we initially discussed measuring talents and we plotted size talents on a bell curve. You learned how talents associated with weight/size might be directly related to work success. It was obvious that a 115-pound person was not going to play in the NFL; nor was someone of 300 pounds going to be a jockey.

Then we used the bell-curve concept to look at behavioral talents. Using the personality profile model, we saw that key behavioral talents could be measured and displayed on a graphic continuum, with everyone in the world having a natural "go to" position (score) on that scale. You will recall that we said that at least two-thirds of the population will have clearly defined Left-Side or Right-Side talents, and the other one-third (Mid-Range) will be less defined but more flexible.

Now I'll admit that the subject of talents is very complex. There is much we don't understand about them, but we do know that behavioral talents are usually among the most important for long-term success in most lines of work. So if we can measure behavioral talents, then we can know something about a person's shape (for simplicity let's just say square or round), and thus we are able to gain insights to apply conventional wisdom. At the same time, we need to measure the shape of the job, using similar criteria—behavioral talents. Without that knowledge, we will never know if we have a match.

You would think that you could read through a job or position description and learn about the shape of the job. Of course that's rarely the case because, generally, they are not written in behavioral terms. Unless the person who is developing the job description has considerable experience at measuring behaviors and has extensive knowledge of the job, they wouldn't know which behaviors were most important. Even then it would be a subjective process.

After several years of working on this problem, we came up with the idea of developing a statistically derived template or benchmark of the position, using the profiles of those who are highly successful performers. The idea was to analyze the successful performers group and identify behaviors that had a high frequency of occurrence within a narrow scoring range.

Going back to the analogy of the NFL linemen, if we determine that 95 percent of them weigh in the range of 270 to 350 pounds, then we know that the likelihood of someone making it in that position who weighs 200 pounds is extremely low. If they had good athletic skills, then we might want to look at them for other positions, where their size talents were a better fit.

Further, a related action that we can take is to look at those who are below average or unsuccessful performers, to see how they compare on these same talents. If the shape (template of key talents) of low performers is noticeably different in some traits, we know that the common behaviors of high performers are indications of key talents for success. Using this process, we have now built a template that provides measurable insights into the shape of the position. And, as you know, you build a template to replicate something. In this case, our goal is to replicate success in a particular position.

Let's now take a look at how this information can be used to see how well the person matches the position. We are going to look at four different graphics. The first graphic below shows a benchmark profile (or template) for an outside sales position. The second graphic shows a comparison of a person named Denny Detailist to the sales benchmark. The third graphic shows a comparison of the sales benchmark to Mindy Motivator. And finally there is a comparison of Denny to a bench-mark for a position in the operations department. Here is the sales position benchmark.

RightPATH 4 Benchmark Report
Position: Sales Associate

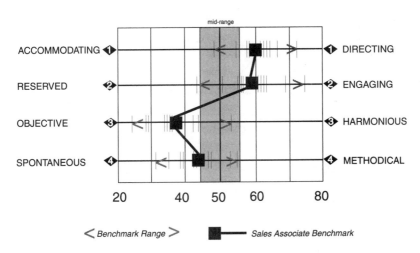

© 2002 RightPath Resources, Inc.
All rights reserved. Used with permission.

In the sales position graphic above, the chevrons mark the range of scores for the top performers in each factor. The tics or hash marks indicate individual scores, which form a scatter plot. As you can see, most of the scores tend to cluster in the same general areas of the graph. The clustering of scores indicates that the people used to form this successful sales profile benchmark were behaviorally quite similar. Also, note the benchmark average scores for this group, indicated by the dark squares and solid lines in the graph.

We see that the template indicates that the successful profile for this particular sales position is someone who is Directing, Engaging, Objective, and Spontaneous. Let's keep that in mind as we look at the next graph that compares Denny to the sales benchmark. (Note: Sales position benchmarks will vary, depending on the product and the situation.)

RightPATH 4 Benchmark Comparison Report
Position: Sales Associate
Individual: Denny Detailist

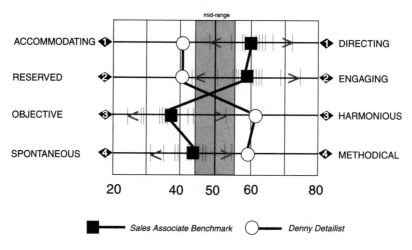

© 2002 RightPath Resources, Inc.
All rights reserved. Used with permission.

As you can see, Denny's shape is quite different from that of our sales benchmark. He is Accommodating, Reserved, Harmonious, and Methodical, so we know that his talents do not seem to match our sales profile. We can further validate his talents through other information and during the interview. If these other insights confirm Denny's results, it would be wise to begin looking for another position that would be a better fit for Denny's strengths. Next, let's compare Mindy Motivator to the benchmark.

RightPATH 4 Benchmark Comparison Report
Position: Sales Associate
Individual: Mindy Motivator

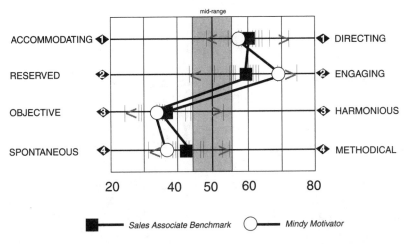

© 2002 RightPath Resources, Inc.
All rights reserved. Used with permission.

Mindy's profile above seems to be a fairly close match to our sales template. She's a little less Directing and a little more Engaging than the average for the group. She also will be slightly less patient and less organized, but her scores on all four factors are within the chevrons that indicate the range of scores for our benchmark group. There are other things to be considered, but we do have a very good indication that Mindy has the natural talents needed to successfully perform in this sales position.

Since Denny is a high-quality person that we would like to have on our team, let's consider him for other jobs where he might fit. One such position is an opening in the operations department. Let's take a look and see how he matches up.

RightPATH 4 Benchmark Comparison Report
Position: Operations
Individual: Denny Detailist

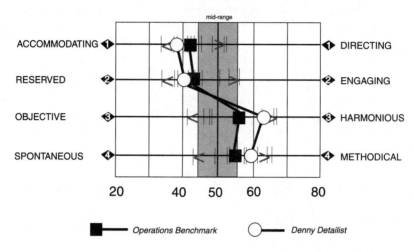

© 2002 RightPath Resources, Inc.
All rights reserved. Used with permission.

At a glance we can see that Denny seems to be a good match for this position. His talents seem very similar to those who are successful performers in operations. As with Mindy, this does not guarantee that he will be successful, but it does give us a high confidence that he has the natural talents that are needed. The odds are that Denny is going to be much more successful and much less stressed in this position than in the sales job. And, with this talent-to-task match, he is much more likely to know the joy of swimming downstream, with the grain of his natural bent, than swimming upstream in the sales job.

These illustrations are designed to show, generally, the powerful concept that underlies the conventional wisdom of matching the talents of the person to the requirements of the job. For those who are sports fans, remember when Michael Jordan left basketball and tried to make it in baseball?

We all know that Michael is one of the most phenomenal athletes of all time; but, as talented as he is, baseball was not the best fit for him. Maybe with a lot of work he could have been an average minor leaguer. Fortunately, for him and all of us who have enjoyed seeing him play, he went back to basketball, the sport in which his natural talents enabled him to be a top performer.

As we close out the formal discussion on talents, I trust that you have a much better understanding of yourself and others. I also hope that you feel much better prepared to be a talent scout and talent manager. Some of the most satisfying things I've ever done were to help people understand their talents and start using them to swim downstream. It's times like those that I feel like I'm also going with the flow.

Coach's Clipboard

Key Point: Matching the talents of the person to the needs of the job gives the greatest likelihood for success. With current employees, if a position change is not possible, try to realign some of their duties to better match their talents.

Action Items

1. How well are you matched to the tasks in your work?
2. How about your team? Who is not fulfilling his or her potential because of being mismatched in his or her job?

Caution: In this chapter, I've provided a basic explanation, intended to show you how behavioral talents (one element of shape) can provide an effective way to help implement the conventional wisdom that we all know works best. However, this process should never be used as a cookie-cutter approach to hiring.

Although profiles provide accurate and powerful information, and benchmarks are a very good tool for identifying key talents, there are other important elements in the hiring or career decision-making process. The behavioral piece discussed here is very important, but it is just one piece of information among many that should be used. (For more information on this, see "Due Diligence for Hiring" in Appendix D.)

❖

TEAMWORK

Have you stopped to think, *Why teams in the first place?* Fundamentally, there are three primary reasons why individuals band together. First, to provide the *strength of mutual support*. There is strength in numbers; and, whether it's in platoons, work teams, tribes, neighborhoods, or nations, individuals seem to realize that the odds of survival and success increase when they're part of a group.

In addition to protection, mutual support enables a joint effort that provides the power needed to do work projects that are too large to be done by one person. Remember how our ancestors teamed up to raise heavy beams and stones to build houses, barns, and bridges.

Also there is the issue of *companionship*. Generally, people want to be part of a community. We all have some innate needs for friendship and a sense of belonging, so we tend to form associations with others to meet our social needs; and, many of these are met through our relationships at work.

Teams also provide us the opportunity to gain efficiency and effectiveness through a *division of labor*. By banding together, a group of individuals can blend an assortment of unique individual talents and skills to achieve what would not be possible working alone. Just think of the way a football teams uses 300-pound linemen and 190-pound wide receivers.

These three basic advantages of teams (strength of mutual support, companionship, and division of labor) have remained unchanged throughout history and are the impetus for teamwork in today's workplace and society.

It may have been somewhat of a surprise for many that the advent of technology has brought more, not less, importance to teamwork in the workplace. It's a hot item in the business world and it should be. The more we can improve our teamwork, the better will be our results and relationships.

In this section, we'll consider *diversity* first and see the importance of different talents and viewpoints for team success. Second, we'll address the impact of *unity* on team effectiveness. Next, we'll observe the role of *trust* in both unity and diversity. Finally, by examining several case studies, we'll look at *team dynamics*.

CHAPTER 14

DIVERSITY:
Capitalizing on Differences to Build Strong Teams

A fundamental reason for assembling a team is to have a division of labor. By bringing together two or more people, you have the opportunity to focus multiple talents and maximize both effectiveness and efficiency. Thus, in team building, one of the essential challenges is to capitalize on differences and use a diversity of talents to build strong teams.

However, whenever you assemble a team, you have a built-in potential for conflict. One only has to watch a few minutes of the nightly news or read a few pages of history to know that differences cause most of the strife in society. Just think for a moment about the current conflicts related to religion, culture, language, economics, geography, sex, age, political parties, and education. The list could go on, but the basic truth is that wherever two or more are gathered there will be differences and, consequently, there will be a high potential for conflict.

So, we have a real dilemma: *teams need both unity and diverse talents, but differences (diverse talents) have a natural tendency to divide and prevent unity.* The mutual trust that teams need is continually undermined by their diversity, and this brings a significant and ongoing challenge to teamwork. That's why one of the major goals of this book is to help you better understand, accept, and value others who are different and thus neutralize the divisive power of differences.

Diversity in many forms

Diversity is a wonderful word that has come to have a somewhat narrow use in American culture in the last thirty years. Most often, it is used to refer specifically to having a good mix of race and gender (and good relations among them) at all organizational levels in the workplace. As the baby boomers' hair turns grayer, diversity will increasingly relate to age as well.

Typical diversity programs play an important role in the American business culture. They educate and remind us of the need to identify and remove any prejudice and bias that undermines fairness and respect for others in the workplace. These programs can help us change our attitudes and behaviors to match our professed values. Clearly, all of us can benefit from personal growth in this area. However, challenges of diversity are much broader than race, gender, and age.

This became obvious during a team session at a plant, when I noticed that there were worldviews from the following different camps.

Management and union: They need each other, but because they think they have different priorities they sometimes forget that they have a common goal.

Racial and ethnic: Anglos and African Americans were predominant at this somewhat rural location. In metro areas, it would include at least Hispanic, Asian, Middle Eastern, and European. Different ethnic groups often have different traditions, approaches, and diverse ways of looking at problems.

Geographical culture: Northerners and Southerners had different ways of viewing things but, in general, they had learned to adapt to each other. (Sometimes this can be more of a challenge than racial differences.)

Provincial culture: Most employees were locals and had worked/lived in the community all their lives, but some were outsiders.

Experience: Seasoned veterans who know the tried-and-true methods had to work alongside "new people" who wanted to try different ideas.

Age: The steadiness and wisdom of senior workers was at times a sharp contrast with the boldness of youth. (Also, there can be significant culture and values differences among those who grew up in the 50s, 60s, 70s, 80s, and 90s. In previous eras, these changes occurred at a much slower rate.)

Gender: Males and females had different agendas and worldviews in several areas. Both sides can feel threatened.

Natural talents (personality): This was one of the major areas of conflict. Different talents took different approaches to issues of control, people, conflict and pace, structure, and details.

These eight areas of differences offer at least sixteen worldviews that affect teams in the workplace. (We could add others, such as parents versus non-parents, single versus married, and well educated versus uneducated.) So, at any point, a team member has many possibilities for being different from someone else in the group. During one session, I observed one team member attribute problems to no less than four of these "different-from" groups.

Because some of these areas of differences are so difficult to talk about, behavioral issues provide a more acceptable and workable way to learn and value differences. And the more we can get people to see that diversity means valuing all people, regardless of their differences, the faster we will see fears and prejudices disappear and the more we will see diversity with unity.

If we can get people to take a broader understanding of the word *diversity*, it will also help us achieve diversity in a broader sense, i.e., capitalizing on the advantages of different talents and ideas to build highly successful teams.

Overcoming the problems of differences

An important goal of the earlier chapters was to help you gain a more objective viewpoint of yourself and others. If you have identified and removed some of your old filters and distorted lenses, you will be able to see others with a more accurate and balanced perspective. This type of awareness will enable you to experience the powerful and positive benefits of individual differences. Now let's examine other ways that teams can overcome the divisive nature of differences and capitalize on them to build stronger teams.

Clarify areas of unity and diversity. One of the problems teams typically have is in understanding areas in which teams need unity and in which they need to allow for individual differences. Consider the lists below.

Needs to be the same (Unity)	Can be different (Diversity)
• Mission	• Talents, struggles
• Commitment, loyalty	• Motivations, ambitions
• Corporate values	• Ideas, interests, passions
• Opportunity	• Needs, expectations
• Policies/discipline	• Styles, worldviews

Typically, teams should encourage diversity and individuality as much as possible and have a minimum of core items on the "Unity" list. These conceptual lists will suit most organizations; however, the nature of some organizations and their missions may require tighter unity and discipline, and some areas on the right column may move to the left. Regardless of the situation, it's always important for there to be a common understanding and acceptance about what needs to be the same (unity) and what can be different (diversity). When there is disagreement or confusion on these two lists, there is likely to be a breakdown in trust, commitment, and team unity.

Recognize that a diversity of talents and ideas is powerful. For an eye-opener on the richness of this word, type "diversity" in your word processor and then select the thesaurus. Here are a few of the synonyms for that word: *variety, innovation, assortment, difference, multiplicity, range, mixture, variance, change,* and *turnabout.* When we view diversity as an infusion of different talents and ideas, it takes on a much broader perspective than just equal opportunity.

Almost all the research on successful companies today emphasizes the importance of having different viewpoints and a constant influx of new ideas for business success. One of the common themes presented by Jim Collins and Jerry Porras in *Built to Last: Successful Habits of Visionary Companies* (forerunner to *Good to Great*) is that visionary companies seek unwavering unity in the area of "core ideology" (core values plus purpose), but at the same time they seek diverse ideas for new methodologies and products.[1]

Relationships that will unite different talents into successful teams

The graphic below provides a conceptual view of some of the essential components in uniting diverse individuals to form a successful team. By now you should have a good understanding of the different behavioral talents. Here and in subsequent chapters we'll look at how to move individuals toward trust, unity, and team success.

Team development: from diversity to unity to success

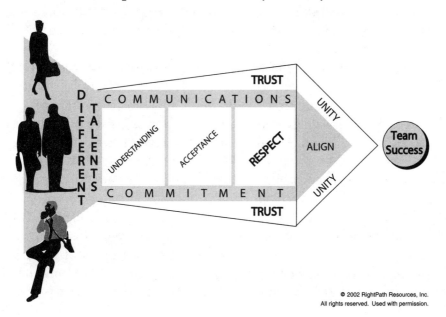

© 2002 RightPath Resources, Inc.
All rights reserved. Used with permission.

Communications: make sure everyone is on the same page.
The POWs learned from our unique experience in the camps
that communications are the lifeblood of any organization.
Without adequate and clear communications, individuals cannot remain focused on the same goals and cannot coordinate
their activities for mutual support. In essence, most of the advantages of teams are lost if communications break down. Our
captors knew this well and went to the extreme to prevent our
communications, but they never stopped us for long.[2]

Can you imagine what would happen to an orchestra's performance if it could not see the conductor? Or what about the
football team that can't hear the quarterback's signals? It's the
same on an office team when people are not getting the information that they need to do their jobs. Communications must
flow smoothly in all directions—vertically and horizontally—
to include peers, customers, and vendors.

Communications problems plague every team to some degree. In nearly every team-dynamics session we conduct, the
group consensus is usually that communications need improvement. Although it does take time and energy to improve
in this area, better communications bring positive gains in all
areas of teamwork and organizational effectiveness. Most important, it's also the only way you can keep team members on
the same frequency and moving toward or maintaining a state
of togetherness and unity.

**Understanding: view differences as just different—not
wrong.** Again, we need to reflect on the concept of objectivity.
As we come to see ourselves as being imperfect (having struggles as well as strengths), we are empowered to see others in a
better light. The challenge of seeing ourselves honestly, rather
than focusing on someone else's differences, has been around
for centuries. An Arabian proverb says, "The camel never sees
its own hump, but its neighbor's hump is ever before its eyes."[3]

Likewise, the wisdom from Jesus was to get the logs out of
our own eyes so that we could see clearly to help the people who
have specks in their eyes.[4] But you and I know this is not an easy
process. Typically, we have looked through the logs so long that
we don't even realize they are there. Yet, dealing honestly with

our own shortcomings can have a leveling effect that positions us to see others with more balance and kindness. And by setting aside our judgmental viewpoints, we are able to move from seeing different as wrong to seeing different as just different and then to valuing differences as complementary.

Acceptance: value different strengths and accommodate different struggles. With understanding, we are able to move to acceptance and begin to work with those who are different. We don't have to be threatened by "different" being better than we are; we can see it as being an addition to who we are. We begin to see that those who are different bring talents and ideas to our team that we will never have in our own repertoire. We can begin to capitalize on our differences, because we see how different talents fill different roles and functions. We see how struggles, others and ours, are just a part of the package that comes with strengths. We give our teammates room to be themselves and are not surprised or offended by their struggles.

Whenever I think about valuing differences, I am reminded of an "aha!" experience by one of the participants in a senior leadership team. During the "take-aways" discussion at the end of the day, a man I'll describe as a senior statesman shared, "I've learned that I need to listen more to the goofy ideas of some of these 'creative' people. Eventually, one of them may make us a lot of money."

From the kindness in his voice and the look on his face, I knew he had indeed learned a way to communicate acceptance and value to some of those "different" people. And I knew that it would be detected, and some people would feel more valued and more united with their leader.

Respect: honor others and celebrate differences. First, we need to respect others because it is the right thing to do. Second, by showing respect, we give unconditional acceptance that lifts other people and empowers them to achieve their full potential. This issue of respect is so important that it would be worthwhile to stop for a moment to consider what it looks like. Recently I've given surveys to several groups of people—to ask what behaviors and attitudes make them feel respected and disrespected. The following is a short summary.[5]

People feel respected when you	People feel disrespected when you
act like they're important	act like you're superior
encourage them	put them down, cut them off
show interest in them	focus mainly on yourself
accept them "as is"	try to change them
seek their input	force your idea on them
listen with genuine concern	ignore or interrupt them
honor their views/opinions	minimize/discount what they've said
allow them to make decisions	try to control them
are open and honest	are evasive, two-faced
recognize their turf	ignore proper boundaries
believe in them	criticize

In comparing these two lists, you can see that the behaviors that communicate respect demonstrate honor to others by giving (or giving up) something to the other person. Those that communicate disrespect, in effect, take something away (usually in order to protect or build up the person who is being disrespectful). This giving/taking concept is very helpful in identifying whether your behaviors are communicating respect.

Generally, those who are always trying to protect or boost themselves are less trusted. Conversely, those who focus on others with attitudes and behaviors of respect are more trusted.

An others-oriented attitude also enables us to see that those who are different have qualities that we can admire and even want to emulate. They can be role models for our personal growth and can help us overcome some of our struggles. Our humility about ourselves, combined with our respect for our teammates, forms a powerful bond for building relationships.

Align: adapt to work together and meet each other's needs. If we are significantly different, then we need to learn how to adapt our behaviors to align with others. I relate this to the way a fast fighter aircraft and a slow-flying tanker have to adapt to align and carry out an in-flight refueling operation. (Ships at sea taking on replenishments also have to make similar uncomfortable adaptations to accomplish their missions.)

To make the refueling connection, both aircraft have to be

at the same speed, on the same heading, and at virtually the same altitude. At the rendezvous speed, the fighter has slowed down to the point of being uncomfortable and the tanker has increased speed above its normal comfort level.

Flying in such close proximity with limited maneuverability is uncomfortable for the fighter pilot even under the best of circumstances. During night and bad weather conditions, it's an even greater challenge. Ultimately, only when each pilot/crew makes appropriate (usually uncomfortable or awkward-feeling) adjustments to align are they able to team up for a successful refueling.

The issues of alignment are similar for an office team. For example, an Accommodating person like Denny (see the following graphic), working with a Directing person like Mindy, may need to speak up more forcefully to communicate opinions and ideas. Likewise, a Directing person like Mindy may need to withhold some of her opinions and work harder at becoming an active listener. She should also encourage Denny to share his ideas.

During a team session, a real "Denny" and "Mindy" related how difficult this was, because it felt awkward and unnatural. However, they both agreed that these adjustments had enabled a significant improvement in their working relationship.

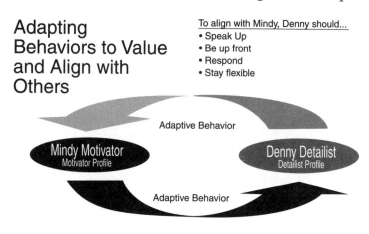

Adapting Behaviors to Value and Align with Others

To align with Mindy, Denny should...
• Speak Up
• Be up front
• Respond
• Stay flexible

Adaptive Behavior

Mindy Motivator
Motivator Profile

Denny Detailist
Detailist Profile

Adaptive Behavior

To align with Denny, Mindy should...
• Seek his input and actively listen without disagreeing
• Provide a supportive environment
• Acknowledge his talents for order and detail
• Recognize his need to work uninterrupted

© 2002 RightPath Resources, Inc.
All rights reserved. Used with permission.

Trust: guard your commitment to each other and the vision.
Trust enables teams to realize synergy and achieve more than
the sum of their talents would indicate. *With alignment and mutual trust, individuals don't have to spend time defending themselves or apologizing for their struggles. Rather, they anticipate
and accept each other's struggles.* Individuals know that they
can depend on their teammates to guard their blindside and
look out for their interests. Their energy is freed to focus completely on the challenges of the tasks ahead. The team is positioned to achieve its goals with maximum success.

On the other hand, trust is a two-edged sword. When it's
broken, the effects are very destructive and can quickly destroy
the ties that are holding a team together. When trust breaks
down, unity unravels and every component of teamwork starts
to collapse. Communications become more difficult, people
quit trying to align, respect falls away, acceptance is replaced
by criticism, and understanding breaks down. Commitment
to the team quickly deteriorates and what is left is a group of
talented individuals in a survival mode with an every-person-
for-himself (or herself) attitude.

Trust is such an essential and powerful ingredient in the
teamwork formula that it must be continually developed and
protected through conscious efforts. Because it is such a major issue on corporate teams, we'll look further at trust in the
next chapter.

Coach's Clipboard

Key Point: Trust is an essential that must be cultivated through acceptance, understanding, and respect. Capitalize on diversity by accepting and valuing differences.

Action Items
1. Use the list on page 156 as a starting point, and make a list of areas essential for unity in your organization and a list of areas in which diversity can and should exist.

2. Review the components of team success: commitment, communications, understanding, acceptance, respect, adapt/align. Which are affecting your team's trust, unity, and success positively? Negatively?

1. James C. Collins and Jerry I. Porras, *Built to Last, Successful Habits of Visionary Companies* (NY: Harper Business, Division of HarperCollins, 1994), Chapters 3 and 4.

2. For the most extensive history of American POWs in NVN, see Stuart I. Rochester and Frederick Kiley, *Honor Bound, The History of American Prisoners of War in Southeast Asia, 1961-1973* (Historical Office of the Secretary of Defense, Washington D.C. 1998).

3. Les Parrot III, Ph.D., *The Control Freak* (Wheaton: Tyndale House, 2000), 30.

4. Matthew 7:1-5, *The Holy Bible.*

5. For a more expansive list of relationship attributes, refer to the Attributes of Great Leaders in Appendix E.

CHAPTER 15

UNITY:
Committing to Common Goals and Each Other

Real teamwork begins when two or more individuals commit to give up some of their independence in order to *unite* to accomplish a shared vision or goal. Unity is not the absence of difference; it is the respect and coordination of differences.

Because so much has been written about teamwork in sports and the military, these two fields offer a ready source of information on teamwork. We'll take a look at some of their common elements of teamwork and then see how those teamwork lessons transfer to business and to society in general.

Sports teams focus on unity

Sports provide a tremendous learning lab from which we can learn many aspects of team dynamics, especially the importance of unity on team success. As outsiders we can observe a great deal, but it's also helpful to hear from the experts:

the players, coaches, and leaders who've experienced great team success.

Jennifer Trosper, recently inducted into the Academic All-America Hall of Fame (volleyball star at MIT), works in the Jet Propulsion Laboratory in Pasadena, California and is one of the nation's leading aerospace engineers. Trosper was prominent in the Mars Pathfinder project and cites her sports experience as having helped her significantly in her career. She says, "You have to know who to go to for specific things and utilize the whole team to get the job done. It's the same in sports. To learn how to work with people is very important, and sports was invaluable for that."[1]

Mike McCoy was an All-American defensive lineman at Notre Dame, a first-round NFL draft choice, and a ten-year veteran who played with the Packers, Raiders, and Giants. Mike is a friend who lives in the Atlanta, Georgia area, so I asked him to share his experiences.[2] He quickly identified four essential aspects of highly effective teams. He said first, "Good teams are usually made up of very diverse people who can come together for a common goal—for example, win the Superbowl."

Mike also pointed out that "it's important for individuals to have personal goals that support the team goals. For example, as a lineman, I might have goals for making a certain number of tackles and sacks during the season." He also said there is an understanding that "in addition to achieving your own goals, you help your buddies accomplish theirs, and you cover for them when they need help." Finally, he said, "Adversity plays a key role in bringing a team together. Good teams are usually energized and drawn together by adversity."

So from an NFL star we can take away these important insights about good teamwork. It includes the following:

➤ commiting to a common goal
➤ having personal goals that support the team goal
➤ helping teammates with mutual support
➤ coming together in adversity.

Another sport in which teamwork is extremely important is auto racing. During a typical NASCAR race, the difference in the first eight cars at the finish line can be less than two seconds. After several hours and 500 miles of racing, the trophy goes to the team that executes with the greatest precision and coordination between the mechanics and driver.

Successful race drivers have to be extremely competent, courageous, competitive, and confident—the kind of people we commonly think of as very self-sufficient. Yet, when interviewed they typically attribute much of their successes to the supporting cast that makes up their teams. The typical NASCAR team involves the efforts of more than fifty people working long hours each week to prepare the car.

On race day, nine members of the team form the pit crew, and by regulation only the pit crew is allowed to service and work on the car on the trackside of the pit wall. This crew can change four tires and refuel the car in less than sixteen seconds. During a typical race, the cars usually pit for service at least six to ten times. A small mistake by one person on the team can seriously affect the outcome of the race.

The importance of the entire team is underscored by driver Ernie Ervan's comment: "NASCAR has gotten so tough, it's easier to pass people through the pits than on the racetrack." (Ervan's remarks related to an announcer's comment that one second lost in the pits means three seconds lost on the racetrack.)[3]

Jeff Gordon, who won his third Winston Cup championship in 2001, is always quick to point out that success is a team effort. As a car owner and driver, he pushes teamwork to the maximum. Robbie Loomis, Jeff's crew chief, was kind enough to share some insights on teamwork from inside NASCAR and the Hendrick Motor Sports racing team that owns Jeff's car. When I asked Robbie how he viewed teamwork, he replied, "It means that everyone is involved and we're using their input."[4]

Robbie went on to say, "I like to use the analogy that when things are working well if one person spills a drink a teammate will jump down and start cleaning it up and another one will run get another soda. That's what it's about, making the next guy's job a little easier. Get everyone pulling *together* toward a common goal."

When selecting people for the team, Robbie believes, "It's important to pick people of strong character who will be willing to work with the other personalities of the group." During the difficult times of a thirty-six-race season, he reminds the team: "We're all in this together." Robbie said that he often shares his personal philosophy with the team: If you "work hard, give much, and expect little, good things will come your way." His words are consistent with the profile of Level 5 leaders described by Jim Collins in his popular book, *Good to Great*.

Sports coaches and athletes often use expressions like "togetherness" and "our team is really coming together now" to describe good teamwork. Legendary coach John Wooden said about UCLA's 1963–1964 undefeated season: "They worked so well together. I don't think I've ever had a team that worked so well *together*."[5]

Coach Lou Holtz is famous for his ability to motivate teams to achieve high goals. After taking over at the University of South Carolina in 1999, his team lost every game that first year. To build team unity, the next summer Coach Holtz held daily sessions before practice, during which players shared their life stories to include both victories and tragedies. This open sharing (transparency) appears to have had a dramatic effect on his team that fall. In one of the greatest turnarounds in college history, the team finished the season with a 8–4 record and defeated Ohio State in the Outback Bowl, followed by a 9–3 record in 2001 and another bowl victory at season's end.

When questioned about their success, South Carolina starting quarterback Phil Petty said, "I don't know what it is, but this team just plays very well *together*." He went on to say, "We believe in each other and we never, ever give up."[6]

Petty's comments about playing well together and believing in each other are consistent with the wider recognition that togetherness is important. If great coaches like John Wooden and Lou Holtz spend time working on togetherness, maybe we should all take note and do the same.

Coaches and players also know that not being together is a serious problem. Internal conflict on the Los Angeles Lakers basketball team during the playoffs of 1996 prompted basketball great Magic Johnson's comments: "So much has been going on, we never could get on the same page; we never could be as one."[7] A *USA Today* article on the same subject wrote that Johnson had said that "he was disappointed by his team's lack of *cohesion* and its finger-pointing in the series."[8]

Cohesion for team success

Military leaders have long known that cohesion (the military expression for togetherness) is an essential component of unit effectiveness. Cohesion is the glue that bonds people in a type of togetherness referred to as *ésprit de corps:* a spirit of unity that will withstand the physical and emotional stresses of military life in general and combat in particular.

Traditionally, the military uses both hardship and fun to build high morale and teamwork. Hardship in training is essential because it builds confidence in people's ability to persist through adversity into victory. Fun and revelry are important, because they enable people to get to know each other in a very transparent way and thus build the camaraderie that is so essential to teamwork.

During my military career, we regularly enjoyed social events, such as softball games, picnics, and parties at the military clubs, as a way to draw people together and build cohesion. These events allowed people to relax some of the formality of their roles and rank and relate as just real people. Looking back I can see that much of the respect, trust, and commitment we had for each other was developed during these social hours away from work.

One of my favorite authors (and a good friend), Laurie Beth Jones, emphasizes the important role of social life and fun as team-building tools. In an interview about her best-selling business book, *Jesus CEO*, she pointed out that with Jesus and His staff, "Everything seemed to be an occasion for a party." She goes on to say, "When people are playing, their defenses are down. You cannot play with someone you don't trust. So by engaging others in meaningful and non-agenda-oriented fun, a special kind of bonding occurs that cannot be measured or duplicated in any other way."[9]

The famous military strategist of the early 1800s, Prussian General Carl von Clausewitz (recently popularized as a source of management strategy), talked about cohesion: "An army that maintains its *cohesion* under the most murderous fire; that cannot be shaken by imaginary fears and resists well founded ones with all its might; . . . such an army *is imbued with the true military spirit.*"[10]

General S.L.A. Marshall did extensive research during and immediately following World War II on the ability of individuals to function in combat. His findings documented the critical importance of this spirit of togetherness for soldiers. Marshall noted, ". . . it is far more than a question of the soldier's need of physical support from other men. He must have at least some feeling of spiritual *unity* with them if he is to do an efficient job of moving and fighting. Should he lack that for any reason . . . he will become a castaway in the middle of a battle and as incapable of offensive action as if he were stranded somewhere without weapons."[11]

General George S. Patton also had strong opinions on teamwork and made it clear that he would not tolerate those who would undermine the cohesion on his teams: "Staff officers of inharmonious disposition, irrespective of their ability, must be removed. A staff cannot function properly unless it is a *united* family."[12]

Our leaders in the POW camps knew quite well that cohesive teamwork would be key to our survival. Unfortunately, so did our North Vietnamese captors, and this was the basis for a daily battle. They followed the standard communist tactics of torture and threats, followed by isolation and daily propaganda to try to split us and break the bond of our POW team.

We resisted with a strong commitment to each other and our mission: to live up to the Fighting Man's Code of Conduct and return with honor. It took that commitment and every ounce of creativity at our disposal to establish and maintain communications in the camps. But the winner of those battles was clear. We maintained great unity, with over 98 percent of the more than 600 POWs in the North remaining loyal to the team and returning with honor.

What fosters this unity?

Before proceeding, let's stop to review the terms that have been used to communicate this concept. It's been referred to as believing in each other, pulling together, playing well together, in this together, on the same page, as one, togetherness, oneness, cohesion, ésprit de corps, military spirit, spiritual unity, united family, and team unity. What they all seem to be describing is a special relationship in which team members make a commitment to the team and to each other that supersedes at least some of their independence.

We could say that unity is then a by-product of what can happen when individuals realize that they can only achieve their personal goals by achieving team goals and that they can't achieve either unless they support each other and share their talents. Unity, togetherness, and cohesion are likely to be present only to the degree that team members respond to this awareness with individual commitment.

The word *commitment* is certainly an appropriate word, but it can sound somewhat abstract and heavy. To make it more real and personal, we could also use the words *caring* or *caring about.*

Caring about what you're involved in is very important to Coach Holtz. In talking about his philosophy on caring, he says, "I don't know how you can be involved in anything and not care. I hate to be around people who don't care, and when they don't care they don't try to do things the right way. The greatest thing in the world is to be around people who genuinely care about what you are doing—there's enthusiasm and positiveness. I don't care if it's important to anybody else, as long as it's important to those who are involved in it."[13]

Whatever your role on a team is, it will be helpful to examine these three areas of commitment: to team goals, to personal goals, and to teammates. They encompass many of the necessary conditions for unity. Remember, the word *commitment* includes the idea that "I care; it's important to me."

Committed to team goals *(I care about the team goals.)*
- Team goals are important to me and to others on the team.
- Team purpose and specific mission are consistent with the goals of our organization, our team, and our personal careers.
- Team values are consistent with those of our corporate culture and our personal values.
- It is in my/our interest to participate on this team.

Bottom line: *Multiple talents are committed to the team goals.*

Committed to individual goals that are a subset of the team goals. *(I care about my own future and see this as a good thing for me.)* Realistically we have to consider this because, as my business partner Jerry likes to say, "We all listen mainly to one radio station, WIFM (What's Init For Me)." So it's important that there be a payoff for the individual; and there are many, such as the following:
- opportunity to achieve results that are not possible working alone
- opportunity to use talents in a more focused/specialized way
- opportunity for talents to be seen by more people
- opportunity for a diverse talent pool (help cover tasks I don't do well, don't enjoy)
- opportunity for teammates to provide encouragement to me
- additional opportunities for personal development.

Bottom line: *If the team wins, I win; and if I win, it helps the team.*

Committed to the people on the team *(I care about you, and I am for you.)*

➤ have a genuine interest in the welfare of teammates

➤ value what they bring to the table in terms of talents, energy, and so forth

➤ see their potential and regularly encourage them

➤ willing to actively listen to their ideas and solicit their input

➤ willing to accept that others are imperfect and give them room for error

➤ willing to set aside or delay some of my own agenda to help teammates succeed

➤ willing to share my talents and energy with the team

Bottom line: *In unity there is a powerful message: We are together.*

In July 2002, when nine miners unknowingly drilled into an abandoned mine in Sommerset, Pennsylvania, they were trapped almost 300 feet below the surface. Their underground chamber immediately began flooding. They remained alive in extreme conditions for three days until they were rescued. When they were back on top, they told the story of how they tied themselves together and vowed that they would die together or survive together. To avoid dying of hypothermia, they had taken turns huddling around each other to keep warm. Unity saved their lives.

If you review the three commitments above and then read the accounts of these miners, you will see that these were exactly the commitments they made. They are also the ones you need for unity on your team.

The best team situations offer an alignment of all three of these commitments: to team goals, to individual goals, to team members. Admittedly, getting these types of commitments is not easy. Commitments of any kind require a person to give up something, and we usually don't give up to people unless we know and trust them. Building an environment of trust is first and foremost the responsibility of leadership. We will examine both of those subjects (trust and leadership) in subsequent chapters.

Coach's Clipboard

Key Point: A commitment to common goals and each other brings a spirit of togetherness—a powerful unity.

Action Items
1. To what degree do your personal goals support team goals?
2. How committed are you to your teammates?
3. What can you do to support others and promote unity on your team?

1. Jack Carey, "Former MIT athlete earns Hall of Fame," *USA Today* (May 16, 2001).
2. Mike McCoy, phone interview, April 27, 2001.
3. Television interview, "NASCAR Racing," NBC (August 16, 1998).
4. Robbie Loomis, phone interview, April 9, 2002.
5. John Wooden, radio interview, "The Legends," ESPN (February 21, 2002).
6. Tony Barnhart, "Gamecocks Rally Keeps Perfect Run Alive," *Atlanta Journal-Constitution* (September 24, 2000) G1.
7. "Johnson Says Infighting Doomed Lakers in Playoffs," *Atlanta Journal-Constitution* (May 4, 1996) G8.
8. David DuPree, "Smith's Fun Night Ousts Lakers, 102-94" *USA Today* (May 3, 1996) 11c.
9. Tom Brown interview with Laurie Beth Jones, *Industry Week* (March 6, 1995).
10. Carl von Clausewitz, *On War*, (Princeton University Press, 1976/84), Chapter 5.
11. General S.L.A. Marshall, *Men Against Fire* (Peter Smith Publishers, reprint, 1990), 42.
12. Alan Axelrod, *Patton on Leadership: Strategic Lessons for Corporate Warfare* (NY: Simon & Schuster, 1999).
13. Lou Holtz, as quoted on Web site, Lou Holtz Hall of Fame, "His Philosophy," (http://members.tripod.com/~LouHoltzOnline/).

❖

CHAPTER 16

BUILDING TRUST

If you have the impression that trust is a major theme of this book, you're right. It is, and I think for good reason. Every day I become more convinced that trust is one of the essentials for effective leadership and teamwork. Evidently, corporate leaders see it the same way. We are seeing a significant emphasis in efforts to strengthen candor and trust among their teams.

With that in mind, let's delve into the concept of trust to gain more understanding of the basics. To do that I'd like to share some of the insights we've gained in working with teams at various levels in a number of companies.

Earlier, we looked at the following graphic to illustrate key components of teamwork.

Team development: from diversity to unity to success

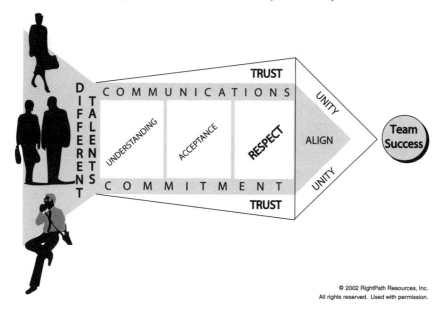

© 2002 RightPath Resources, Inc.
All rights reserved. Used with permission.

Reflect on these components and you can see three important principles about team development.

- Team success is directly tied to relationships.
- Good relationships require that people give to each other in order to align with the other person.

Give

- ☐ understanding
- ☐ acceptance
- ☐ respect
- ☐ commitment
- ☐ effort to communicate, and
- ☐ alignment by adapting

- To do all this giving requires an increasing amount of trust; we normally don't give when we don't trust.

Because trust is so fundamental, I recommend that you develop a habit of approaching every decision and action with the question, "Will this increase or decrease trust in the relationship and among the group?" This up-front awareness of the impact you are having on trust will go a long way toward building a stronger team. The information that follows is designed to help you evaluate that question.

Understand and anticipate personality differences to build trust.

We've talked about the value of understanding personality differences, but let's explore the subject specifically related to trust. One of the main reasons we need to understand others is so we won't be blindsided by their struggles. By now, you know that talents *always* have a shadow side.

There is an old word of wisdom about buying and investing that says, "If it sounds too good to be true, it probably is." That concept applies to people as well and should help you gain an objective view of potential hires and teammates. No one has it all together, so we must expect the other shoe to fall and their struggles to eventually emerge. As we saw in Chapters 5 through 12, for every strength there is generally a corresponding struggle.

It's good to remind ourselves that a person does not have to be perfect to be trusted. In fact, it's usually easier to trust someone when you know how he or she is likely to let you down. By anticipating others' struggles, we adjust our expectations accordingly and we are not surprised or disappointed.

One CEO told us that he knew his COO was not as initiating as some of his other staff, but he went on to say that he was quite happy with him. He understood and even anticipated this struggle and could give him a nudge when needed. He valued his COO's other talents so much that he could manage this struggle quite easily.

Expecting reality instead of perfection from our teammates increases candor and openness and promotes honesty and respect. If people know that you will accept them, even with their faults, they are more likely to give you their trust. They are also more likely to try to live up to yours.

In a similar manner, when we see that someone's irritating behaviors are just the struggles that go with their best talents, we are far less likely to take it personally or see it as a character flaw. More often than we realize, the behaviors that offend us have nothing to do with us but have everything to do with the struggles and insecurities of the other person. With this perspective, we are better equipped to maintain trust and respect in the relationship.

The tendency to trust or distrust is related to personality.

Some personality traits naturally are more distrusting than others are. If we plotted a scale of trust—distrust it would look something like the following.

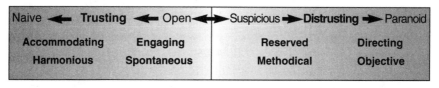

© 2002 RightPath Resources, Inc.
All rights reserved. Used with permission.

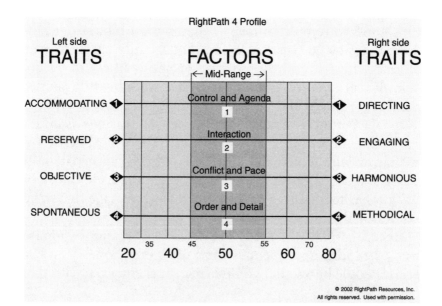

© 2002 RightPath Resources, Inc.
All rights reserved. Used with permission.

Tendency to distrust. As you can see, Directing and Objective people are naturally much more inclined toward *distrust* than their behavioral opposites. You will recall from the personality chapters, the Directing group tends to be more concerned about control and therefore sensitive to power. They are naturally on guard toward others who might be a threat. They tend to be independent and trust themselves more than anyone else. In some cases their distrust borders on paranoia. If you've seen this at the extreme, as I have a time or two, you know it doesn't make for a good work environment.

Those with Objective traits also are likely to be suspicious and distrusting. Their natural tendency toward being skeptical, judgmental, and critical undermines their efforts to trust. Their nature is to confront to find out how "strong" others are and determine if they are "worthy" of their trust.

Reserved/Introverted and Methodical/Structured people also give trust slowly. Introverts typically are somewhat private and carefully guard access to their inner world. They like to keep their distance and are reluctant to open up to others until they know them well. Trust is usually given step by step over a period of time, as relationships develop.

Methodical/Structured people tend to be cautious by nature; they don't rush into anything. They also are skeptical because they want perfection and don't trust others who might get involved and mess up their "system" or their "stuff." Worse yet, the others might drag them down into the muck of imperfection. For Methodicals, it often seems better to not take the risk than to trust others.

Now, pause for a moment and think about senior leaders. What traits do you think make up the majority of executive leadership teams? I'm sure you can guess that Directing and Objective are the most common traits at that level. When you add to this a number of other factors that undermine trust, such as ambition, competition for promotion, and pressure for results, you can see why it's so difficult to build trust on leadership teams.

We have been fortunate to work with a number of senior leaders who are willing to tackle trust building. Generally this is neither an easy nor a welcome process for their team, because these groups tend to be predominantly suspicious and distrusting. Additionally, trust building sounds touchy-feely, which this group typically disdains immensely. They also fear being out of control in an unknown experience—like "trust building."

In spite of the initial resistance, these efforts can work surprisingly well, especially when a secure leader initiates the effort and the people on the team are committed to a common core of values. As in most other areas, character plays an essential role in determining the degree that trust can be expanded. Secure and well-adjusted people can move toward trust, but those who lack those characteristics will have great difficulty in doing so.

Before moving on, let's not overlook one more especially important perspective on the non-trusting side. The people who are the least trusting also tend to be the most task oriented and are more driven for results. Thus, there is an irony that when it comes to carrying out big responsibilities and major challenges these folks are the most trustworthy and reliable to deliver.

We've given them a pat on the back for producing results, but in the end getting results is not enough. To survive in today's environment, companies and organizations need genuine trust at all levels and especially at the top. Those who hold themselves accountable to actually walk their talk about trust and values are going to be the long-term winners.

Business books, such as *Good to Great,* point out the importance of intentionally developing leaders for smooth transitions in executive succession. By its very nature, development of others requires that they be entrusted rather than controlled and micromanaged. Aside from the struggles to increase revenues and maintain integrity, it seems that there are two significant and related challenges for corporate leaders today: "How do we build an environment of trust among leadership teams?" and "How do we let go of control enough to develop and retain our replacements?"

Tendency to trust. Now let's move to the other side of the trust continuum. The personality traits listed on the Right Side (Harmonious, Accommodating, Engaging, Spontaneous) are more open, less concerned about power and control, and by nature more relationship oriented. Consequently, they are able to give trust more easily. Their nature is to want to trust and to think that others feel the same.

The positive effect of this group is that they are helpful and enjoy cooperation. They also are more likely to delegate and trust that others will fulfill their responsibilities without being controlled. As such, they are usually better at developing others for leadership responsibilities.

Of course, those on the *trusting* side have their problems too. Sometimes they trust when trust is not warranted, and things don't go well. This can hurt the larger team if expected results are not delivered. Also, they are likely to lose focus and get distracted on to another project. So now, we have another irony. The people who are the most trusting are likely to be those who are least trustworthy for delivering results and keeping their promises.

Much the same as with talents, we find that both sides of the trust continuum have their advantages and disadvantages. This means that no matter where you are you have something positive to share, as well as some areas for development. This will be important, because issues of trust on teams turn out to be a bigger challenge than you might think, as we're about to see.

Trust busters are more common than you think.

Because trust has become such a hot topic for teams, we developed a survey called the "Trusted Teammate Exercise." By using this exercise in corporate settings, we have learned that the quiet politeness that you see in staff meetings can be misleading as to what's really going on in terms of trust. By giving people an opportunity to share their experiences and concerns with candor and anonymity, reality emerges in this exercise. Let's take a look at some of the common trustbusters that people identify as undermining trust on their teams.

Common Trust Busters

- **Selfish.** Take care of self at the expense of others. Self-promotion takes precedence over working with the team.
- **Ambitious.** Too focused on positioning self (looking good) for the next job at the expense of teamwork.
- **Insincere.** Not up front, withholding/distorting information. Tell one person one thing and another person something else.
- **Controlling nature.** Want to control all the decisions. Want to control the information and use it for their own benefit.
- **Defensive.** Defend own opinions and do not listen to others. Move ahead without adequate facts.
- **Distrustful.** Don't show trust or consideration for teammates. Leave them out if they think they might disagree, even when it's obvious they have a stake in the decision/action.

These trust busters are present on nearly every team, especially at the higher levels of leadership. I suspect that distrust is more common at the higher levels, because of the personality factors discussed earlier and also because of more expansive ambitions, bigger egos, and higher stakes. At the same time, there is greater pressure for results and the competition to stand out is more intense.

In extreme cases, some leaders have been known to play on the natural fears and insecurities of their people and encourage these type of behaviors. Their thinking is that by playing people against each other they can heighten competition and increase productivity. Sadly, some leaders want to see who is Machiavellian enough to do the dirty work they think is necessary to succeed at the top. In other words, it's a type of survival of the fittest (meanest) succession plan. But those type of leaders are probably becoming more rare in today's environment.

The good news is that most leaders want to promote trusting relationships that will facilitate good teamwork. Let's look at some trust builders and see how that can be done.

Trust builders are basic (un)common courtesy.

Of course, everyone wants others to trust him or her; however, there is another irony associated with this trust business. To get trust, you have to give trust. This is a consistent message from leadership books, published research, and our experience in working with teams. Additionally, you build trust by making yourself vulnerable to others. This makes sense, because in order to give trust you are, in effect, giving that person the power to break trust and let you down.

Here are some of the key trust builders as revealed by our "Trusted Teammate" survey.

Key Trust Builders

- **Trusting and open.** Candid. Share their true feelings, not spin.
- **Honest.** Exhibit integrity and authenticity. Act the same no matter who is around. Walk the talk.
- **Transparent.** No private agenda, no surprises. What you see is what you get.
- **Genuinely care.** Concerned about the needs of others as evidenced by actions, not just words.
- **Listen.** Listen carefully, nonjudgmentally, with empathy.
- **Seek and value other opinions** (before making decisions).
- **Support.** Reach out to help others.
- **Build relationships.** Socialize, engage in fun activities.

In looking at this list, it seems apparent that people who are confident within themselves are the best equipped to give trust. A person will not normally exhibit these trust-building, others-oriented behaviors unless they feel secure. That's why leaders (and parents) have such a high responsibility to build an environment in which people know they are cared about, where they can feel safe to express their opinions, and where they are allowed to make mistakes.

In General Colin Powell's autobiography,[1] he relates how his boss handled Powell's first big mistake. As a young lieutenant in Germany, he lost his Colt 45 automatic pistol. Losing a weapon is an extremely serious infraction for a soldier, especially an Army officer. Powell's commander scared him half to death, but he used it as a learning situation and allowed it to pass without damaging his career. No doubt that example was crucial, not only in saving the career of a bright officer but it also empowered him to give trust during his years as a military leader.

Trust affects the bottom line.

Trusting others appropriately is important because it is the right and noble thing to do. But, if you need a monetary reason to get you to be more trusting, here is some incentive.

A classic study conducted for the Life Insurance Agency Management Association revealed that the major difference between low- and high-performing groups of insurance salespeople was the degree to which they reported they trusted their supervisors.[2] Other studies show that employee trust of senior leaders has a direct impact on morale.

Keep in mind Gallup's findings that employees' productivity and retention are determined by their relationship with their immediate supervisors.[3] This also speaks to the trust issue because common sense and personal experience tell us that trust is at the core of any good relationship. And, in today's workplace, relationships have a direct and powerful effect on bottom-line results.

Considering the damage done to employees, shareholders, and the economy in general by a breakdown in trust, how can any serious leader ignore the need to build trusting relationships? But as one highly capable and ambitious executive told me in a coaching session, overcoming some of these habits (he was facing five of the six issues on the trust busters list) is going to be *hard, very hard*. I told him that one of my old POW cell mates had a saying that applies to changing our old habits: "Pain purifies."

Building good relationships and moving from distrust to trust can be painful; it means a change from the comfort zone of our natural and acquired *modus operandi* to a zone of discomfort. The scientist and sometimes philosopher Isaac Newton taught us that a body at rest tends to remain at rest and a body in motion tends to remain in motion. To change our habits requires that we overcome a similar law of behavioral inertia. And, as we've already said, changing our behaviors is like rerouting a river.

Typically, to increase trust we have to build strong relationships that are built on reality. Reality implies some degree of transparency and vulnerability. Opening up and at the same time giving up some control and putting ourselves at the risk of being taken advantage of by someone else is not going to be an easy move for many people. However, as the authors of *The Leadership Challenge* point out in the following comments, it is essential for leaders to take those risks.

"Trust is built when we make ourselves vulnerable to others whose subsequent behavior we can't control. If neither person in a relationship takes the risk of trusting at least a little, the relationship is inhibited by caution and suspicion. If leaders want the higher levels of performance that come with trust and collaboration, they must demonstrate their trust in others before asking for trust from others. That includes going first in the area of trust; it means a willingness to risk trusting others."[4]

An ancient Chinese proverb reminds us that a journey of a thousand miles begins with a single step. Further, in the classic movie, *What About Bob?*, the psychiatric patient/philosopher teaches us that to make changes we need to take "baby steps." And in moving from distrust to trust, that's good advice. So, overcome your inertia and start moving in the right direction with a few small steps to implement some of the trust builders mentioned above. Believe me, it will make a big difference.

Coach's Clipboard

Key Point: Don't assume trust is in good shape. Develop a strategy to build it on your team.

Action Items
1. Is your tendency to trust or distrust?
2. What can you do to give more trust to others?

1. Colin L. Powell (with Joseph E. Persico), *My American Journey* (NY: Random House, 1995).
2. James M. Kouzes and Barry Z. Posner, *The Leadership Challenge* (San Francisco: Jossey-Bass, A Wiley Company, 1995), 166.
3. Marcus Buckingham and Curt Coffman, *First Break All the Rules: What the World's Greatest Leaders Do Differently* (NY: Simon & Schuster © by the Gallup Organization 1999), 11–12.
4. James M. Kouzes and Barry Z. Posner, *The Leadership Challenge* (San Francisco: John Wiley & Sons, Jossey-Bass, 1995), 166, 167.

CHAPTER 17

TEAM DYNAMICS:
Case Studies

Just like individuals, teams have their own unique personality. And as you would expect, the behavioral traits of the people in the group individually and collectively have a significant impact on how the team operates. As you will see, the information on behaviors presented in Section 2 provides important insights for understanding the team personality and the associated dynamics.

Several years ago, a consultant friend who specializes in team development asked us if we could format a team matrix to display the behavioral traits. We did, and it's been a great tool to understand team dynamics and explain many of the team's strengths and struggles. Since you have acquired some knowledge of the traits, I thought it would be insightful and fun to analyze the personality matrix of two case study teams. This will show you how an understanding of the behavioral traits can be used to anticipate many of the critical issues that affect team dynamics. The final case study is taken from a letter sent by a client/friend who shares her experiences on a team that was totally focused on results, with little concern for relationships.

The Harmonizer Team Case Study

Review the team matrix for the Harmonizer Team shown below and consider the distribution of talents (and struggles).

Harmonizer Team *RightPath 4 Profile*

Accommodating	Mid-Range	Directing
Ed D Mary J **TEAM LEADER** William T Steve Y	Jerry G Ronald G	Susan E John F

Reserved	Mid-Range	Engaging
Jerry G Ronald G John F	Susan E Ed D William T	Mary J **TEAM LEADER** Steve Y

Objective	Mid-Range	Harmonious
Susan E John F	Jerry G Ronald G Mary J Steve Y	Ed D **TEAM LEADER** William T

Spontaneous	Mid-Range	Methodical
Mary J **TEAM LEADER** Steve Y	Ed D William T	Susan E Jerry G Ronald G John F

© 2002 RightPath Resources, Inc.
All rights reserved. Used with permission.

Consider these questions as you analyze the dynamics of this team.

- If the four continua were beams with the balance points in the center of the Mid-Range, in which direction would the team tilt in each factor?
- How would the team personality be affected by this distribution of talents? For example, how would this affect meetings, results, relationships?
- How does this team make decisions?
- How good are they at getting closure?
- How would you expect them to communicate?
- Who is going to stand out as being different?

You can gain powerful insights into team dynamics by applying your knowledge of behavioral traits to answer these questions. Let me guide you through this process.

Factor 1. You can see that there is a definite tilt to the Accommodating side on the control/agenda factor. Additionally, the team leader is on that side and this will tend to give additional impetus toward being Accommodating. We can expect that this team's overall personality will be practical, cooperative, and process oriented. They may struggle with initiative, risk taking, and making quick decisions.

Factor 2. The team is almost equally distributed, which means that they have some talkers and some listeners. With the team leader on the Engaging side, we can expect that they will not hesitate to volunteer for center-stage opportunities. The leader will want the group to make a good impression and will enjoy leading them into the limelight. They are likely to be fun oriented and we can expect that the talkers will prevail. It will be important for each person to have his or her say; and, when they do, the Right-Side, Engaging members will tend to get off subject. The leader may be hesitant to set an agenda and keep them on task, so meetings may run long.

Factor 3. The team has a slight bent toward harmony and cooperation, and the team leader will likely push them farther in that direction. She will set the example for a nonconfrontive atmosphere. The question is how much will "Susan" and "John" hold back when they have opinions that differ from the rest of the group (which they will, because they are Directing and Objective). Additionally, their lack of patience with the slower pace of decisions and results may add to their frustration.

Factor 4. The team is slightly tilted toward the Structured and ordered side and this will be helpful, since the team leader is on the opposite, Spontaneous side. The detailed people can help her get closure. The good news is that with this distribution there will be a good mixture of viewpoints and talents. The bad news is that these opposites can be irritating to each other. If "rigid picky" can value the complementary talents of "flexy messy" and vice versa, they can be a great help to each other.

Now, let's look at some other likely issues. John and Susan are both results oriented (Directing and Methodical). Likewise, they are Objective, which means that they are impatient. But they are somewhat Reserved and may hold off expressing their opinions, especially if they have high regard for the team leader, which is the case.

If you followed the analysis above, then you can grasp the dynamics of this headquarters' marketing team. They have lots of meetings, lots of talk, lots of fun, but they're slow to make decisions. The team leader's natural leadership style is to try to get consensus so that everyone is in agreement and feels good about the decisions. Susan and John are somewhat frustrated, because results are slow in coming. In fact, they are looking for a way out of this team so they can get more challenge, more action, and more and faster results.

Once the team leader reviewed this matrix, she saw what was happening in a new light. She recognized the problems and made changes in her style to become more results oriented and more decisive. She also engaged Susan and John and some of the Mid-Range people from Factor 1 to help get things moving. Additionally, she used some of the talents of the Methodical people to help get closure on some of the projects already underway.

The dynamics of the team changed, because the team leader adapted her style to align with the needs of the situation. She later went on to align the responsibilities of the individuals to better match their talents. These actions significantly increased the morale and effectiveness on the team.

As we will discuss in detail later, these are key characteristics of good leaders. They recognize (Read) the realities of the situation and then take appropriate actions (Act).

The Director Team

Now let's analyze the team shown below. At a glance you can see this is a different animal. In fact, if you were to hang around them you might think they were a herd of wild horses. Let's see why that analogy might fit.

Director Team *RightPath 4 Profile*

Accommodating		Mid-Range		Directing	
Martin M		Lee H		Ben L	Wendy P
		Chet W		Sam B	Lyle W
		Frances Z		Donald D	David K
				TEAM LEADER	Jonathan H
				Patricia L	Derek B

Reserved		Mid-Range		Engaging	
		Martin M	Lyle W	Lee H	Frances Z
		Donald D	David K	Ben L	Sam B
		Patricia L	Jonathan H	Chet W	TEAM LEADER
		Wendy P	Derek B		

Objective		Mid-Range		Harmonious	
Lee H	Patricia L	Martin M			
Sam B	Wendy P	Ben L			
Donald D	David K	Chet W			
TEAM LEADER	Jonathan H	Frances Z			
	Derek B	Lyle W			

Spontaneous		Mid-Range		Methodical	
Ben L	Sam B	Martin M	David K		Wendy P
Chet W	TEAM LEADER	Lee H	Jonathan H		
Frances Z	Lyle W	Donald D	Derek B		
		Patricia L			

© 2002 RightPath Resources, Inc.
All rights reserved. Used with permission.

Factor 1. Because this predominantly Directing group tilts so far to the right, we know they are usually results oriented, decisive, and strong willed. "Don't fence me in" could be their motto, and only the strongest boundaries will contain their independent and challenging behaviors. They are highly opinionated and aggressive. They'll kick up their heels and race at breakneck speed to get what they want. They love to look down from the mountaintop and survey the big picture for the competition. Individually and as a group they are always alert to detect threats to their power and territory.

Factor 2. They also are a friendly Engaging group. And though they are independent, they enjoy romping with other bands of horses around the territory. They make a lot of noise, enjoy merriment, and are good mixers. They are usually great performers and would enjoy the attention that show horses get in places like the rodeo or circus. But they are also like the wind blowing across the open range. They don't like to be harnessed, and they don't want to plow the same fields all day long. They'd rather just roam, moving from one meadow to another.

Factor 3. On this factor, they tilt clearly to the left, which indicates that as a group they like a fast pace and a changing gait. You could expect that they are the most impatient team of horses in the land. Also, they find it natural to dig in their heels and resist going where they don't want to go. They will confront head on when they are cornered. They are quite insensitive and may trample the feelings of others. They would tell you it doesn't bother them because they don't even notice these things called feelings. You see, they come equipped by nature with a very thick hide. But if you want to really make them uncomfortable and get them on edge and nervous, just talk about touchy-feely things. They don't like feelings, but they do have strong reactions to feelings, so be careful what you say. If the conversation gets mushy, they'll break and stampede to the safety of the badlands where the tough hang out.

Factor 4. Spontaneous is the word for this group. Like a bunch of quarter horses, they start quick and finish fast, and they aren't much on those long endurance races. Their strength is their ability to change directions; they can turn on a dime. Flexibility is what they love, so don't expect them to hang around for the confinement of details. They want the wind in their faces and the freedom to roam away from the bridles of rules and regulations.

It's kind of fun to think of this group as a herd of wild horses, and it does describe them exactly. They are actually a very good team, because their work fits their nature. They are a team of sales managers, and each has his or her own herd to lead and range to roam. When they do get together as a team, they have fun and roughhouse each other (with words) like a group of playful ponies. If they had to work closely together on a daily basis—where they did not have power, freedom, and turf—it would be a different story altogether.

"Martin" and "Wendy" are the dark horses. And does this team ever need them! Martin represents the only significantly different viewpoint on the control factor (Factor 1) and will have key insights for the team. He needs to speak up, and they need to listen to him. Wendy is the only one with a Methodical bent, and her approach to systems and organization will be beneficial for the group. Fortunately, the other team members have a good support system to help them keep the records straight, the systems running, and all the other detailed and structured areas in line.

As you can see, team dynamics are extremely important and are significantly affected by the distribution of traits in the group. As much as we have worked with this concept, I'm still amazed at how accurate behaviors are for predicting team strengths, struggles, and related issues. That's why I'm so passionate about the personality information we've discussed. It has powerful application for the issues facing individuals, teams, and leaders.

Kathy's Case Study

When I told a friend about the idea for this book, she offered to share her personal story about a team she had been on some years earlier. I think it fits here and would serve us well because it ties together talents, behavioral issues, team dynamics, and leadership in a way that is all too typical. It's a sad story, but it does have a happy ending, at least for Kathy.[1]

"I first started working with Acme Enterprises as the assistant to John, a vice president in the finance division. I really enjoyed that job and fitted well; however, that position was temporary. At its end I was asked to stay on with another team. It was a new position, and a lot of assumptions were made regarding what the job would entail. My new manager, Tom, along with John and I, assumed that the role would be very similar to what I had been doing previously. We couldn't have been more wrong!

"Soon after I began, I was asked to work on a project that the team was undertaking. I was asked if I would 'manage the office,' which, when outlined to me, sounded like a challenging, rewarding job. However, again, I didn't understand exactly what the job would entail (nor did anyone on the team, unfortunately, as it was another new position). If I had, I probably wouldn't have accepted that role.

"My RightPath Profile is that of a Networker[2], very Engaging and Spontaneous. What this means in the workplace is that in order to function to my full capacity I need to be able to network, inspire, and relate to people, with a minimum of detail work and with 'safe' opportunities to present my ideas to people. My work needs to center on my people skills and be varied. I also need strong acceptance in order to feel confident enough to extend myself, and I am motivated by recognition and appreciation of my efforts. This description is, unfortunately, exactly the opposite of what my job in finance entailed.

"The new project, once established, ended up being a very basic administration role. There were three main parts to the job: firstly, enormous amounts of filing and copying of legal and technical documents; secondly, producing documents for the team; and thirdly, organizing meetings for various teams and committees. I had been hired as an executive assistant, and it constantly frustrated me that I was doing the work of a junior admin assistant. I used to joke that I was the most expensive photocopying machine in the company.

"The first two functions of the job, which took up the majority of my time, were a constant struggle for me, because they demanded abilities that didn't come naturally or easily to me. There was constant 'task' orientation, which is physically and mentally draining for me. Just as introverted people find constant networking a drain, I find isolation draining, because I am energized by relationships and people contact.

"Despite all of this, however, I would have had a much easier time, and possibly even enjoyed working there, had the personal relationships been different. I clashed with two people in the team—namely Tom and one of his direct reports, William. The irony is that I respected Tom a lot, but I found working with him a struggle that I couldn't surmount!

"Tom would probably be a Driver profile:[3] very highly Dominant and also highly Objective. He is very, very task focused; and, because of our differing points of view, we found it hard to understand and relate to each other.

"The things that motivate me to excellent performance in the workplace are feedback, appreciation, and support. And I need that to be spoken or written—otherwise I will not pick up on it. During my year with Tom, I asked him many times for feedback. Each time he replied, 'I don't have time.' What he didn't understand was that this 'time' was not a cost; it was an investment.

If he had been able to invest just fifteen minutes a week into giving me constructive feedback and meaningful appreciation, I would have easily doubled my productivity.

"One other thing that Tom told me several times was 'If I don't say anything, you're doing okay.' I found this lack of direction really difficult. What Tom didn't realize was that if he didn't say anything nothing was being communicated. It was difficult to measure success in my job, so I had no specific goals or targets by which to judge my performance. The result of that was that I set impossible targets for myself, and I struggled constantly to meet them. So when I didn't achieve them I was very tough on myself.

"In addition, most of my efforts at establishing a friendship with Tom were met with disinterest. This was quite hurtful at the time, and I perceived it as personal rejection. I couldn't understand his unwavering focus on work and tasks, because I am focused on people and relationships. Tom is very much motivated by getting results at work, and I think this made it difficult for him to understand that I am motivated by relationships, encouragement, and acceptance.

"The other personality clash going on was that between William and myself. William also has a highly Directing personality, and he found it easy to criticize other people. Unfortunately, he took a pretty instant dislike to me, and I think he found my people-focused personality a useless commodity in a workplace. He also worked on the project, and he was often curt and rude to me in the office. Added to this, he frequently made very cutting remarks about my personality, my looks, and my abilities. He always maintained it was a joke, but his remarks were quite acid and they never got a laugh from me! Often, his remarks were made in front of other team members, but I found them too embarrassing and painful to respond to most of the time.

"I felt that Tom made excuses for William, because William was very good at what he did and he was a very valuable asset to the team. Tom did tell me in a formal appraisal that it was my responsibility to 'handle' William, as though I was responsible for his behavior. I certainly did not respond to William as well as I could have, and I would react differently if I were placed in the same situation again. Nevertheless, his behavior toward me was unacceptable; but it seemed to be okay with the rest of the team.

"After a while in this work environment, I found that my

personality actually changed. I am Mid-Range on the Accommodating/Directing scale, meaning that I can follow others—or be blunt, independent, and assertive—depending on what is called for at the time. However, because Tom and William were so strongly dominant, I couldn't compete with them, and I became overly accommodating and wouldn't stand up for myself. I'm also very independent (to a fault!) but wasn't independent in that environment, because of overwhelming feelings of inadequacy.

"I am also Mid-Range on the Objective/Harmonious scale, meaning that I can make tough calls and work in a changing environment—or just agree with the status quo—depending on what is required. But again William, and to a lesser extent Tom, was extremely Objective. I responded by becoming overly Harmonious, which translated to being too sensitive, unwilling to confront, and resistant to change.

"One of the failings of the team, and the organization, was their inability to use personality differences to their advantage. Most of Acme's management team was highly Dominant: either Drivers, Analyzers, or Strategic Thinkers.[4]

"Rather than adopting a philosophy that people were encouraged to use their natural strengths, I felt I was put down for not being Directing and Dominant. In fact, Tom actually wrote in a formal appraisal 'If you excel in this position, it will be because you move about 75 percent from how you would like to operate to how I operate.' In other words, stop being Engaging and start being Directing.

"The fact is, Tom never purposely made me feel this way. He would probably be quite devastated to know how deeply his behavior affected me, and I'm sure he would be surprised to know how his relationship with me affected my work performance.

"Unfortunately, the company has a culture where people are secondary to profits, and there is no real understanding in the organization of how much the work environment affects the bottom line of the business. People issues are seen as extracurricular, to be focused on after the 'real' work is done. Unfortunately, they don't realize that the "real" work suffers if there's no focus on people.

"I recently visited Acme and was amazed to see about 60 percent staff turnover after only eighteen months. I think this high turnover may be due to the culture. It's costing them productivity and profit, not to mention hiring and training cost; but, unfortunately, the senior management hasn't allowed that to come into their field of vision yet. Managers at Tom's level have so many pressures put on them from higher in the organization that they can't afford to devote time to people issues, and it's actually having a negative effect on productivity and profit.

"My year with Acme Enterprises was the most difficult year in my life, and I left that job with almost no self-esteem or belief in myself. I struggled the whole time with feelings of inadequacy and failure. My new work environment is one where people are put first, and it has made an enormous difference. I am now making innovative contributions to my new company, which I never would have been able to do at Acme because of the environment and how I responded to it.

"I think the saying, 'Whatever doesn't kill you makes you stronger' is largely true. I am currently using my painful experiences at Acme to teach other people about using personal differences to benefit the organization. It's inevitable that personal differences will occur in any workplace, and whether these are assets or liabilities depends on how they are managed.

"When I left, I told Tom that if he were ever doing anything slightly more interesting I'd love to come and work for him again, which is still true. I think he could be a much better manager in a different environment, and I'd love to teach him what I've now learned about personal differences!"

Kathy's story provides several lessons for teams and leaders. Let's review them. When good workers are mismatched to their jobs, productivity and morale go down. Leaders at the highest levels have great power to set the environment, and whether good or bad it flows downhill to the lowest levels. If all the focus is on results, relationships suffer. Exit interviews and extensive research show that good relationships are a central part of good leadership. When people are not valued for their differences, the team suffers. Too often management tolerates rude and harassing behaviors from people who work hard and get results for themselves but undermine teamwork and retention. When differences (talents) are recognized, valued, and managed appropriately, everyone benefits.

Coach's Clipboard

Key Point: Individual behavioral traits shape team dynamics and are a good predictor of the team personality.

Action Items
1. What are the dynamics on your team?
2. Are you making an intentional effort to value differences on your team?

---

1. This is a true story. Like the examples used elsewhere, the names have been changed to protect confidentiality. My thanks to "Kathy" for sharing in such an insightful way. She reports that she is on a good team and has a position that fits her talents well.
2. Refer to Appendix C for more information on the Networker profile.
3. Refer to Appendix C for more information on the Driver profile.
4. These profiles tend to be highly task oriented. To read more about this see Appendix C.

❖

LEADERSHIP

No discussion of talents, teams, and top performance can be complete without also focusing on leadership. Someone has to take the responsibility to unite the diverse talents into a team and move things along toward achieving the goals. In some mature teams, the responsibilities may shift from one person to another, depending on the circumstances. However, regardless of the situation, leadership is essential for success.

Leadership is a fascinating subject; it is both simple and complex. We know it is simple, because every day you can observe school children effectively leading their peers at any elementary school playground.

We know it's complex because library shelves and corporate offices are stocked with books and tapes on the subject, and organizations spend untold amounts trying to develop their leaders. The basic tenets of successful leadership seem so obvious, and yet they are so elusive that no one ever reaches the absolute pinnacle of leadership performance.

The old arguments about whether leaders are born or made have fallen by the wayside. There's a consensus that it's probably some of both. The more productive approach in today's environment is that everyone can improve his or her leadership ability through education, training, development, and experience.

If you've done any reading on this subject, you know that there are many leadership models, principles, and traits put forth by various institutions and experts. They all seem to have much in common, and most of them can be helpful.

Because we are approaching this from the coaching perspective, the focus here will be to hit key issues that will point the way in your continued growth as a leader. In the following chapters, we'll examine leadership attributes, the Read/Act leadership model, and control in leading. Then we'll conclude this section with leadership checkpoints.

Let's get started.

CHAPTER 18

❖

LEADERSHIP ATTRIBUTES:
Part One

The word *leadership* has a special meaning and attraction that immediately gets our attention. My first thoughts always go back to my years of military training, when it was ingrained that leaders were entrusted with two primary responsibilities: accomplish the mission and take care of the people.

To achieve the former, the leaders must be willing to employ all the power of their intellect, personality, and position. For the latter, they must see themselves as servants who are watching out for the welfare of their people—down to the lowest levels. These two entities—power and the needs of people—must be carefully stewarded. For that reason, we must treat leadership as a special trust—an almost sacred privilege.

Regardless of your background, this word *leadership* probably brings to mind a broad array of experiences from your past—as a leader and as a follower. It may cause you to reflect on certain principles and techniques you've added to your tool kit. It may also bring to mind memories of leaders who used power and influence for great achievements. Before looking at specific leadership attributes, let's consider some broad definitions of the subject.

The Leadership Challenge, a practical handbook for leaders, defines leadership as *". . . the art of mobilizing others to want to struggle for shared aspirations."*[1] In a similar vein, *Primal Leadership,* Daniel Goleman's latest book on emotional intelligence, opens with the statement, "Great leaders move us. They ignite our passion and inspire the best in us."[2]

The consistent theme in most all definitions of leadership is that it involves people, common goals, and motivation of those people to work together to achieve the goals. It may sound easy, but as we all know, "There's many a slip twixt the cup and the lip." Leadership is always a challenge and, of course, that's why the leader's role can be so rewarding.

During the years 2000 to 2002, our company designed and presented leadership training in two Fortune 200 organizations. These workshops provided the opportunity to gain unique insights into what people consider great leadership.

We usually begin these sessions with the "My Greatest Leader" exercise. Participants are asked to think of all the leaders they've ever had and to identify the greatest one. Next, they are to list two or three attributes of that leader to answer the question, "What was it that made this person a great leader?" Participants share and discuss their responses and they are listed on a flip chart for reference during the rest of the training.

The collective responses of over 300 first-line supervisors and mid-level managers provided more than 120 attributes that people value in leaders. The list is obviously not exhaustive, but it is sufficient to give some distinctively clear indicators of what people respect and remember about their leaders. We have logically grouped them into five general categories. These categories (shown on the following page) provide a meaningful structure that gives good insights into the core factors of leadership.

We also use the attributes within these five "Building Blocks of Leadership" as specific behaviors for individual coaching and leadership development. Let's examine each of these blocks, starting at the bottom.

Building Blocks of Leadership

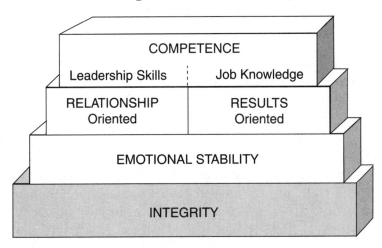

© 2002 RightPath Resources, Inc.
All rights reserved. Used with permission.

Integrity, the foundation for leadership. Leadership must always be anchored in *integrity*, because honesty is essential for sound decisions, mutual trust, and credibility. This list had the fewest number of attributes, but they were the most focused. Among all the individual attributes, the one that encompassed *honesty* was second only to *good listener*. Shown below are the characteristics of people with integrity.

Honest, trustworthy, have integrity
Do what they say they will do
Fair, treat others fairly
Loyal/dedicated to their companies
Wise, use good judgment
Accountable
Take personal risks to support people, organization
Willing to stand up to superiors
Strong family values

You'll notice that these are the same traits that are commonly expected of people who have good character. They are also very powerful leadership behaviors, because they naturally inspire respect, trust, and the loyalty of others.

It's possible that the issue of integrity is so fundamental that you may be thinking, "Why even bother? We all know it's important." The reality is, no matter how lofty you or I think our integrity is, we are only a short step from violating the very principles we stand for so strongly.

If you think you are above making a mistake in this area, look out! You are in real danger. Without a clear understanding that people like you and I have the capability to look the other way or intentionally cut a corner, we can get off track. Given the right pressures and circumstances, it's sometimes easy for the-ends-justify-the-means thinking to take over. The drive to achieve goals, pride, fear of failure, greed, or some similar underlying problem will overshadow our principles, and we'll see wrong as right and never even notice. It happens because it's inherent to our nature.

Most of us have heard of the Greek cynic (Diogenes, circa 320 B.C.) who went around in the daytime with a lantern, in search of an honest man. The story may have been a myth, but it was based on the realities of the ages. The biographies of great leaders from Israel's King David to modern business leaders, generals, and presidents highlight the frequency of failures in integrity. We all know this is a problem, but we must recognize that it can be a problem for us if we aren't careful.

The Watergate conspirators provide somber insight into the frailty of the human condition. They were bright, well-educated, successful men; yet they made very serious, almost unbelievable errors in judgment. The root cause was a breakdown in basic integrity that permeated from the top down.

White House counsel, Jeb Magruder, explained this problem quite well: "My ambition obscured my judgment. Somewhere between my ambition and my ideals I lost my ethical compass."[3]

The shocking Enron/Arthur Anderson scandal of 2002 provided an unwelcome introduction to a string of integrity failures in corporate America and Wall Street. For a while it seemed that every week there was another company admitting that it had accounting errors. The extent of these problems underscores what I said earlier: It's much easier than most people think to slide over the line.

I doubt that most of these leaders started out with the intention of violating the trust of others. However, where there is power and pride without oversight, history indicates that it's easy for greed to take over.[4] When you add the pressure to keep looking good and meet the quarterly earnings for Wall Street analysts, the odds of integrity failures soar.

There are two steps that we can take to protect our integrity. First, have an understanding with our teammates that everyone is susceptible to being blinded by both good and bad motives. You've heard the expression "blind ambition," but it may be more appropriate to say that ambition is a blinder. When ambition takes over, we don't see what we are doing objectively.

We must operate with the assumption that we are human and that these temptations are going to happen. (Think back to the people you trusted who let you down.) Next, we must encourage others to question our motives and actions when they suspect that we are being blinded or are headed off track. If we are honest about wanting to guard our integrity, then this won't threaten us. We'll see it as protection.

We must also agree to put everything to the "sunshine" test. Rather than conceal the logic and motives behind an impending decision or action, we seek counsel from others who will be totally honest. We get their assessment of the integrity of the decision or action in question. Admittedly, it can be painful when someone throws cold water on your excitement or idea. But the wisdom of good counsel can keep you out of trouble.

Remember that it's easy to talk about these attributes of integrity and to assume that we have them, but it takes *real* courage and self-confidence to live them out in the pressure cooker of leadership responsibilities. The bottom line is that we must all assume we are capable of violating our professed integrity and to make sure we keep square corners square and walk the talk. We must be proactive.

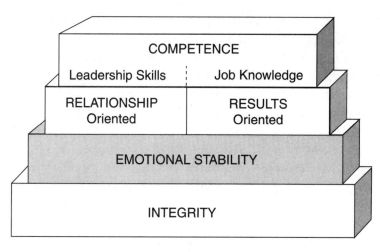

© 2002 RightPath Resources, Inc.
All rights reserved. Used with permission.

Emotional stability (maturity). Emotional stability (maturity) is the next level up in our building block structure of leadership attributes. By emotional stability we mean exactly that: People are stable and consistent in their emotions; behavioral swings are within the normal range of accepted behaviors. (This is not to be confused with emotional intelligence, which also is important and discussed in another chapter.) The attributes listed below often go unnoticed when they are present in the positive, but when they are in the negative range they get everyone's attention.

Loyal	Clear thinking, rational
Positive, good attitude	Do not jump to conclusions
Confident	Keep an even keel
Balanced, good perspective	Levelheaded
Good humor, make work fun	Down to earth
Stable	Maintain objectivity
Consistent	Energetic
Genuine	Enthusiastic
Respected by peers	Flexible
Get along well with others	Know how to deal with others

Transparent	Remember their roots
Calm, professional (even under stress)	Love their jobs
Diplomatic	Never quit
Open-minded	People of faith

In general, these attributes relate to areas of self-control, willpower, humility, good manners, confidence, and a positive attitude. They also attract people, engender trust, and work like a lubricant to reduce friction in the working environment.

When you are around leaders who have good emotional stability, you experience an atmosphere that is light and uplifting, even when times are hard. With the opposite type of leader, it feels "heavy," even in good times.

When I think of these characteristics, several individuals stand out as good role models. Two are presidents of large companies that we have worked with. They always seem level-headed, genuine, stable, consistent, positive, confident, and fun to be around. They also are strong leaders who can make the tough calls, but you also can trust that they are not going to do anything rash.

A public figure who seems to be a good example of emotional stability and maturity is Secretary of Defense Donald Rumsfeld. He became somewhat of a folk hero during daily press conferences following the attacks of September 11, 2001.

Rumsfeld was an attractive figure because he was genuine and positive and remained calm, confident, and balanced under pressure. His good humor in difficult and even annoying circumstances proved to be a powerful tool for handling the press. Several business leaders we work with are using Rumsfeld's style of emotional maturity as a model to guide them in their personal development.

Tiger Woods is another good example of someone who manages his emotions well. In spite of the tremendous pressure from the media, he seems able to smile and keep a positive outlook. His composure following a disastrous third round at the 2002 British Open was remarkable. He bounced back the next day with a final round score of 65, indicative not only of his great talent but his sound emotional stability.

Because Secretary Rumsfeld and Tiger Woods know that people are watching every move they make, they demonstrate emotional stability. That's the special role of a leader.

You are setting the standard for integrity. People are watching every move you make to see if you walk the talk or if you are like so many others who cut the corners to protect or advance their own agenda. Likewise, your emotional stability will determine the environment. Take those responsibilities seriously so that those who follow will benefit from your leadership and also from following your model when they become leaders.

Coach's Clipboard

Key Point: Integrity and emotional stability form the bedrock that supports any leadership effort. Stay straight and keep an even keel.

Action Items
1. Assume that you are susceptible to integrity problems and productivity. Check yourself regularly. Keep the square corners square.
2. Check your attitude and emotional maturity. Are you positive? Stable? Fun to be around? Or, are you frequently criticizing, grumbling, and complaining?

1. James M. Kouzes and Barry Z. Posner, *The Leadership Challenge* (San Francisco: Jossey-Bass, A Wiley Company, 1995), 30.
2. Daniel Goleman, Richard Boyatzis, and Annie McKee, *Primal Leadership* (Cambridge: Harvard Business School Press, 2002), 3.
3. Statement by Jeb Magruder at Watergate Trial.
4. The best-seller, *John Adams* by David McCullough, attributes these very concerns to Addams' insistence on a tri-cameral government. He knew that power could not be trusted to any person or group without checks and balances.

CHAPTER 19

❖

LEADERSHIP ATTRIBUTES:
Part Two

Integrity, the foundation level in our building-block approach, is anchored in character and values, which are typically set at an early age, though they must be cultivated daily. Emotional Stability, the second level, seems to be tied to our psychological adjustment, which reflects our mental outlook and personal baggage. Moving up to the third level, you'll see two blocks labeled **Relationship** and **Results**.

Both of these building blocks encompass essential attributes for successful leadership and both are closely related to natural personality behaviors. Reflecting on the factors described earlier, you will recall that some traits are naturally more relationship oriented and some are more results (and task) oriented.[1] Consequently, people tend to be talented in one of these areas but rarely in both. However, good leaders have to be effective in both. So, most of us have to hold on to the one that comes easy and work hard to overcome our struggles in the other. Let's take a closer look at the attributes.

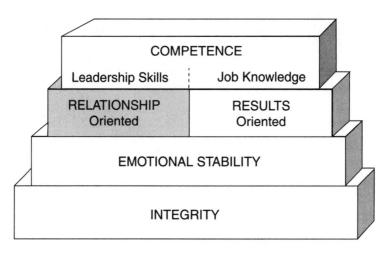

© 2002 RightPath Resources, Inc.
All rights reserved. Used with permission.

Relationship oriented. Individuals who are naturally relationship oriented are those we normally think of as having people skills. They find it easy to take an interest in others and consider their welfare. It's natural for them to trust others and give of themselves in order to listen, encourage, and show empathy.

For those who don't have these strengths, the difficult part of gaining them is that it is not natural and will take extra effort. In fact, it may even feel awkward and uncomfortable. But the good news is that everyone can use the list of specific behaviors that follows to coach themselves into using these powerful relationship-building habits. Perhaps you can remember your experiences with people who have these relationship-oriented behaviors.

Good listener

Cared, concerned, cared about me

Trusted me to do the job

Supportive, lend a helping hand

Respect others and me

Approachable

Friendly

Priority was people first

Got to know me

Gave me regular feedback, reinforcement

Thoughtful, had a kind word for everyone

Observant, responded well to my needs

Had time for me, had time to teach me

Wanted me to succeed

Looked for strong points

Allowed me to develop, learn, grow

Talked to the "little" people

Treated me like a person

Compassionate

Easy to talk to

Solicited and valued my input

Trusted my decisions

People persons

Understanding

Team approach, helped me achieve goals

Gave both positive and negative feedback

Gave recognition for a job well done

Treated me as an individual

Very encouraging

Likeable

Concerned about others

Served people

Believed we could make a difference

Valued me as an employee

Showed interest in what I was working on

Patient, took time to understand

Able to relate

Wanted and acted on my suggestions

Cared about my career

You'll note that "good listener" is at the top of the list. In fact, it was at the top of the entire list as the most frequently occurring attribute of "Great Leaders." If you want to adopt one behavior that would do the most to improve all your relationships, as well as your leadership credibility, being a good listener would be a good place to start.

Although most people think they are good listeners, the truth is that some are and some aren't. Just because a person thinks he or she is a good listener does not make it true. Directing/Dominant and Objective people almost always think they are good listeners but rarely are. (Of course everyone around them knows the reality.) When challenged, they will respond with something like, "I'm a very good listener when I want to be." The problem with that is that they can quickly lose patience and not "want to be" any longer.

In a team session, when we were doing the "Awesome Traits Exercise," one lady responded to my challenge with, "Well, I'm a good listener until I see where they are going, and then I don't need to listen to any more of it. It's just wasting my time; and besides, I already know how I'm going to respond."

A senior manager was more realistic: "I now realize that I'm not a good listener, and I'm working on it. But honestly, it's a struggle. It's difficult to slow down and listen."

Because listening is related directly or indirectly to many of the other attributes on the list, it is very powerful. Let's focus for a moment on two important aspects of listening: a *caring focus* on the other person and *patience*. The pace of work makes it difficult to slow down and express a genuine interest in others, even for those who are naturally people oriented. For those who are primarily task oriented, it can be nearly impossible.

When you show enough patience to listen and care, you are relinquishing your time and your personal agenda for the benefit of the other person. That's the sacrifice that many are not willing to make and the reason that many leaders are not good listeners. But business requires leaders to understand and respond to the critical connection between relationships and financial success in today's environment.[2]

When employees don't see that they are making a difference (with little or no positive feedback) and they don't think anyone cares about them (leader doesn't listen), they are likely to either quit and leave—or quit and stay. In either case, the loss of productivity and the costs of replacement are huge. Either you invest time in those you have or spend big bucks to find and train more and repeat the cycle.

Good relationships improve every area, including the bottom line. In *Working with Emotional Intelligence*, Daniel Goleman cites several areas of research and concludes that those who have emotional intelligence skills for relating to others are three times as productive at entry-level jobs and three hundred times more effective at some of the more complex responsibilities that require teamwork.[3]

For those who need to work on building relationships, I recommend that you pick some of the items from the list on page 211 and start practicing. Intentionally engage people on a regular basis, but do it on their terms. Listen to their ideas about how things should be done without offering any judgment. Set aside your own opinions long enough to see the world from their viewpoints. Learn about their dreams, their families, their struggles, and show an interest in their welfare and success.

Reflect on your greatest leaders and you'll recall how powerful it was when someone on a higher level took time to care about you. Now it's your turn to "repay the bank." Show others that they are important to you, and your relationships will empower them to new levels of performance.

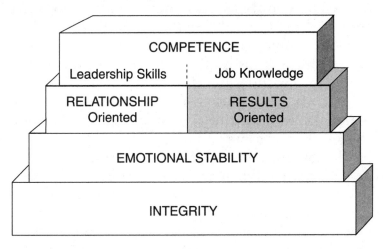

© 2002 RightPath Resources, Inc.
All rights reserved. Used with permission.

Results oriented. The clichés "Leaders make it happen" and "Leaders get the job done" remind us that the report card on a person's leadership performance ultimately hinges on results. The following list shows attributes of leaders who know where they are going and are both capable and committed to taking others with them.

Straightforward, direct	Set high goals
Clear expectations	Take action, initiate, are proactive
Strong work ethic	Good planners
Big picture, visionary, strategic	Organized and well prepared
Decisive, give direction	Create and expect accountability
Good problem solvers	Stern but fair
Firm (but flexible)	Desire to be the best
High expectations of self and others	Challenge others within their capabilities
Very focused (on the mission, goals, tasks)	Committed to excellence
	Pay attention to detail
High standards	Single-minded focus on customer service
Results oriented	

As the items on the list point out, leaders are expected to communicate the vision, define the goals, ensure high standards, resolve problems, make key decisions, hold people accountable, and keep projects on schedule. Ultimately, the leader's role is to ensure success.

We are attracted to those who get results, so winners are usually popular in every endeavor. In college sports, winning teams have a clear edge in recruiting the top athletes. The same is true in the corporate world, where successful companies have an edge in attracting the most talented candidates. Likewise, when it comes to promotion, those who produce (get results) attract attention at all levels.

However, results-oriented leaders often struggle with relationships. Thus, it should not surprise anyone that the higher up the corporate ladder the more likely leaders are to be more focused on results than relationships, even at the expense of their people. This problem often causes chaos at the lower levels, but all too often it is tolerated at the top because of the intense focus on short-term results.

In *Beyond Ambition: How Driven Managers Can Lead Better and Live Better*, Robert Kaplan (Center for Leadership Development, Greensboro) discusses the problems of "destructive productivity" for those who focus on results and personal achievement at all costs.

Kaplan's research found that "The principle drawback to the extremely expansive executive who obtains good bottom-line results is that he or she harms the organization in the process. These executives reduce the organization's talent pool by driving people away and demoralizing some of those who remain. For the subordinates who are chronically exhausted or demeaned in the mad dash for results, success proves to be an inadequate tonic."[4]

The question comes, "Can the leopard change his or her spots; or, in this case, can the destructive leader become more *sensitive* to people?" The short answer is, "Yes, but it's not easy." Such changes are sometimes unnatural and uncomfortable because they require letting go of deeply ingrained behaviors.

Competitive, strong-willed, independent, tough-minded people usually don't make such changes voluntarily. Those of good character will make efforts to change when they are made aware of reality and the consequences to themselves and others of not changing. Also, when senior leaders set examples of personal change, it makes it much easier for others to follow.

On the other hand, some people will never change until they run headlong into reality—a reality that not only will not give in to them but also actually will bite back. When the pain outweighs the gain, they will consider changing; and their success is usually in direct proportion to the sincerity of their repentance from the old ways.

During a team development session, we listened as an experienced manager confessed, to his shame, that in the past he had publicly badgered and humiliated people as a way of getting results. He explained that this was the leadership that had been modeled for him; and, by personality, he took to it well. Fortunately, his leadership had changed to the point that his team could hardly believe he was capable of such behaviors.

Another highly results-oriented executive friend recently shared that he was on his third career and third wife. But, with a pained look on his face, he went on to explain that he was beginning to learn how wrong he had been for so many years. His concluding comment was, "You know, I've learned that being happy is better than being 'right.' "

Relationship-oriented leaders may struggle with results. Those who are naturally sensitive to people often struggle with the tough side of leadership. Because they are so sensitive to the needs of others, they typically like to lead by consensus. There are situations in which this works well; however, it's unrealistic to think that everyone will agree on a regular basis. Eventually, the decision process usually slows and results lag when the leader is trying to please everyone,

We've seen this on a number of teams, and it usually causes problems for the more results-oriented team members who get frustrated when things are moving slowly. They may become rebellious, motivationally check out, or actually quit the team. To prevent this from happening, the team leader must have the courage to adapt his or her style sufficiently to take charge and act more decisively.

Because relationship-oriented leaders typically want to be liked and dislike confrontation, they often struggle with holding people accountable. They sometimes undermine their leadership credibility because they avoid difficult personnel actions, such as disciplining and replacing problem employees.

Leaders who know they are too soft when toughness is needed can learn to adapt their behaviors, once they see that they are doing no one a favor by letting things slide. Avoiding tough issues hurts the team, undermines the leader's role, and actually delays the correction and possible improvement for the problem person. Tough love is just that, and it's tough for everyone. But when it's needed, it's the kindest thing to do. Also, when done right, it usually gets results. Interestingly, if it's done right, it may save the relationship as well.

I hope you can see how almost all of us naturally tend toward one side or the other of the relationship/results equation; and that's the rub. If we focus primarily on relationships, results will suffer and people will not be challenged. If we focus too much on results, we neglect, grind up, or run off valuable people resources. The great leaders are those who are somehow able to master their unnatural side sufficiently to walk both sides of the street. They build relationships. And they get results.

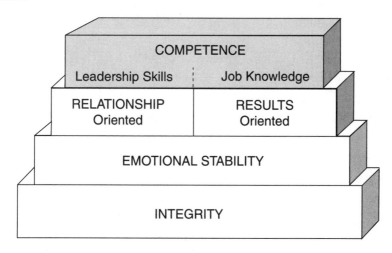

© 2002 RightPath Resources, Inc.
All rights reserved. Used with permission.

Competence in leadership skills and job knowledge. The top level of our leadership building blocks combines two different areas of competency: job knowledge/experience and leadership attributes not covered in other areas.[5] Leadership is often considered as both art and science. The following list of items cover both disciplines but seems to be more oriented toward science, i.e., the skills that are learned along the way. As you read the following list of attributes, see if you recognize yourself or leaders with whom you have interacted.

Knowledgeable	Share knowledge
Intelligent, smart	Competent, effective
Lead by example	Provide resources to do the job
Delegate, then allow me to do my job	Good judge of people, assessed abilities
Empower employees	Not too political
Good communicators	Able to prioritize among departments
Innovative, think outside the box	
Experienced, record of high achievements	Could navigate through information glut
Match people to tasks	Share information
Able to resolve conflict	Able to filter politics
Guide but do not control	Able to lead and follow
Put effort into supervisory relationship	Know when to listen and when to act
Provide environment for success	Willing to teach

This final group covers a broad array of competencies that can serve as touch points to remind us of what great leaders know and do. Leadership touch points can play a valuable role by helping us keep fresh in the many facets of this complex subject.

When I think of using touch points, the picture that comes to mind is the experience of flying an aircraft totally on instruments. The key to good instrument flying is a timely cross-check so that the pilot is visually and mentally connecting with all the key instruments on a frequent basis.

When flying an instrument approach in the weather, leaving an essential component out of your cross-check can be disastrous. If a pilot focuses too long on one area (airspeed for example), another area (like altitude) may get out of control. In the leadership role, it's the same. Although the priorities shift, depending on the situation, leaders must also touch base on all the important areas on a regular basis. Leaders must be careful not to become so immersed in the issues of the day that important functions are overlooked. A regular leadership cross-check can keep you on course to your destination with your crew intact.

Use the leadership attributes. Looking back at these five groups and more than one hundred attributes, we can see that the supervisors and managers we polled have provided a wealth of information on what it takes to be a great leader. The lists also remind us that the bar is high and we all have room to grow. You can use these attributes to design and carry out your development plan.

Coach's Clipboard

Key Point: Relationships and results are both important. You are probably good at one but will need to work on the other.

Action Items

1. Identify your weakest building block on the third level: Is it relationships or results? Go back to the personality chapters and review your strengths and struggles and see how they relate to your weak side.

2. Select key behaviors from the Leadership Attributes and begin to practice. Keep at it. Get feedback on your progress.

---

1. See Appendix B for more on this.

2. Marcus Buckingham and Curt Coffman, *First Break All the Rules: What the World's Greatest Leaders Do Differently* (NY: Simon & Schuster, © by the Gallup Organization 1999), 11–12.

3. Daniel Goleman, *Working with Emotional Intelligence* (NY: Bantam Books, 1998), 35–37.

4. Robert E. Kaplan with William H. Drath and Joan R. Kofodimos, *Beyond Ambition: How Driven Managers Can Lead Better and Live Better* (San Francisco: Jossey-Bass, 1991), 111.

5. Keep in mind that these five building blocks are intended to provide a general model for understanding the actual attributes that were submitted as characteristics of great leaders.

CHAPTER 20

READING AND ACTING
LIKE A LEADER

We've just covered five blocks of leadership and more than one hundred attributes of great leaders. That alone should remind us that leadership is a complex activity. But the complexity becomes more obvious when you take into account the difficulty of acquiring and processing information into decisions and actions. As we're about to see, our abilities to successfully function as leaders are intricately tied to our abilities to read people and situations and act appropriately.

The Read–Act leadership concept

During the mid 1980s I was assigned to the leadership team at Squadron Officer School, the Air Force's eight-week leadership school for lieutenants and captains.[1] A major emphasis of the course was on what we called the Read–Act leadership model.[2] We taught these officers that good leaders read people and situations and then take the appropriate action. This concept provides a manageable way to approach a complex subject.

The following matrix illustrates the basic idea of Read–Act. It underscores why reading and acting appropriately is so important for everyone, especially leaders.

	READ	DON'T READ
ACT	**Performers** • Effective • Successful • Reliable/Responsible	**Dangerous** • Impulsive • Bull in the china shop • Rash
DON'T ACT	**Self-Protectors** • Political • Timid • Grumpy	**"Happy"** • Clueless • Lazy • Dreamers

We used this Read–Act model as a way to evaluate student responses to various leadership laboratory situations. It proved to be a simple but very effective way to get people to analyze the effectiveness of their leadership processes relative to outcomes.

Several other well-known leadership theories parallel this basic concept of reading and acting. For example, Ken Blanchard's Situational Leadership® model focuses on the need for leaders to assess (*read*) the level of competence and commitment of the individual and then use the leadership style that fits the situation (*act*).[3]

Daniel Goleman's emotional intelligence model also is oriented toward reading self and others and then acting appropriately. His four major domains of emotional intelligence are Self-awareness, Self-management, Social Awareness, and Relationship Management.[4] In other words, reading self and others (awareness) and acting (managing each) appropriately.

At RightPath Resources, all of our training follows a similar concept: *understand* self and others, and *apply* that knowledge to be a more effective teammate and leader. Let's look at some specifics of reading and acting and some of the barriers to gaining an understanding of self and others.

Reading: we must face reality to understand ourselves. Our minds are much like computers: garbage in means garbage out. To render meaningful decisions and actions, we must have clean, accurate data. But here's the rub: To get this type of information requires a keen and *objective* awareness of self, the environment, and others.

It's no accident that objectivity is a recurring pattern throughout this book. Consistently, we observe that a lack of accurate information and/or objectivity is the Achilles' heel of most leaders. Too often, either they don't get or don't accept input from others or they don't regard their own inner voices.

Winston Churchill is reported to have said, "Men occasionally stumble over the truth, but most of them pick themselves up and hurry off as if nothing had happened."[5] Churchill had some insight into this phenomenon (heeding what we want to heed) and its effect on himself, because he knew he wore people out with his high energy and excessive talking. Yet, he continued to keep his guests and staff awake well past midnight with his nonstop storytelling, lecturing, and manic workaholism. One Churchill biographer wrote, "Those invited to 'dine and sleep at' Chequers quipped that they had been invited to dine and stay awake."[6]

For all of his greatness, Churchill was notorious for ignoring the problems caused by his own extreme behaviors. For instance, his habits of micromanaging and generating paperwork were demoralizing. It caused one of his contemporaries, General Kennedy, to express the military view that, "I don't see how we can win the war without Winston, but on the other hand I don't see how we can win with him." And some in the bureaucracy were known to say that it was "easier to win the war against Hitler than the war against Churchill."[7]

Reading: we must get feedback from others to understand ourselves. Blind spots are a major problem for all of us. For leaders, they are the source of legendary horror stories. Yet, somehow, as people attain higher levels they tend to forget what they saw when looking up the ladder. Since we cannot see ourselves clearly, we need input from others. But many leaders don't get the candor they need because their people are afraid to tell them the truth.

Robert Kaplan from the Center for Creative Leadership (Greensboro) divides the reasons that executives don't get totally objective feedback (criticism) into two general categories: *power* and *ego*. The power of the executive poses barriers to criticism, as follows:[8]

- *Isolation at the top of the hierarchy.* Limited exposure to those who know what's really happening.
- *Executive prerogatives.* May be exempt from feedback.
- *Position.* Subordinates defer because of high position.
- *Misuse of power.* Subordinates may be actively intimidated.
- *Executives may need to be flattered.* Subordinates ingratiate themselves. Executives hire people who will agree with them and people who think and operate like themselves.

Perhaps an even greater problem is that many leaders have egos that are so fragile they can't bear to hear the truth, especially about themselves. Not that it's always so bad; it's just that they don't want to hear anything that could be negative. Kaplan's list of ego-related barriers to criticism is summarized as follows. Senior leaders have the following:

- *A strong need to be perfect.* This is reinforced by others' expectations of them (it is not okay to admit flaws).
- *A need to justify themselves.* Even when they acknowledge problems, they try to explain them away.
- *A need to appear competent.* This need is exacerbated by their high visibility (criticism is discounted because it would undermine their image).[9]

As you can see, these power-and-ego blinders relate to the insecurities that most of us have. People who truly feel secure and self-confident inside are actually somewhat rare. One way you can spot them is by their ability to deal with reality about themselves and others. Furthermore, secure people are much more aware of their own feelings and emotions and what is causing them. *Insecure leaders who are quick to defend their image of always being right need to look within to identify the sources of the fears and deal with them.*

Leaders (especially at the executive level) must establish and aggressively promote a culture that values people over power and personal growth over a perfect image. This approach sets an environment that builds trust and empowers people at all levels to look honestly at themselves and accept realistic feedback from others.

Reading: we must get feedback from ourselves to understand ourselves. We also tend to ignore important data from ourselves when it tells us what we don't want to hear, even at our own peril. Some leaders violate their own leadership principles and ethical codes when they are under the gun to meet certain goals and expectations.

Jane Doe, a senior manager we worked with in the past, is a typical example. She had big responsibilities, yet she didn't have hands-on control and didn't really trust the people who did. Because of the pressure of her job, she partitioned off her internal feedback loop and operated as a critical, micromanager and control freak. Jane ignored the professional leadership principles she had been taught and trampled on the very corporate values she was promoting. Of course, her people learned to keep their heads down and do as they were told. In effect, she neutered her staff of most of their initiative and creativity.

It's likely that the controlling "Janes" (and "Johns") can spot these leadership breakdowns in others, but it's a different story when it's their reputations or results at stake. Their blind spots can be so large that they block out reality, leading them to deny, defend, or in some way rationalize their behaviors.

It's also common for people to silence their own self-feedback messenger (conscience) so they can talk (lie) their way out of a commitment or an embarrassing situation. Most often, this evidences itself as what we call selective memory. The individual remembers details in the way that suits his or her needs in the current situation. When money, pride, or professional reputation is at stake, the still small voice that says, "this is violating your ethics" is often ignored.

While completing my master's degree practicum at the federal prison in Montgomery, Alabama, I talked with inmates who were judges, lawyers, doctors, stockbrokers, business owners, and politicians. Rarely did I meet one who admitted to having done something illegal.[10] These ex-community leaders were still denying the feedback that could have protected them in the first place.

If prison examples sound extreme, just reflect on some of the companies that had to restate their earnings in 2002. Logic would say that you have to be intentionally ignoring or discounting your own internal feedback to think you can pull off a shell game in a publicly traded company by hiding expenses to the tune of a billion here and a billion there.

These examples should be a warning of how difficult it is to get a consistent and accurate read on ourselves. Let me encourage you to practice stepping back from your fears, ego, power, filters, and biased lenses to hear and observe yourself. Check to see if your emotions, words, and actions are consistent with your self-perception. Take the approach that it's quite possible that your talk and walk are incongruent. After all, if it were true, then wouldn't you want to be the first to know?

Remember, the more accurate your self-awareness, the better you will be at reading yourself, the higher your emotional intelligence will be, and (most important) the more appropriate your actions will be as a leader.

Reading: understanding others is also a challenge. Good leadership also requires insights (data) regarding others. For example, what is motivating them?[11] What are their passions, priorities, and purposes? What are their immediate cares and concerns? Where and what do they sense as the sources of power and the sources of threats? In other words, we need to know the flow of the river that we are dealing with so that we can have some hope of influencing its course. But, how does one go about gaining this awareness of others and the environment?

The information on personality in Sections 1 and 2 will be a significant tool in helping you accurately understand others, but "reading" people goes further than naturally motivated behaviors. It requires you to listen carefully, not only to what people say but also to what they don't say. One of the most important ways you can read others is to observe their body language as you interact with them. Their words may be saying one thing while their bodies are saying another. If you are really reading them, you'll know which to believe.

Perhaps the greatest challenge in reading others is that you have to listen with empathy—see the world from their point of view to comprehend their meaning and perspective. In *Primal Leadership*, Goleman explains empathy as "Sensing others' emotions, understanding their perspective, and taking active interest in their concerns."[12]

He goes on to say, " . . . Empathy means taking employees' feelings into thoughtful consideration and then making intelligent decisions that work those feelings into the response." Then he tops it off with, "Empathy is the *sine qua non* [an indispensable condition] of all social effectiveness in work."[13]

It seems clear that the sensitive and caring perspective of empathy is essential for understanding (reading) the other person, and thus it is a requirement for good relationships and good leadership.

Now, with all this talk about sensitivity, feelings and empathy, I imagine that one-third of you, the Objective/Detached group are feeling a bit queasy and may want to throw down this book and run out the door. Don't do it! Just trust me. And if you don't trust me, trust Daniel Goleman. Developing empathy likely will improve your leadership abilities more than anything you've done in a long time.

Goleman and his team explain why leaders must gain this ability to perceive the emotions of others and respond with empathy. They also make a compelling argument that empathy in relationships is the key to retention.

"Empathetic people are superb at recognizing and meeting the needs of clients, customers, and subordinates. They seem approachable, wanting to hear what people have to say. They listen carefully, discerning what people are truly concerned about, and they respond on the mark. Accordingly, empathy is key to retaining talent. Leaders have always needed empathy to develop and keep good people, but whenever there is a war for talent the stakes are higher. Of all the factors in a company's control, tuned-out dissonant leaders are one of the main reasons that talented people leave–and take the company's knowledge with them."[14]

These last comments on retention are consistent with Gallup's research and Buckingham and Coffman's conclusion that retention is directly tied to the individual's relationship with his or her supervisor.[15]

Empathy, relationships, and retention have a huge impact on the bottom line, but there are other reasons why leaders need to read people. In reality, every interaction with another person is an opportunity to gather data that can be used in carrying out the myriad of leadership attributes discussed earlier.

No matter what your current level of expertise at reading people, improving your awareness of others and the environment will significantly enhance the quality of your decisions and actions.

Acting, responding to what we've read.

Managing ourselves and our actions. Gaining insight is not enough; we have to apply this information to act more appropriately. Often, self-management is the most difficult thing we have to do. One of my peers recently pointed out that a study of successful and unsuccessful people found that the main difference was that the successful people were able to make themselves do the things they really didn't want to do. In many ways, this is the essence of self-management and a key characteristic of successful people.

Self-management really is management in every sense of the word, because it involves setting goals and establishing priorities. It involves using the information acquired from "reading" and applying it in the stewardship of time, talents, money, etc. Self-managing is also about self-control, i.e., how well you are able to control your words, emotions, and actions in relationships with others.

In recent years, I've learned to use self-coaching as a powerful tool for talking myself out of negative behaviors and attitudes and into those more positive ones to which I aspire. Often, I can read a situation, decide it isn't headed the way I want it to go, and make changes in my thinking and actions. But it's not as easy as it sounds. Self-coaching requires courage, confidence, and a commitment to do what you may not feel like doing. However, the payoff is worth the effort, because reading and acting appropriately does bring better outcomes.

Some of the most rewarding work I've done has been helping executives use self-coaching. Terry, president of a business division of a Fortune 500 company, shared with me how he had coached himself to hold back his own comments and opinions to hear what others have to say. He is now coaching himself to encourage some of his Reserved and Accommodating staff to speak up. James, an Extroverted, Dominant, and Detached vice president, shared how he had been able to remain quiet and stay out of a conflict with his boss and peers during a staff meeting.

These incidents of reading self and acting appropriately were significant victories in the continued development of two established and respected leaders. An interesting aspect of this is that the better they get at managing themselves the better they are at managing their decisions and actions with others. The payoff from reading and acting appropriately (and self-coaching) is huge and extends in all directions.

Reading and acting does sound simple, and at times it is but it can also be the ultimate challenge. We tend to have a bent (natural and learned) that is not easy to change. As mentioned earlier, changing these ingrained behaviors/responses can seem as difficult as trying to divert the channel of a river. So, if we desire to be the best leaders we can be, we must commit to continual personal growth and development in order to improve our ability to read and act in relation to ourselves and others.

Expanding the Read–Act into the Team Decision-Making Process

Before leaving this subject, I'd like to offer an expansion of the Read–Act model. Let me emphasize that these types of models are intended only to provide a framework for communicating concepts in a general way. They are not a formula for success— just a graphic way of conveying ideas. With that said, let's look at a model for the Team Decision-Making Process.

Making decisions and taking actions in relation to people and situations is both an art and an inexact science. There are endless possibilities and permutations, but any good response usually follows a process similar to the following.

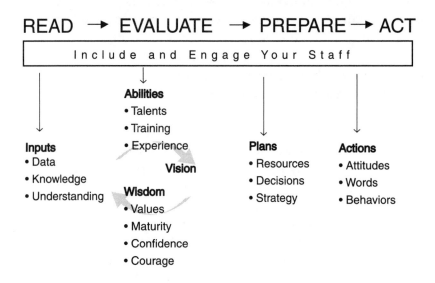

Team Decision-Making Process

READ → EVALUATE → PREPARE → ACT

Include and Engage Your Staff

Inputs
• Data
• Knowledge
• Understanding

Abilities
• Talents
• Training
• Experience

Vision

Wisdom
• Values
• Maturity
• Confidence
• Courage

Plans
• Resources
• Decisions
• Strategy

Actions
• Attitudes
• Words
• Behaviors

The Team Decision-Making Process allows us to expand the Read–Act model by inserting two additional steps—**Evaluate** and **Prepare**—and these are the two that I want to focus on briefly. Keep in mind that for simple situations this entire process can be cut down to a microsecond. For example, if someone asks you to do something obviously illegal, you don't need to consult others or spend much time processing your response. Your values system and your experience would immediately cut short the deliberative process, and you could respond immediately by saying "No" and be confident that you had done the right thing.

When you get into more complex situations, a leader's success in making the right decision is highly dependent on the process that the leader uses to gather and evaluate the data and reach decisions. Central to the evaluation process are the **Vision, Abilities, and Wisdom** of not only the leader but of the entire team.

The leader's *vision* provides a framework in which the evaluation and ultimate decision and actions must fit. The *abilities* will vary from individual to individual, depending on talents, training, and experience. Likewise, different leaders will have varying levels of *wisdom* and maturity in applying personal and corporate values. Now here is the point: Good leaders are able to augment their evaluation process by tapping into the abilities, wisdom, and vision of others—teammates, peers, and their own leaders.

What I've just said sounds so obvious as to be trivial, but some of the most common problems we see come from experienced leaders who act on the spot and make impulsive decisions and commitments that have not been adequately evaluated by their teams. These knee-jerk responses often result in dumb decisions that cause problems, embarrass the organization, and misuse resources. Just as important, skipping this type of decision-making process tends to demoralize the team/staff. When left out, they typically feel devalued (i.e., "Why are we here?") and resent not having the opportunity to provide input.

Inexperienced managers often don't fully avail themselves of their staff/team resources either. They may not know to use them or they may think they are not acting like confident leaders if they get others involved in the process. To reach the best conclusions, make the best decisions, and take the most effective actions, secure leaders—no matter what their experiences—will want to get others involved. Insecure leaders will operate like warlords who, to protect their "positions," will hang on to every ounce of power.

So, as you refine your leadership, take a look at the Team

Decision-Making Process chart on page 230 and critique your-self. Are you using the people resources on your team to full advantage? Ask them what they think and see how they evaluate your use of *their* abilities and wisdom. If they have a generally consistent response, you can expect that they are giving you accurate feedback.

Coach's Clipboard

Key Point: Good leaders learn how to be intentional about reading self, others, and the environment and then acting appropriately.

Action Items
  1. In which quadrant of the Read–Act model do you typically operate?
  2. What will you do to be more intentional in your reading and acting?

---

1. Now limited to captains only. In the1980s we educated/trained 4,000 officers annually (five eight-week classes of eight hundred officers).

2. The Read–Act model originated with the late Professor Gus Ecomomos, from DePaul University, who introduced it to Squadron Officer School in 1972. Faculty members, Captains Len Daley and Jack Veth, developed Read–Act for school application, and Major Lee Storey implemented it into the curriculum. My description here varies somewhat from the original words.

3. Ken Blanchard's Situational Leadership, *The Article*, 1994, Blanchard Training and Development, Inc.

4. Daniel Goleman, Richard Boyatzis, and Annie McKee, *Primal Leadership: Realizing the Power of Emotional Intelligence* (Cambridge: Harvard Business School Press, 2002), 39.

5. Quotes by Winston Churchill, CreativeQuotations.com.

6. Piers Brendon, *Winston Churchill: A Biography* (NY: Harper & Row, 1984), 158.

7. Ibid., 158.

8. Robert E. Kaplan with William H. Drath and Joan R. Kofodimos, *Beyond Ambition: How Driven Managers Can Lead Better and Live Better* (San Francisco: Jossey-Bass, 1991), 36.

9. Ibid., 42.

10. This was the same minimum-security prison where several of the Watergate conspirators had lived. A former state governor and some of his staff were "guests" during the time I was "practicing" my counseling skills.

11. Those who rule through power and control may not be concerned with any motivations of others except fear. However, to ignite passion, inspiration, and influence, the source of motivation becomes a key input.

12. Daniel Goleman, Richard Boyatzis and Annie McKee, *Primal Leadership: Realizing the Power of Emotional Intelligence* (Cambridge: Harvard Business School, 2002), 39.

13. Ibid., 50.

14. Ibid., 50.

15. Marcus Buckingham and Curt Coffman, *First Break All the Rules: What the World's Greatest Leaders Do Differently* (NY: Simon & Schuster © by the Gallup Organization, 1999), 11–12.

CONTROL

Control has been a recurring theme in this book, because it is at the core of so many issues of leadership and teamwork. It is also another one of those good news/bad news subjects. It is an essential element of management, and yet when it's overdone it undermines leadership more than almost any other problem. Understanding how to walk that tightrope between some and too much is the challenge that all good leaders must consciously face. Let's examine this issue, and you can check yourself to see if you have controlling tendencies.

Some forms of control are essential.

The more complex the responsibilities and the higher the stakes, the more supervision and control is needed and expected. For example, those involved in launching ballistic missiles are highly restricted by a formal command-and-control system. Other high-risk occupations and environments, such as prisons, operating rooms, firing ranges, and power plants, are also highly controlled—and for good reason. Likewise, when individuals have low capability for the task, more oversight is appropriate.

Modern civilizations use various forms of control to govern and regulate society and business. Consider the following ways that we control and are controlled in our everyday lives: performance management; technical manuals; supervision; playbooks; policies; guidance; directives; corporate values; federal, state, and local laws and regulations; safety guidelines; operating instructions; contracts; letters of agreement; covenants; and rules for everything imaginable. From cradle to grave, we experience control, and so it's natural for us to turn to control as a management tool.

Overcontrol can be deadly

Because control is such a normal part of our lives, often it is overused. Then the problems come. In *The Leadership Challenge*, Kouzes and Posner express it this way.

> Traditional management teaching suggests that the job of management is primarily one of control: the control of resources, including time, money, materials, and people. Flesh-and-blood leaders know, however, that the more they control others the less likely it is that people will excel. They also know that the more they control, the less they'll be trusted.[1]

Overcontrolling does not work; it ignores human potential and disregards the boundaries of others. With a focus primarily on themselves and their own agenda, controllers don't notice when they are trampling over someone else's legitimate personhood, territory, and related privileges. Typically, they justify their actions by the "good" work they do or the "crisis we are facing." However, those on the receiving end do not feel empowered and more capable as a result. On the contrary, they feel less valued and then they take less ownership for their work.

I have personal knowledge of the problems of overcontrol from all angles. As one who has been overcontrolled and as one who has overcontrolled, I know how demoralizing and debilitating it can be. I also know how difficult it can be to not be in control and feel out of control. Let me share a few personal insights in this area.

Since I'm on the Directing side of the control factor, I like to set the agenda, make the decisions, and run the show. I feel that's when I'm the most productive. But the tendencies can be problematic.

If you take someone who has this natural bent to control and has grown up with high control and then goes into a highly controlled environment like the military, it gets reinforced. Next, consider the five years as a POW where I was controlled by an enemy; and, at the same time, as the communications officer I used control to keep from getting caught and punished. Then add several years as an instructor pilot and supervisor of flying, where control is a matter of life and death on a daily basis, and you can understand why I like to be in control.

But control can be a matter of life and death in other ways. Without freedom to explore, take risks, and make mistakes, growth dies also. I got my first lesson in this from one of my student pilots one day when I was over-instructing him on how to lead a formation landing. This nineteen-year-old Danish lieutenant stopped me cold in the middle of our flight with these simple words: "Sir, I can handle it myself." He was right, and he did fly it better than any first attempt I'd ever seen. This was a revelation to me, and I began to back off from telling my students how to do the things they knew already. That kind of freedom from micromanagement brings life to people and gives them the opportunity to really learn and build their confidence. It also frees them to reach their highest levels of productivity and creativity.

There were some key steps that we learned in the flight instruction business that apply to all fields of management and development. A good development sequence (and the process of giving up control) follows a building-block approach. First, the students studied the books on the maneuvers we would fly. Then the instructors would talk them through the tasks, using model airplanes and hands. Then in the air we would demonstrate the maneuvers. Next, we would let the students practice the maneuvers, with us monitoring or perhaps riding along on the controls with them. Typically, we would demonstrate again and re-explain points in the maneuvers and let them practice again. Shortly, though, they had to digest all this information and do it by themselves. They had to make it "their thing."

When the students could develop their own concepts and transfer them into safe and acceptable replications of the maneuvers, then we knew they had learned it. If they could do it consistently and safely (not perfectly), it was time to make their solo flights. I would climb out of the aircraft, give him or her a pat on the back, a big smile, and a thumbs-up, and walk back into the flight operations building. With that, a twenty-two-year-old, right out of college, would taxi out and take off all alone in a multimillion dollar supersonic jet. Yes, there was still some control around the student, such as a runway supervisor to monitor the takeoff and landing; but the student had complete control of the aircraft.

I gave the students the control (authority), but I did not and could not give up responsibility. My career was riding on the training that we had given the students, my assessment of their capabilities to handle the challenge, and their performances. It's the same in any leadership scenario. When you delegate and empower others with meaningful responsibilities, you take risks. But effective leaders don't take foolish risks; they take calculated risks.

The students had received careful screening for their aptitudes, had been given the proper training, and had demonstrated that they were capable of doing the job safely. There were no guarantees for any of us, but at some point leaders have to trust their own judgment and others' capabilities.

In the flight training business, there are only two alternatives: You either delegate and empower or you eliminate them from training. In that environment, micromanaging is not an option. If they meet the criteria, you have to get out and let them fly alone. But in most organizations, micromanaging is an option, and some leaders choose it. And when they do, people hate it because it's degrading and eventually sucks the motivation and creativity from both them and the organization.

One of the questions in our "Awesome Traits Exercise" is "How does your group like to be managed?" The responses are almost universally the same, regardless of the group's traits. "Give us the task, give us the resources and guidelines, and get out of our way. Don't micromanage us or tell us how to do our jobs." It's instructive that we've never found one person that likes to be micromanaged. It's also true that most people who are micromanagers don't realize how negative their management is.

Overcontrolling out of fear

In psychology, there is a saying that "awareness is curative." Since leadership also deals with human nature, let's assume that more awareness on your part will be either preventive medicine or an incentive for healing. If you will accept that, then let's look at the source of our controlling nature and some of the ways these behaviors are manifest.

We control either to keep something from happening or to make something happen. In either case, controllers are determined to make sure things are done their way. Granted that some control is necessary in certain situations, but what motivates people to become control freaks?

The most common sources of controlling behaviors are fear and anxiety. In describing controllers, psychologist and author Dr. Les Parrott points out, "They are not nearly as self-assured as they often appear. Terrified of being criticized, rejected, or exposed in any way, they try to protect themselves by staying in control of every aspect of their lives—and everyone else's. . . . The soul of control is fueled by anxiety and nurtured by feelings of extreme vulnerability and a fragile self-confidence."[2]

Dig deep enough in most of us and you will find embedded in the dark rooms of our fragile egos the source of most of our problems: feelings of inadequacy, insecurity, insufficiency, imperfection, and inferiority. For some, the associated feelings of shame are so great that they will do almost anything to keep these feelings of vulnerability hidden from view. On the other hand, those who are emotionally healthy learn

to deal with reality as they mature and shed the illusion of perfection. They are able to accept their frailties with grace, humility, and sometimes even humor.

But when the vulnerability is extreme and the ego needs extra protection, watch out. From these dark rooms of shame come
the four horsemen that bring death to the management style of
controllers: fear of failure, fear of looking bad, fear of not
being perfect, fear of being judged. Control is usually about gaining some form of power, with the idea that power will eliminate the possibility of these fears becoming reality. With power,
we can prove that we're okay and cover those feelings of inadequacy.

Most everyone has at least a mild form of these fears. In
some ways, they can actually be helpful to stimulate us to be
productive and successful. But when enough fear is combined
with a high ambition, big responsibilities, and a fragile ego, you
have the recipe for high control. This is one of the most common problems for controlling leaders, because they are typically ambitious but have to depend on the performance of
others for their own successes. But when they resort to overcontrolling others to protect themselves, it's out of the norm
and it's dysfunctional.

Doug, a senior level manager, is a very intelligent leader who
has great potential in many ways. But, the competition in his
organization is very keen, and he thinks that the slightest mistake or problem in his area could take him out of the running
for the next promotion. Doug has always been motivated by
those deadly twins—fear of failure and a high need to achieve—
so his situation reinforces his natural directing tendency to control others. He's a good guy and his people like him as a person,
but his micromanaging, pinging-off-the-wall style of leadership
is slowing their productivity and undermining teamwork.

It will not be easy for Doug to master his fears sufficiently
to change his behaviors and quit micromanaging and controlling. In order to do so, he will have to believe in himself, his
people, and his leadership enough to let go of his death grip
on the control stick. Since he has no absolute assurance that
he won't be disappointed, it comes down to a philosophical

(and in some ways a spiritual) matter. Doug has to be willing to do the very best he can, using his experience, professional knowledge, and the best techniques of leadership; and then he must have faith that everything is going to turn out all right.

When I stepped out of the cockpit with the student pilots and sent them on solo flights, I had to give up control and operate on faith. I trusted my judgment and experience; I trusted their capabilities and strong motivation to survive another day and have successful careers. I knew that they were motivated to do the best job possible. Given the circumstances, that was all anyone could ask. I could not guarantee that they would not crash and burn, because that did happen from time to time. I always risked the possibility of an accident investigation that would probe every detail of my instruction and decision to empower the students with such a big responsibility.

Ultimately, Doug cannot control as much as he thinks he can either. He needs to see that although he thinks he's in control of his life, that's somewhat of an illusion. For example, he cannot control his promotion; that's up to his leaders. By micromanaging, he can make his people miserable, but he cannot keep them from making a mistake. He also needs to trust in himself and his people. He has a great record and many superb leadership qualities. He really doesn't have to prove anything to anyone except that he can be a wise and respected leader. If he does that, even a mistake in his area is not likely to kill his career.

Surviving a problem is more common than people think. I've observed this in the corporate world, and it was true in the military. As a colonel, part of my job was deciding (in collaboration with my boss) whom to select to command the eight squadrons in our organization and which captains we would recommend for promotion to major. These experiences taught me that leaders pick leaders whom they trust to be responsible, get results, and take care of their people. They typically look at the whole picture, rather than at one incident. Perfection is usually not a criterion for a promotion or a successful career—at least not in my experience.

As a major, I was in charge of a deployed flying organiza-

242 ✧ LEADING TALENTS, LEADING TEAMS

tion and was directly responsible for qualifying a rated pilot (not a student) to fly, who subsequently did crash and die. The investigation board determined that it was pilot error, with high crosswinds a contributing factor. I had flown with the lieutenant earlier in the day and he had done a fine job under similar conditions. In the morning, he had demonstrated the capability to handle the situation; but in the afternoon he made one mistake that led to another, and that cost him his life. It was a sad and tragic event that left a widow with a small child. It was something I'll never forget.

I tell this story only to make a point. Things under my control didn't turn out right, but it didn't ruin my career or affect my next promotion. In fact, within a year I was given the coveted position of chief of standardization and evaluation, responsible for conducting annual flight evaluations for all pilots on the base.

These and other experiences reinforced my belief that you can only control and protect yourself and your career so far. There are limits, and one of them is the legitimate boundaries of others. Leaders must learn to deal with the dilemma of being responsible. Yet, to some degree, they have to trust their future to the performance and decisions of others. Solving that challenge with each unique individual and in many different situations requires extraordinary discernment and judgment—the essence of reading and acting.

Egocentric Controllers

Now let's look briefly at some of the outward manifestations and rationalizations of highly egocentric control freaks. They operate as if the world revolved around them, and therefore they need to be at the center of control.

Some people control out of a fear that something will go wrong if they are not involved to make things turn out right. If operations are a manager's background, she may want to be involved in all the details of operations. If sales are his background, a manager may feel that he has to accompany his people on every important call. Similarly, if you have ever been a parent of a teenager about to take the car out for the first time, you may have struggled with that type of fear. But at work or at home, eventually you have to rely on the capability, judgment, and training of others and let them go. Much like soloing a student in an airplane, you do the best you can and trust that person to do likewise. But it is a calculated risk in judgment that you have to take, and it requires a level of faith.

In a similar vein, some people *control out of a need to be the rescuing hero*. They have inflated views of their own importance and feel a need to rescue all those poor, inept people around them. They get their psychic income by being needed, and of course they can think of many reasons why those around them need their help. This can be very subtle at first, because they operate as some of the nicest, most thoughtful people you've ever met—until you feel the arms and tentacles of the octopus start to constrict.

There is also a selfish need by some people to *control because they take excessive ownership or they enjoy the tasks and don't want to let go*. They don't want to turn loose and miss out on the gratification they get. This is especially common in situations in which special skills are required. Of course, it's difficult to get practice and develop the needed skills when someone else controls all the opportunities.

Others *control because they know best and it has to be done their way*. They are the experts and want everyone else to do it exactly the way they think it should be done. Since they always know the best way, they insist on others following their instructions. Of course, they often do know a very good way and perhaps they may know the best way, but that's not a reason to undermine the learning process of others.

Not taking over can be very difficult, because to not control means that you must stand back and watch someone make an error or do something stupid in order to learn on his or her own. But usually, the so-called experts have such good knowledge and techniques because they learned through experience, even bad experiences. As painful as it is, we must allow others to learn from the school of hard knocks. For most people, this is not only the best way to learn but it's the only way to learn.

Recognizing controlling behaviors

The book on control, quoted earlier in this chapter, is an excellent resource on this subject for those of us who are recovering controllers. It's also helpful for those who have a control freak for a boss, teammate, or family member. In it, Dr. Parrott offers the following ten qualities of controlling people.[3]

- Obnoxious
- Tenacious
- Invasive
- Obsessive
- Perfectionist

- Irritable
- Demanding
- Rigid
- Critical
- Close-minded

There are passive controllers too. We normally think of controlling people as being active and somewhat aggressive in their behaviors. But passive people can be very controlling as well. For example, of the ten behaviors above, a person can be tenacious, obsessive, perfectionist, rigid, and close minded without displaying assertive and pushy behaviors. A passive controller often operates by shutting down and not cooperating: "If you are not going to play by my rules, I just won't play." Or perhaps, "If you won't give me what I want, I'll go to my room and pout until you feel guilty and give me what I want." The intended result is to exert power and change the behaviors of others. If you find yourself having to walk on eggshells, you may be dealing with a passive controller.

Passive controllers tend to be much subtler, so they usually run undetected under our regular control-detection radar. And because of the way they operate, passive controllers probably affect fewer people—primarily, their immediate teammates and family.

Finding our place on the control continuum. A starting point for you to identify the degree that you control others would be to review the list above and make an assessment. Then, get some truly honest feedback from other people who know you well. It won't work to ask them if you are a good person. Most controllers are good people with good intentions, so that's not the issue here; and it's not the way you assess controlling behaviors. Also, don't ask someone who has weak boundaries. He or she won't be able to give you an objective answer.

The road to recovery for "controlaholics." The discussion earlier about Doug provides several insights for dealing with controlling tendencies. As with alcoholism, the first step is to admit the problem and take responsibility for it. Doing so takes some of the power away from its hold and allows controllers to begin coaching themselves into more trusting and healthier lifestyles. Most people are going to need someone to point out specific examples of their controlling behaviors and hold them accountable for change. Some, even senior executives, have baggage that is so serious and so entrenched that they will need professional help before they can let go of their death grip on control.

As a leader, I'm a big believer in a loose/tight approach. Loose in that everyone doesn't have to do things the same way that I would. People are allowed freedom to choose their methods and means to achieve the assigned goal. Yet, tight in that everyone is working toward the right outcomes and aligned on the same values and same overall vision and mission.

Our leaders in the POW camp were wise enough to employ this loose/tight strategy. We were tight on our mission, goals, and values. Yet, within those broad commitments, each person had the latitude to operate in his own way—sometimes just the best way he could. Each one of us faced different circumstances and we had different talents and capabilities. Some were physically stronger and healthier, some were tougher emotionally, and some had greater courage. Some had more creativity and some had more consistency. Together we made a great team.

For most of those years, the POWs of North Vietnam had only a few guidelines. Primarily, these were the military code of conduct for combatants, our vision statement (Return with Honor) and our motto ("Resist, Survive, and Relax"). There were a few clarifications along the way, and some policies were added in the later years, but in the end it all came down to the vision: *Return with Honor.* If you did all that those three words encompassed, you didn't have to worry about what others might think.

The POW leaders expected loyalty in the core areas and allowed latitude in how each person lived it. I know that some of the camp leaders came in with controlling tendencies, but they really weren't a factor in that environment. Faith, hope, and love abided on this team, and the love was powerful enough to overcome most of our fears and controlling natures. My experience is that these same qualities will work quite well in the corporate "camps" as well.

Coach's Clipboard

Key Point: At the root of control is insecurity and fear. Exercise your best judgment and then allow faith, hope, and love to cover those things you can't control.

Action Items

1. Is it possible that you have controlling tendencies?

2. Ask your teammates if they sometimes feel like you are micromanaging or pushing into their boundaries.

3. If you have controlling tendencies, what are your fears? What behaviors do you need to change?

1. James M. Kouzes and Barry Z. Posner, *The Leadership Challenge*, (San Francisco: Jossey-Bass, A Wiley Company, 1995), 16.

2. Les Parrott III, *The Control Freak* (Wheaton: Tyndale House, 2000), 51.

3. Ibid., 34–35.

❖

LEADERSHIP CHECKPOINTS

To round out our leadership discussion, I'd like to walk you through some of the common issues that I've faced—personally as a leader and professionally as a consultant and coach. My assumption is that you are a good leader who has been successful. We are not trying to remake you but to move you down the leadership path with increased awareness, renewed focus, and perhaps some new ideas and tools for the journey.

These checkpoints may keep you from taking a dead-end detour or being ambushed along the way. With that understanding, please allow me to talk very straight with you about leadership. Of course, by now you've figured out it's difficult for me to do it any other way.

 Leadership always makes a difference.

Leaders make things happen, and good leaders make the *right* things happen so, ultimately, responsibility for success always comes back to leadership. As someone who gets an inside look at a number of companies, it's rather easy to spot organizations in which there is good leadership. The first things you notice are positive attitudes and that people are aligned—headed in the same direction. The corporate vision is well understood, people are focused, and they're meeting their goals; or, if not, they are taking action to get back on track.

Communications are open and honest, and leaders show respect for individuals at all levels. A basic level of trust is evident, and there is a team attitude across departments with peers at least attempting to cooperate with each other. Morale is high, and even though people are working hard they seem to be having fun. Accountability is strong at all levels. The organization resembles a well-oiled machine, except with a head and a heart. These are the markers of good leadership.

Tom, a regional manager for a national company that I've worked with, is a good example of a highly effective leader. His leadership is especially impressive because he's been under heavy pressure. His team has faced some significant challenges in the past three years due to financial problems in their headquarters: a merger and then reorganization.

Tom's team has worked at a frenzied pace to increase revenues and, at the same time, incorporate a number of new systems. Through it all they are getting the job done: revenues have grown, morale is good, and teamwork seems to be flourishing. Tom has a razor-like focus on his organizational and personal goals, *and* he builds strong relationships. He is totally engaged with his team, his boss, and his peers.

Poor leadership is usually just as obvious. The bottom-line may still be written in black ink, but there is also a black cloud overhead and shadows are evident on the people's faces. We can tell from the signs that trouble is brewing. As we meet with the staff, our suspicions are usually confirmed. Through carefully worded responses, body language, and sometimes even horror stories, we see that people are walking on eggshells or they have withdrawn to the survival mode. People's talents and energy are not fully engaged, and enthusiasm is missing.

When there are significant problems like these, the leaders typically have some or all of the following problems: not dealing with reality, not clearly focused, not listening, not communicating, not committed, overwhelmed, indecisive, withdrawn, disrespectful, totally self-focused, lack courage, insecure, afraid, angry, emotional, pushy, and controlling. When these issues are obvious, we know that the organization is either treading water or on the way down.

Organizations can't afford these leadership qualities, even when the leader appears to be getting results, especially in today's competitive market for talent. The top performers—especially from the younger generations—are not going to stay the course with a tyrannical or incompetent captain.

However, sometimes it may not be that the leader is bad; it might be bad chemistry or timing. Leaders have their limitations, and at times the problems may be that he or she is just a bad fit for the needs of the situation. No matter what the situation, it always comes back to leadership. If things are not working right, the leader needs to do something; if not, then someone at a higher level should. *Are you and your leaders making a positive difference?*

☑️ **Leadership is rarely easy.**

Tom's success under difficult circumstances reminds us that leaders typically face incredibly complex problems for which there is no clear course or guaranteed solution. They often must chart a course through a wilderness of competing issues and priorities. They must lead and inspire even when they face challenges over which they have little control.

This is a lesson I learned as a squadron commander that I wish I had fully grasped earlier in my career. There was an aircraft accident at another base, and the follow-up investigation brought inspectors digging through our unit. They were taking sworn testimony and generally disrupting morale, as well as normal operations.

None of our people had any firsthand contact with those involved in the accident, so I was complaining to my boss about it. His face took on a chastising look as he said, "Lee, anyone can steer the ship through calm waters; the real captains can pilot it through the storm." His comment hit me like a hammer, and it has inspired me many times when forces outside my control were threatening success.

Tom was a good example of a real captain, because he did

not cause any of the challenges he faced, but he had to overcome them in order to succeed, and he did. *Have you accepted it as your role to take the team through the storms regardless of what they are or where they come from?*

☑ Leaders must walk the talk.

One of the clearest tests of the leadership is the degree to which lower-level supervisors and employees in general perceive that the corporate values are carried out. For example, most organizations today have a formally stated set of values regarding the company's commitment toward integrity, fairness, quality, and the way customers and employees are to be treated. The very presence of such value statements calls for accountability when those values are not upheld.

However, too often loyalty to fellow leaders and, in some instances, remnants of the good-old-boy system are still causing serious problems. When leaders at any level wink at violations of policy and corporate values because of relationships or even performance, the corporate wellspring of trust is poisoned.

When the walk does not match the talk about corporate values, the slick brochures, pretty posters, and closed-circuit television speeches by senior leaders only serve to point out how out of touch management really is. Credibility—a must asset for effective leadership—takes a hit when this type of disconnect occurs. *Are you and your leaders walking the talk?*

☑ Leaders must be held accountable.

Fortune magazine recently looked at several big name corporations—Enron, Arthur Anderson, Kmart, Lucent, Global Crossing, and others that have undergone near collapse—to analyze what happened. They summarized the problems as "the familiar stuff of human folly: denial, hubris, ego, wishful thinking, poor communication, lax oversight, greed, deceit, and other Behind the Music Plot conventions." The authors went on to say, "Chances are your company is committing some of them right now."[1]

Sounds scary and perhaps even insulting, but it's not far-fetched. Many well-known companies have had serious financial and morale problems in recent years due to poor leadership at the top. By pretending that everything was all right, not listening to their employees and other good counsel, and especially "drinking too much of their own Kool-Aid," they've given their customers, employees, and stockholders a rough ride and a lot of heartache.

These well-publicized leadership failures are examples of what has happened to many companies. But, it can happen to anyone. Ever heard of Solomon, the richest and wisest man in the world? He started well but found that success is hard to manage. Likewise, the companies that have had problems were run by very intelligent and, in most cases, well-meaning people who started well and had much success but somehow got off track.

What this all seems to suggest is that we must carefully tend to our leadership garden. It starts with the individual, and we can't assume that just because we're smart, well-meaning people we won't get off track in our leadership. We all must be on guard and we all need others who are providing accountability.

Those who provide oversight to senior leaders can't assume that everything is okay; rather, they must ask the hard questions and find out how okay things really are. This starts with boards of directors who must take it as their duty to know what's happening and hold senior leaders accountable. In turn, it's vital for senior leaders to know what their managers (and others down the line) are doing. I'm not talking about a witch-hunt—just the need to be sure there is oversight and accountability.

Accountability means little or nothing if there are no consequences when leaders are failing. This does not mean that people have to be removed the first time they make mistakes. In fact, leaders should be expected to make mistakes if they are doing their jobs well, because risk taking is part of their responsibilities. But when there is incompetence, or when the same mistakes continue, or when there are integrity problems, the overseeing authority must take action—and the sooner the better.

In the final analysis, *leadership at every level must be able to withstand reasonable scrutiny.* Good leaders should welcome this type of accountability, because it helps them succeed over the long haul. Bad ones will try to avoid it because they know it will expose their true colors.

☑ Leaders must be objective about the people around them.

Ironically, one of the most difficult challenges in corporate consulting is getting senior leaders, even some who have a reputation for being tough, to make objective decisions on key personnel. This is especially true concerning employees who have been personally loyal but don't have the talents for the position they are holding and are not performing commensurately with their level of responsibility. It's our human nature to rationalize and overlook more than we should when the relationships are strong.

Objectivity is always an issue when there is a transfer of control or money or when families are involved. For example, the challenges of a leadership transfer (succession planning) are compounded if the retiring leader's offspring are involved. After all, who can be objective about his or her children? If you are like me, you may be saying, "I honestly believe I can." But, without exception, every experience I've had indicates there is no way any of us can be totally objective about our kids. In these situations, without objectivity (getting the facts and good counsel) it's always possible to select an unqualified leader with serious or even disastrous consequences for the organization. *Are you totally objective about all your team or are you carrying someone who is not carrying his or her load?*

☑ Leaders must be willing to make difficult choices.

When emotions are involved, it can be painful to make an objective choice. As we gain age and experience, we know this is true. I think I first realized this during my experience as a POW. I had been a captive for about two years and had never received a letter from my family (I was still a bachelor) when one day they called me into the interrogation room and offered me a package from home. Of course they had opened and inspected it, so I could see the contents: candy, vitamins, dried fruit, and pictures from home.

You can imagine my elation at the prospects of receiving something from home in these circumstances. But there was a catch: I had to sign a receipt for the package. Looking over the form, I saw a sentence: *In accordance with the policy of humane treatment of the government of the Democratic Republic of North Vietnam, I acknowledge receipt. . . .*

As I realized the significance of those words, I knew I faced a hard choice. I wanted that package from home so badly that my stomach ached with hunger. However, I couldn't help but think back to some of our harsh treatment. Just a few months earlier, one of my roommates had been tortured and my heart had ached much worse. Signing the receipt seemed like a whitewash of the treatment in the camp and could potentially be used as part of their propaganda.

I explained my objection to the receipt and offered to sign a revised version. They didn't accept, and I was escorted back to the cell with empty hands. Not everyone chose the same path that day. Some men who were much braver than I was signed and got their packages, and that's okay. Those were difficult circumstances, and we didn't always have the luxury of a staff meeting to decide on policy.

I never saw that package again, but about six months later another round of packages came, and this time there was not a "humane treatment" statement in the receipt. As we enjoyed some of the candy from home, it was doubly sweet for me. Not signing that first receipt was one of the most painful decisions of my life; however, looking back, I knew I'd done the right thing. That and many similar experiences in the camp taught me that making an objective decision often requires making what at the moment is the most painful choice.

More often than you would expect, I find myself having to coach leaders on making an uncomfortable decision to remove someone on the staff. One CEO said words to the effect, "I know we could increase profits by putting someone else in, and I shouldn't keep putting it off, but it's just hard to do." Realistically, if it's not working, it's not working for anyone, so fixing it will make it work better for everyone.

One of the most useful pieces of advice that I ever received was from my commander who said, "When things aren't right or when you feel uncomfortable, dig in, get the facts, and if needed take action before things get worse." As a leader, I still find myself having to frequently replay this advice. You see, for a number of reasons, it's human nature to put off the difficult or hard decisions, especially when it concerns people who work for us.

As a consultant, I've experienced all of these situations from the inside of the organization and also from the outside. Regardless of the reasons, when leaders ignore the real world evidence and don't make the hard choices, the entire organization suffers.

Leaders face difficult decisions almost every day, and that's why the reading and acting with the team decision-making process is so important. When you go through the right process, you have the best possibility of coming out with the right decision. The right choice is often the one that at the time seems the most painful but in the end proves to be the best for all concerned. *What difficult choices are you ignoring or delaying?*

☑ Leadership development should be an ongoing process.

In the last few years I've read and/or listened to biographies about a number of great leaders and have been impressed not only with their successes but also their leadership failures. Looking at history, it's clear that leadership is truly a process, because no one ever arrives at being the perfect leader. Yet, people deserve the best leadership possible, so it behooves us all to continually be sharpening our skills. You've probably noticed the same in your leaders. There is always room for improvement.

Leadership is mostly about how a person influences others.

Influence is a function of credibility, and credibility is directly tied to both results and relationships. Results-oriented leaders are going to naturally stay abreast of the business and technical changes in their profession. But, developing leadership skills related to people usually gets short shrift. It may be just dismissed (I'm good at this) or ignored, because it sounds soft or elemental. In any case, leaders must hone their interpersonal skills in order to increase their influence.

Many companies recognize this need and are providing leadership coaches all the way up to the top leaders. When you consider the level of responsibility and the pressures that go along, it makes good sense (and cents) to have someone who can provide personal, confidential coaching to senior executives. I have worked with some of these leaders and have been impressed by their willingness to engage in the coaching/development process.

It's been rewarding to see them get positive feedback from their staff and peers that they have become better listeners, or more patient, or more empathetic. This may sound somewhat like soft-skill training, but as we now know, these behaviors open the door for leaders to build more trusting relationships, which leads to better teamwork and better management information coming up the chain.

The genuine effort to improve leadership starts at the top and flows down the chain. In a meeting of plant managers, one corporate leader exhorted that "we need new perspectives and a new approach to leadership. In many ways the old ways we led our people do not work in today's environment."

He expanded his comments by explaining how important it is to develop people and provide an encouraging place to work. Like so many others, he realizes that to be competitive his company must take full advantage of the talents available and recruit and retain better than ever before. This thirty-year company veteran concluded by saying, "Ladies and gentlemen, we the leaders have to change."

Growth always requires change, and change is never easy. The old saying that "You can't teach an old dog new tricks" speaks to this difficulty, but it should never be accepted as truth—at least by those who call themselves leaders. We must regularly take a brutal assessment of our performance and look for areas in which we can grow. We can benefit from it, and those who give us their loyalty deserve nothing less. *What are you doing to develop and grow as a leader?*

☑ **You lead teams, but performance management and individual coaching are one-on-one activities.**

This tendency to deal with the entire team for issues that only affect a few individuals is a common leadership fault. It's an understandable one, because of the speed of business and workload that leaders are facing. Group management is an easier and faster way to cover the exceptions. But it's a big mistake to hit the entire group in a staff meeting, rather than meet individually with those who have the problems. It's also a natural trap for inexperienced leaders who don't know better, and sometimes the leader is just modeling what he or she has seen. In any case, it causes problems, because it does not connect with good performers and often causes them to respond defensively.

Leadership, at any level, requires some amount of one-on-one time in which the leader coaches, mentors, consults, counsels, trains, encourages, manages, corrects, and disciplines. Good leaders focus time on the things that apply to the entire group, such as passing on the word from higher echelons, policy, strategy, and discussions of important issues that have broad common involvement. *Think before you speak/act and you'll know what's for the group and what's for the individual.*

☑ **Leaders must be flexible in order to respond appropriately.**

We've said that leadership is complex and that good leaders need to read and act appropriately. Therefore, it's obvious that leaders need a wide array of talents (behaviors) in their tool kits. In fact, the best leaders are those who are able to live in paradox. Looking at this next list of behaviors, you can see the flexibility needed to walk both sides of the street.

This	and	This		This	and	This
Visionary		Practical		Independent		Team player
Generalist		Specialist		Persistent		Know when to quit
Strategic		Tactical		Realist		Dreamer
Confident		Humble		Chaos		Order
Detached		Sensitive		Serious		Fun
Tough		Compassionate		Results		Relationships
Decisive		Get counsel		Leader		Servant
Opinionated		Good listener		Strong		Vulnerable
Bold		Cautious		In control		Delegates
Quick		Patient		Competitive		Supporting

Laurie Beth Jones, author of *Jesus CEO*, explains this ability to shift our focus as the picture-in-picture approach. She says that we must learn to keep more than one channel on the screen. For example, a leader needs to be able to expand the "vision" onto the full screen in order to develop strategy. At the same time, the practical details of reality should be in the smaller picture. At any moment, he or she may need to swap pictures and bring the details of "here and now" into the full screen with the future vision reverting to the small frame.

This level of flexibility may sound like "nailing Jell-O to the wall," but it is possible by overcoming some of our struggles. The other option is to rely on our natural go-to strengths and use the same tool for every situation. Of course, then you are back to being a carpenter whose only tool is a hammer, and we know how dangerous that is.

For most people, flexibility comes from professional development and learned behaviors. Young people have the opportunity to learn from mentors how to be more flexible. As you get older, flexibility gets harder and usually requires personal growth that is also difficult but still worth the effort. *What do you need to let go of in order to be more flexible?*

✅ **Leaders must set aside time to lead.**

Leaders usually get to be leaders by working hard and

achieving their goals. As they go up the ladder to greater responsibilities, it's difficult to quit doing the work and delegate. But that's exactly what is needed in order to spend more time doing what leaders should be doing. I don't think anyone knows what the ratios should be. For discussion, though, let's say that a first-line supervisor might be working 70 percent of the time and leading 30 percent. As a mid-level manager, it might be 50-50, and at the senior levels it moves more toward 80 percent leading, 20 percent doing hands-on work. Put another way, leading must become the leader's hands-on work.

Leaders must schedule time to think comprehensively about the future, the big picture, the competition, and the business or professional environment. They must also dedicate time for building and shoring up their relationships with bosses and peers. This quality time will build trust and provide a basis for some give-and-take when they have conflicting priorities. I know it's easier said than done, but it's like the old commercial: "Pay me now or pay me more later." *Schedule time to do "leader work" and you'll be more effective in the long run.*

✅ Leaders give encouragement.

Leaders generally get their rewards from seeing results, so they are not highly dependent on outside feedback. Typically, it does not occur to them to give encouragement to others, because they don't even think about it. And if they did, they would probably discount it as unnecessary (and probably too uncomfortable). However, we are all human beings and we do need encouragement from time to time. Reassurance and reinforcement build a storehouse of positive feelings that sustain leaders in difficult times and continually flow out from them to their people.

By its very nature, leadership tends to be a lonely responsibility. Let me encourage you to reach out to the leaders around you (especially those who work for you) and encourage them. Tell them how much you appreciate their contributions, their dedication, and their support. Regardless of how much you think you are encouraging them, it's probably not enough. *Increase your level of encouragement and leadership to others. It will make a difference.*

☑ Everyone is leading somebody.

Regardless of your role, you are leading others, even when you don't know it. People are watching you, and they are keying their ideas and responses from your example. Think about your own life and reflect on the people who influenced you the most. Many of them were not your formal leaders but were people in your environment who were role models, mentors, friends, or teammates.

As the youngest and most junior officer in most of the POW camps, I was surprised to discover (then and after release) the influence that I had over others. Sometimes in supporting my commander I influenced others to do the same. Sometimes I challenged him and got him to reconsider and do what he should have known to do. At other times, my role was to mediate or to push someone to initiate, take a risk, or stop doing something that was too risky. Most of the time, it was probably just having a can-do attitude and being a good example for others. Of course my associates were also influencing me, and I am much better for it.

It's this very power of influence that should cause us all to pay attention to the way we conduct ourselves. Every day we make choices that will keep us moving on or toward the straight and narrow path or take us off course. It would be bad enough if it were just ourselves that we were taking into the quicksand, but we must always remember that others are watching us and they are going to follow our lead. *Have you thought about your influence over others? Are you setting the right example?*

Coach's Clipboard

Key Point: Leaders must constantly be checking on themselves, lest they get off the path. Use markers and checkpoints to guide your course.

Action Items

1. Do you have your own list of checkpoints? If not, you can use these as a starting point.

2. Do you currently have a leadership mentor? If not, who could serve in that role? When will you ask that person?

---

1. Ram Charan and Jerry Useem, *Fortune* (Time Inc., May 27, 2002), 53.

❖

PERSONAL GROWTH:
Key to Leadership Development

The greatest likelihood for you to improve your leadership ability is not through gaining more knowledge about leadership but through your own personal growth. Accordingly, one of the main goals of this book is to help you understand yourself better, because you need that information to make good decisions about growth.

It's now time to deal with some of the uncomfortable issues that get in the way of applying what we know to manage ourselves and our relations with others. Let me forewarn you that this section may seem like I just pulled you through the self-help aisle at your local bookstore. Actually, self-coaching is self-help and it's also about the best way I know to improve your performance. In fact, for most of us it's about the only way to improve.

Still, I know that some of you just can't stand this sort of stuff. I understand where you are coming from, but let me share an insight about wanting to avoid something that I also thought I couldn't tolerate.

When I was a major, my commander told me I should get an assignment as a staff officer. I told him straight up, "Colonel, I'm a pilot and I need a staff job like I need another hole in the head."

He responded, "Lee, trust me. It's something you need to do if you are going to become the leader that you want to be." I did trust him and, looking back, that was about the best career advice I've ever received.

So I say to you, "Trust me." As a consultant and coach, my job is to understand people and their teammates and then help them overcome some of the roadblocks to performance and relationships. As your coach, I can tell you that to get where you want to be you will need to grow as a person. To do that, you'll have to overcome several big challenges.

In the next three chapters, we'll examine two key roadblocks (feelings of inadequacy and personal baggage) and then look at change: the path to personal growth.

FEELINGS OF INADEQUACY:
The Source of Our Problems

Inadequate, insecure, insufficient,
and inferior—shining the light in the dark rooms

At this point you may be saying, "Whoa! I may have said that I was interested in being objective, but this is not what I had in mind. Those dark rooms don't sound like anyplace I'd like to visit."

That response is quite normal. Most of us have no desire to look at things like inadequacy or insecurity. But, to be honest, it's a crucial step on the journey to understanding self and others. We all have some of those feelings, and without facing them squarely you can't be real with yourself. Further, if you aren't real with yourself, you can't operate with total integrity with others. Without integrity, how can you be a good teammate, coach, or leader?

The word *integrity* is an appropriate word for this discussion. In the previous paragraph, it was used to mean honesty, and we used it in that context earlier when discussing leadership. But to explore the problems of inadequacy let's focus on the other meaning of integrity, which relates to the term *wholeness*. Synonyms for wholeness are completeness, perfection, and soundness. Unfortunately, none of us are whole people, and that's why we feel inadequate and all those other "in-" words: insecure, insufficient, inferior.

This lack of wholeness or integrity (the same as a problem with structural integrity in buildings and airplanes) causes major problems in every area of life. If you will take a moment to reflect on what you already know, you will see that most of our negative behaviors ultimately can be traced back to this one source of not feeling whole or sufficient. Consider the two extremes of low self-confidence and egotism. Both have their beginnings in feelings of inadequacy.

You would expect these "in-" feelings from those who say that they have low self-confidence, but it's just as big a problem for those at the other extreme. In fact, it's no secret among high achievers that their key motivators are often fear of failure, fear of rejection, fear of looking bad, fear of being financially poor, fear of disappointing people who believe in them, and fear of not achieving perfection. When people feel inadequate, they often are fearful (even ashamed) of being seen just like they really are.

It's not just high achievers though; most all of us are trying to prove ourselves a success to someone. These motivations can be used for good, but if the fear is strong enough and there is enough of a threat, or goals are blocked, it's easy for the negative behaviors to show up.

Think back over some of the worst leaders and teammates you've had and recall the behaviors that put them in this category. You'll probably come up with a list that includes terms like dishonest, bullying, cowardly, jealous, manipulative, withholding information, deceiving, not trusting of others, unwilling to delegate, controlling, passive, unappreciative, overly cautious, indecisive, gossiping, critical of others, selfish, envious, and procrastinating.

For some, these behaviors are aimed at building up self (power, money, control, reputation, etc.) to gain a feeling of being adequate, secure, sufficient, or superior. For others, it's an attempt to hide conscious feelings that they are weak and don't have it all together.

Even those who are the most secure display some of these behaviors, as well as others that are less severe and more acceptable. Think about the underlying drive in so many of our efforts to *look good*, whether it is through clothes, trim figures, athleticism, intelligence, our cars, or our homes. I bring this up not to give anyone a guilt trip (though we are all guilty) but to point out that these underlying feelings are powerful motivators of our behaviors.

The issue we want to keep focused on is that these self-oriented behaviors can have a major disruptive effect on leadership, team unity, and performance. So the question comes, "What can we do about it?" Before looking at how to work on this problem of feeling inadequate or lacking in wholeness, let's explore a little deeper and find the source.

We didn't get all we needed but we're still trying.

If it were a perfect world, we would have received everything we needed to feel whole and secure. But since it's not, we all have some degree of insecurity. What we needed and did not get is called unconditional love; and for those who get squirrelly when they hear the word *love,* call it *acceptance.* We may have gotten some unconditional love/acceptance, but no one has received enough. Therefore, no one is capable or whole enough to give it adequately to others.

All too often, the love/acceptance we have received is mostly conditional love (it has to be earned by doing something), and that just doesn't fill our need for security and adequacy. In fact, it does just the opposite. We become conditioned to *perform* to get the love/acceptance we so desperately need. Thus, at a very early age we get unmistakable messages that our worth comes from something we do or don't do.

We learn to *do* in order to *be,* rather than *be* in order to *do,* and that causes problems. Let me explain. For my last assignment in the Air Force, we moved to a college town, in which most of the community was centered around the university. Many of our new friends and neighbors were professors at the school. They were very nice people, but they were extremely different from the people we had known in the Air Force.

For starters, they were cautious, typically reserved, and their work was usually specialized in a narrow field. In church and community affairs, they seemed especially dedicated and faithful, but they were often reluctant to speak up or take the lead. Comparing these people to my military friends seemed like comparing night and day or winter and summer.

The one thing that stood out to me was their obvious insecurity; I'd never been aware of anything like it. I saw these professors building their security in a castle of knowledge. It seemed to me that their goals in life were to become the world's leading experts in their narrow fields. They started early in their careers and laid their foundations by getting the highest educational degrees possible. Then, with each published paper or book and each research effort, they could add more stones or bricks to the walls of their fortresses.

If these academicians worked hard enough and kept their focus narrow enough, they could eventually build castles of expertise so strong that no one could penetrate them and challenge their superior knowledge. And having a fortress of knowledge, even on some obscure subject, was so important because it was their security—emotionally, vocationally, and financially.

I used educators for this word picture only because they were so different from me that I could actually see what was happening with them. But, in reality, we in the military operated about the same, except that our insecurity was covered by bravado and aggressiveness. And we used forts like tanks, guns, and airplanes, rather than fortresses of academic knowledge and research.

After retiring from the Air Force and spending some time away, I could look back and see some of the same bricklaying going on in the military, as people scurried to fill all the squares for promotion and work for all the right people—to get their "tickets punched." Like the professors, much of this was so they could meet their needs for security and adequacy.

No profession is exempt from these bricklaying, castle-building efforts to gain feelings of security and adequacy. If you want to see it at the extremes, just watch some of your local high-income professionals compete with each other—to build their fortresses by having the biggest houses and most expensive "toys." Once you see it at the extremes, you'll begin to notice that almost everyone else is really doing the same thing; it's just on a smaller scale.

In one way or another, we're all adding blocks to our fortresses to make us feel sufficiently adequate to be accepted or more accepted. I have to say that life has been exceptionally good to me, and I'm probably more satisfied than many. But I must confess my own struggle in this area. There is a part of me that would like to write more books, develop new assessments, make more money, have more expensive toys, and build my fortress just a bit higher.

> ### Give your teammates acceptance—
> ### it's a great filler for inadequacy.

You may be saying, "I get your drift, but what am I supposed to do?" Okay, let's take it back to the team level. Teams are made up of people, so we know that no matter how together our teammates appear, they're not. A layer or two below the surface they have feelings of inadequacy and insecurity that have a profound effect on the way they interact with others.

At times, this lack is going to cause them to act in ways that disrupt good teamwork. You know that they are good people, so here's what to do. Give them unconditional acceptance, no matter whether you think they deserve it or even if you don't want to do it.

You may be wondering, "What does it look like to give acceptance to others?" Let me share some of the coaching I have used with leaders.

- Determine to ignore some of the struggles of others that have been irritating you. Instead, learn to value their strengths. Give kind words of encouragement.
- Look for areas in which you may be in a power struggle with someone and give it up. This may be difficult for you

to recognize; so, in confidence, ask someone else on the team if he or she has seen examples of this. Remember, there are few areas where it's important for you to be right. Also, keep in mind that being right is often about filling your own need for adequacy at the expense of someone else's.

- Take the focus off yourself and put it on others. Stop usurping others' time, attention, and energy to meet your needs. Instead, start giving those things to others.

- Be more transparent. Share with a teammate some of your own feelings of falling short in certain areas. Ask him or her for help in those areas.

- Recognize the high potential in someone's talents. Give that person a vision of a bright future.

- Give someone your trust and let that person know that you are confident that he or she will succeed. Of course, this should be commensurate with the knowledge and abilities, but it probably should be to the point that it feels like somewhat of a risk for you.

- Give your loyalty. That doesn't mean that other people don't have to be held accountable or accept consequences from their actions but that, no matter what, you care about them and their future.

These are just a few areas to give you an example of what "fills people's tanks" with feelings of acceptance.

When I look over this list and think about giving acceptance to others, I am reminded of a book entitled *The Gift of the Blessing*. In it the authors offer five ways that parents can give the blessing for life to their children. These are: *meaningful touch, spoken words, expressing high value, picturing a special future, and active commitment*.[1] These same actions will provide a blessing to teammates as well.

For the team setting, handshakes, pats on the back, and occasional group hugs (when appropriate) will be adequate for the meaningful-touch item. Beyond that, the others are really more like giving an *emotional* hug: valuing people so they know that you accept them just as they are.

Someone has called this the *Platinum Rule:* "Do unto others as they would like to be done unto." It means reaching out to them in the ways that they need to be reached. For some, it means being sensitive enough to ask about their pain. For others, it will mean encouragement. For all, it will mean giving them a vision of their greatness—their God-given potential. This is a key leadership attribute that Jesus used. He showed people a bright picture of who they could become, and He communicated His confidence in their future.

Passing along a vision of high value and high potential is the way you can do the most to fill in those holes of inadequacy. Nothing is as powerful to fill another person as knowing someone else thinks highly of him or her just as he or she is. That's what we needed more of in our early years, but to some degree we can still fill in some of the holes of inadequacy for each other, even in our adult lives.

We never totally gain the fulfillment we need in this life. However, by giving acceptance to each other and also receiving it through our spiritual connection, we can make progress. But, when you spend your waking hours putting mortar and bricks in your own castle—to keep it solid and build it higher—you're not putting much thought toward giving to others.

In addition to our lack of focus on others, there seems to be a natural fear: *If they gain, then I must lose.* Giving of this type is not a zero-sum game. In fact, the real irony is that it's a gain-gain scenario. When we give unconditional acceptance to each other, we all become more whole. Now that's real team-building at a low price!

Coach's Clipboard

Key Point: Feelings of inadequacy and inferiority are the source of our problems. When we give unconditional acceptance to each other, it makes things better for everyone.

Action Items

1. Where or when do your feelings of inferiority and inadequacy manifest themselves? How can you deal with them in a constructive way?

2. Who on your team needs unconditional acceptance right now? Can you give it? How? When will you do it?

---

1. Gary Smalley and John Trent, *The Gift of the Blessing,* (Nashville: Thomas Nelson, 1986).

❖

HEAVY BAGGAGE TAKES ITS TOLL

We've just seen the problems of "traveling light" in some areas; now let's examine the burdens of heavy baggage. Baggage can be seen as the negative behaviors that are not covered or explained by the normal personality behaviors discussed earlier. Baggage may be similar to some of our personality struggles, but it's much more extreme; it stands out like a sore thumb.

When you see someone on your team acting illogically or being weird, you know it's because of baggage. Actually the more psychological term *dysfunction* also describes the problem well. Baggage really does keep us from being fully functional in some areas.

You've probably had enough training to know that baggage or dysfunction is typically the result of past painful experiences. It could be as simple as being embarrassed in front of a group. It could come from being let down by someone you trusted. Or, it could be from the pain of verbal or physical abuse. Generally, it's a protective or defensive (over)reaction to bad things that have happened.

Every one of us has some degree of baggage or dysfunction, because no one had perfect parents, grew up in a perfect home in a perfect neighborhood with a perfect school, or experienced a perfect work life. Along the way, we all have painful experiences and go forward with the accompanying baggage. The good news is that the less baggage in the family of origin, the less baggage we carry as adults. (There's a message there for all parents: Get as much healing as possible as fast as you can, and you'll give your kids a gift for a lifetime.)

Baggage often hitches a ride with personality traits.

Although personality factors don't identify baggage, the way people display baggage is somewhat related to personality traits. When we did our original research in the area of personality factors, it included a factor we called **Stress**.[1] This factor included many of the typical behaviors that relate to anxiety, tension, or depression. Using statistical analysis, we found that this factor was composed of two subfactors that we called **Tense** and **Ashamed**.

The Tense subfactor contained all the items (feelings) that were primarily outward focused and could be actively aimed at others. It included words like resentful, discontent, bitter, jealous, and angry. The Ashamed subfactor was entirely inward or self-focused and included such emotions as feeling ashamed, guilty, embarrassed, discouraged, inadequate, and disheartened.

Now, I bet you can guess which personality groups from the earlier chapters are most likely to be outward focused and aggressive toward others with their baggage. If you said the Directing/Dominant and the Engaging/ Extrovert folks, you are right. When they display their baggage, it is usually to blame or attack someone else. They also are more likely to use active-aggressive behaviors to control others.

On the other hand, the Harmonious/Compassionate and the Methodical/Structured groups tend to be inward focused and are much more likely to blame themselves when something bad happens, even when it's not their fault. Even though their outward-focused teammates are likely to have problems with anger management, these latter two groups are much more likely to have problems with depression. Their negative behaviors tend to be more passive, so their tendency is to hold back, hide out, and pout. (It is this group that is most likely to explode with massive workplace shootings.)

There is one more apparent link between baggage and personality that doesn't have much to do with teams, but it may help you understand yourself better. There seems to be a tendency to inherit the way we express our baggage from the parents whose personalities are most like ours. So two siblings who experience the same painful situation may come away with entirely different responses.

An active-aggressive controller usually passes along those tendencies to the child who is most dominant. And likewise, the parent who is passive and avoids even reasonable risks will likely pass that baggage on to the child whose personality is similar. Perhaps this is a fulfillment of the biblical admonition that the sins of the parents extend to the third and fourth generation. Here is another encouragement to parents to gain insights into their own behaviors and perhaps make changes so that their children's burdens will be lighter on their life journeys.

Dysfunctional teams carry extra baggage.

It's not unusual to see dysfunctional teams in the workplace, and most often the underlying cause is the personal baggage of one or more individuals. Perhaps you've seen a team in which everyone walks on eggshells because of an angry, controlling person. I've consulted with several managers who were facing that very problem: a smart, capable, team leader who cannot get along with people

Or maybe you've been a part of the opposite situation, where the leader is unwilling to confront the inappropriate behaviors of certain individuals. In either case, the results are a dysfunctional team that operates at much less than optimum effectiveness and efficiency. Equally important, from a financial perspective, retention takes a hit as the healthiest people and top performers often move on to a more productive and enjoyable place to work.

Baggage always drags the team down and usually consumes

an inordinate amount of management time. Since leaders are not really equipped to solve these kinds of problems, my counsel is first to communicate clear expectations: that the job must be done, that teamwork is important, and that others must be treated with dignity and respect. Then, when someone's baggage interferes with those guidelines, apply swift, logical consequences.

Each person must claim his or her own baggage.

Now that you've reflected on your own experience with the baggage of others, you can remember how much of a roadblock to good teamwork it really was. It could be that you're all fired up to "go fix 'em." If so, you took the bait, and it's time to set the hook. The reality is that the only person's baggage that we can even begin to fix is our own.

In their landmark book *Boundaries,* the authors point out the impossibility of changing someone else: " . . . remember the Law of Power: You only have the power to change yourself. You can't change another person."[2]

Even though in the last chapter we saw how we could fill in some of others' feelings of inadequacy by giving unconditional love/acceptance, in reality, we cannot get rid of their baggage. We might say that we are able to at least contribute somewhat to the healing of others, but when it comes to actually fixing someone else about the best thing we can do is set or enforce the logical and natural consequences and let the people decide to fix themselves.

For an extreme example, think of the alcoholic or drug addict. If you have been through the difficulties of trying to help an addict, you know that ultimately they only change when they decide that the payoff of not using is better than the payoff of using. A bright, likeable, and now successful businessman who is a recovering addict explained it this way: "I loved it all. If you could drink it, smoke it, shoot it, or sniff it and get high, then I wanted it. I've been shot at and put in jail because of my addictions; and the only reason I stopped is that the pain of doing finally exceeded the pain of not doing."

Most of our baggage can be just as difficult to recognize and deal with. Typically, we block out or rationalize the pain that it's causing us and we don't notice the pain that it is causing our teammates. Also, it's almost impossible to have empathy for others when we are operating in our own areas of dysfunction. At those times, our total focus is on ourselves and trying to meet our own needs of the moment.

To identify the baggage, look for the pain tags.

Do you remember the filters we talked about in Chapter 3? Well, our baggage always includes filters that preclude us from seeing the situation with others or ourselves objectively.

If you want to unload some of your baggage, you first have to identify it and claim it; and that's not easy. By now, I think you see that it's difficult to be objective about ourselves; so, if you really want a look into your dark rooms, you'll probably have to get someone else to shine the light. Outside the family, just ask someone whom you trust to give you some feedback on situations when your negative behaviors and responses seem to stand out. Often, those inside the family system can't be objective; but you may be able to identify your baggage by observing the pain they experience at certain times when they are in relationship with you.

Some baggage requires special handling.

How we deal with feelings is a major area of baggage for many people in the workplace. Let's look at this logically so we don't let our feelings about "feelings" cause a push back. Contrary to what some people would like to think, people are not machines; they do have feelings and emotions. Having a broad range of feelings, including joy, excitement, sadness, fear, and anger, is a part of the normal human psyche. Thus, the sharing of feelings is an integral part of normal relationships. As mentioned in Chapter 10, it's normal for people to differ significantly in their comfort level for shared feelings.

Many of us learn to deny feelings; it's a defense mechanism

that works very well in many situations. In wartime, it can be a convenient tool to block out the emotions of fear, death, and loss. In business, when a leader has to carry out very difficult decisions—like layoffs—he or she may have to set aside personal feelings to do what is necessary. But when we begin to rely on it as a way to avoid dealing with the sensitive realities of life, the results can be disastrous at work and at home.

If feelings are a normal element of people and relationships, then they are an essential part of normal teamwork and good leadership. We also know that feelings are critical in the workplace. Six-month, post-exit interviews consistently show that the number one reason people leave their companies/jobs is because of their relationships with their supervisors/managers. The general thrust is that they don't feel they were cared about or valued.

Now, let's link this back to the broader subject of feelings and, in particular, not having feelings. Even when you believe in someone strongly, if you don't show feelings how can you have a relationship that communicates acceptance and value? How can you have the empathy that we've seen as being so critical to work relationships and retention?

A few years ago we were conducting a team session for the president of a large company and his ten vice presidents. This company is a leader in a male-dominated industry. There were only men in the room, and most of them were over fifty. This was as fine a group as I've ever worked with, but as you might imagine they were crusty businessmen—almost all on the Objective/Detached side of the continuum. As we discussed this third factor of personality, I wanted to point out that they could be more effective by being more sensitive to the feelings of their people. I paused, and then I said, "I need to use the 'f' word, but I'm afraid you guys might run out of the room."

As you might imagine, my reference to the 'f' word got their attention big time, as well as the attention of my partner. They had no idea where this was going, so I continued, "The thing you men fear most is 'feelings.' You get uncomfortable in any situation where feelings are brought up, and it's hurting your impact on many of those who work with you who are different in this area."

It was a real encouragement to me at the end of the session, as we recapped with their "take-aways," when one of the more detached and reserved participants shared that he was going to commit to sharing and being more open with his feelings with his employees. He said he could see how trust and teamwork could be improved by doing so. Now, there's a courageous man in my book and someone who is dedicated to being a better leader.

If you have a problem with dealing with feelings, you are a handicapped teammate and leader. You have a low emotional intelligence and need help. Since you tend to rely heavily on logic, I recommend you start with some of Goleman's books on emotional intelligence mentioned earlier. Perhaps his research can convince you to develop this area.

Destructive tools in these bags

Abraham Maslow, best known for "Maslow's Hierarchy of Needs," had a classic analogy (word picture) that explains why our baggage is so difficult to identify and resolve. He said, "If the only tool you have is a hammer, you'll tend to see every problem as a nail."[3] In essence, if shutting down feelings has worked well in the past, then you'll see that as the solution of choice when you encounter uncomfortable feelings and emotions. If getting angry and roaring back got the bad guys off your back, then why not use it to get results from the staff? And if retreating and pouting gets attention and results, why not continue to do it?

The answer, of course, is that every problem is not a nail; and when you use a hammer to polish your finest china, valuables get shattered.

Bringing the baggage home

I've touched on home issues several times because that's where our most valuable and dearest teammates reside and, ironically, where our baggage usually does the most harm. Also, when there are problems at home, it usually affects job performance and teamwork. However, over the years I've counseled with many people who are very successful at work but are failing at home because of their baggage.

For many career-oriented people, their ambitions and political savvy actually can serve as a restraint that keeps much of their dysfunctional behaviors out of sight in the workplace. But, at home, often there are no such restraints and, under the stress of a difficult work life and the need to have a perfect family, their worst comes out. The outcome of their baggage is a dysfunctional family system, and the symptoms are often depressed spouses, divorce, rebellious or problem children, daughters living with drug dealers, sons dropping out of school—and the list goes on.

There is one last insight relating to baggage at home that I'd like to share. My wife Mary and I jokingly call this theory, "Lee's Law of Relationships": *People marry to their own level of dysfunction—usually different baggage—but equal in level of total dysfunction.* For example, people who are 90 percent healthy don't marry people who are 30 percent healthy. They find spouses at their own level. If you think you are seeing something otherwise, you can expect that one of them has a type of baggage that is not observable in public.

As a counselor, Mary's practice focuses primarily on family counseling. She has a real talent for being a "baggage handler" and says her experience is consistent with this theory. So here's another way to get insights into your own condition. If your spouse has significant baggage, then you can assume you do also.

Unloading the baggage

Okay, if we've all got this baggage, and it's bad, how do we get rid of it? There's only one way, and that is through the process of change.

All aboard! Get ready to leave your bags at the next station.

Coach's Clipboard

Key Point: Everyone has baggage. To improve your leadership and teamwork, identify yours and unload it.

Action Items
1. What is the baggage that's holding you back in your work and relationships?
2. How important is it to you to turn it loose?
3. Do you agree that you have a choice, or do you just see yourself as a victim?

---

1. This Stress factor is not used in the business version of the RightPath 6 Profile.
2. Henry Cloud and John Townsend, *Boundaries: When to Say YES, When to Say NO, To Take Control of Your Life* (Grand Rapids: Zondervan, 1992).
3. Abraham Harold Maslow and Robert Frager, *Motivation and Personality* (NY: Harper & Row, 1987).

CHAPTER 25

CHANGE:
The Path to
Personal Growth

Once we come face to face with our personal roadblocks, we have two choices. We can say, "That's just me; that's just the way I am and I'm not changing." Or we can take the path to growth. All too often we choose the former, because the latter requires brutal honesty about ourselves and the challenges of change. The importance of change has not been lost on many great minds of the past.

Heraclitus: *There is nothing permanent except change.*

Richard Hooker: *Change is not made without inconvenience, even from worse to better.*

Henry Steele Commager: *Change does not necessarily assure progress, but progress implacably requires change.*

Tolstoy: *Everybody thinks of changing humanity and nobody is thinking of changing themselves.*

Ghandi: *You must be the change you wish to see in the world.*

Abraham Maslow: *What is necessary to change a person is to change his awareness of himself.*

Denying our need for change

We intelligent humans deny reality and assume the world is or will be the way we want it to be rather than see it the way it really is. Our understanding of who we really are is deceived by our images of who we want to be. A leadership article in a recent *Harvard Business Review* spoke to this problem.

"A grandiose sense of self-importance often leads to self-deception. In particular, you tend to forget the creative role that doubt—which reveals parts of reality that you wouldn't otherwise see—plays in getting your organization to improve. The absence of doubt leads you to see only that which confirms your own competence, which will virtually guarantee disastrous missteps."[1]

Because we are prideful creatures, all too often we deny the feedback coming from our environment that is telling us we need to change. You may have noticed that many who have anger problems (active and passive) accept their behaviors as perfectly normal, even when there is abundant evidence to the contrary.

Unfortunately, I was in my late forties before anyone ever confronted me with my anger. During a family counseling session, my teenage son dropped this bomb in my lap. Of course, I calmly (and honestly—from my own perspective) responded, "I don't have an anger problem." I would have continued to deny the problem if it had not been for a wise counselor who turned to my son and asked him if he could give an example.

I'm sure there were signs of this problem, but if so I had discounted and rationalized them away. This is typical, because often even when we see the evidence that we need to change we may stay in denial. To take ownership of those behaviors that need to be changed also means that we must take responsibility for the problems they have caused. It's not a pleasant thing to look into a mirror and see that we are not who we thought we were. In fact, at times we are the very opposite.

Most of the time we don't acknowledge this incongruity until we are stopped in our tracks by the realities of the physical world. Journalist Terry Anderson, who was held hostage for almost seven years (1985-1991) in Lebanon by an Islamic radical group, gives a powerful description of how frightening it is to see ourselves objectively. In *Den of Lions*, Anderson's book about his ordeal, he describes his reactions when he learned that his friends saw him as the source of many of the relationship problems in their small group.

"I've been sitting here thinking about all that. It's not a view of myself I like—argumentative, bullheaded, trampling on other people. Especially in a situation like this. It's hard to accept, but I have to, since both Father Martin and Tom agree. Have I been taking out my frustration and anger on David? Can I do anything about it? Once again, I'm faced with the contradiction between what I believe I am and what others see me as. This place is like living in a hall of mirrors. There's no hiding from the others, and there's no ignoring the reflections they give me of myself."[2]

I had a similar experience during my captivity. Although it's been over thirty years, I still have a vivid memory of the day someone held a mirror up for me. One of our roommates was doing something that irritated me, and I gave him a verbal lashing. Ken, our senior ranking officer and my close friend, turned to me and asked, "Why don't you quit acting like such a baby?" As I reflected on it, I saw that the "baby" behavior that he referred to was my self-centeredness that was unwilling to "share the road" with my fellow POW.

In a bizarre way, people who've had experiences like Terry Anderson and me are blessed, because someone kicked open the dark rooms and shined in the bright light of truth. Most of the time, our self-protection and fear of facing reality are so strong that we reject feedback until we are cornered and confronted by the physical realities of what we have done. Consequently, without such a self-confrontation we and our teams and families will continue to reap thorns when we really could have an abundance of beautiful flowers and delicious fruit.

Why we resist change

There are many reasons we resist change, but the underlying

factors seem to focus on a combination of fears. We are afraid to move away from what we know (even when it's uncomfortable) and afraid of what something different might bring. Any change typically means getting out of our comfort zone, and it usually involves taking risks. Serious changes often require dealing with the risks we fear the most.

Usually, our decisions related to change are governed by the way we see the risks and rewards that result from change. If we believe that the expected benefits of change are greater than the perceived risks, then we will likely embark upon change. But often we don't see things as they really are; hence, we aren't able to evaluate the risks or the benefits adequately to see the positive rewards of change.

To put this in perspective, consider the reasons why a person who is being physically abused continues to stay with the abuser. These situations are usually complex, but a common thread is often the combination of sticking with the known (inertia) versus the fear/risks of the unknown. The abused person fears the risks of change (new situation, financial insecurity, being alone, repercussions from the abuser) more than they believe in the benefits of getting away from the abuse.

Admittedly, physical abuse is an extreme case, but it makes it easy to see the point. Consider a more common issue. Why do people continue in career fields or jobs they dislike? They know they're wasting their talents and that time is running out, but they hang on. The fear of change is stronger than the pain of staying.

There is also a large dose of stubbornness tied to our resistance to change. Sometimes, even when we suspect things would be better if we changed, we are unwilling to move. I am reminded of the supposedly true story of how a monkey trap works. A coconut is placed inside the trap and the trap is closed. There's a small hole for the monkey to slide its hand inside. But once the monkey grabs hold of the coconut, the only way to withdraw his hand through the opening is to turn it loose. But rather than let go and be able to get away, the stubborn monkey hangs on to the coconut until he's trapped.

Like the monkey who won't turn loose, our basic nature is

to hang on to behaviors even when we know they are leading us down a path that does not take us where we want to go. The same persistence and determination that brings us success in life can have a flip side of stubbornness that keeps us mired in the areas that are our personal quicksand. To commit to change, and to change to something new, we have to be willing to let go of behaviors and attitudes that have become part of us. If you think that letting go is the same as giving up and that giving up is for quitters, maybe you need to remember the monkey. Successful growth is about giving up (quitting) old/bad habit behaviors and acquiring good ones.

What are the costs of change?

The greatest challenge in the process of real personal growth and change is that it requires us to learn to see ourselves objectively, to acknowledge and grieve over the bad in the same way we celebrate the good.

The apostle Paul provides one of the best descriptions of this challenge. He got a good look at himself and observed, "*I do not understand what I do. For what I want to do I do not do, but what I hate I do.*"[3] He seemed to understand quite well the struggle of knowing he was not what he wanted to be.

By reading Paul's epistles, it's clear that he had a huge ego, before and after his Damascus road turnaround experience. Reflecting on Chapter 5, on behavioral traits, you will recall that the strong confidence of Directing and Dominant personalities often brings struggles of egotism. Paul could be the poster boy of the Dominant personality, and it's obvious from his writings that he realized he had an ego problem.

Paul says that he was given (or had) an affliction, and many scholars have speculated on what it might have been. In his writing he states that he prayed that it would be removed, but God would not remove it—to keep him humble.[4] Could it be that his affliction was that he had to live every day facing the reality that he wanted to be perfect, and yet he saw clearly that he was terribly flawed? Living in this tension caused him great pain, but it also continually refreshed his humility. Paul provides a classic example of what one has to live with in order to continue to change and grow into the person he or she is called to be.

Jim, one of my Marine Corps roommates in Hanoi, used to say, "Pain purifies." That seems to be another paradox of change. Something that can be so painful in the process can actually rid us of undesirable habits and free us for greater success as leaders and teammates.

Shakespeare, who was both philosopher and writer, packed great wisdom into Polonious's farewell speech to his son Laertes: "To thine ownself be true; thou can'st not then be false to any man."[5] We've heard it often, but here it has a special meaning. To begin to see oneself in truth (reality) is a challenge, but it is the price of real integrity and the entry fee into the path of personal growth and change.

How do we go about making changes?

Generally, there is no quick fix for change. We can buy instant coffee and instant oatmeal or turn a switch and instantly have cool or hot air, but we can't buy instant change. My mom, a lifelong teacher, had a four-foot wide wooden sign in her classroom that said, THE ELEVATOR TO SUCCESS IS NOT RUNNING. YOU'LL HAVE TO TAKE THE STAIRS. Change is kind of like that; we have to follow the slow and old-fashioned, low-tech way. How ironic that the process of change seems to never change.

Perhaps you've heard the expression, "No change means No Change." And, there is the definition of insanity that emerged in the nineties: "Insanity is doing the same thing today that you did yesterday and expecting different results." It's clear that change involves behaving or acting differently than we have in the past. But we have to act by letting go or giving up the old way and stepping out in a new way, trusting that it is going to work out.

Recently I had the opportunity to hear Dr. Jerry Linenger (Capt. USN Ret.) speak about his four-and-one-half-month adventure as a NASA astronaut onboard the Russian space station Mir.[6] Dr. Linenger said that one of the greatest challenges he ever faced was during his space walk when he had to let go of his white-knuckled grip and float in space. The natural fear was that once he let go he would fall away and go flying through space or fall back to earth. Forcing himself to look at the situation objectively, he realized he had to trust his training and knowledge in order to overcome his fears.

To his credit, he was able to adapt and change his mindset from fear to faith and act on what he believed to be truth. He did overcome his greatest fears, stepped out, and began his walk. Within minutes, he went from experiencing stark terror to one of the most glorious events of his life. Likewise, to change we must begin to act, based on truth knowledge and not on our old habits, fears, and feelings.

Change is a process

Unfortunately, behavioral changes are usually not onetime events; rather, they are a process. The process starts with knowledge or awareness (in business we call it management information). Then comes a plan (includes the decision). Then we take action (execute), get feedback, analyze and critique, gain new insights, refine the plan, and then execute again. When doing individual coaching, I've found it helpful to use this model as a way to focus on the development process.

Typically, with each cycle we make a little progress. Things get a little better, performance improves, behaviors change a little more, and the resulting feedback provides encouragement and insights for continued improvement. We repeat the cycle over and over again until the new behaviors have become second nature.

If you look closely, you will see that this is really the identical process that is used in all training programs. It is the foundation for merit-badge progression in Scouts, and it's used in areas from music lessons to military training. It is the process I used as a flight instructor, and it's the same for the Blue Angels and Thunderbirds. Nearly every athletic team and performer follows the same concept.

Admittedly, this is a simple explanation of a very dynamic process, so expect there to be lumps in the flour and sand in the gears. Change is not easy, life is difficult, and sometimes we just mess up. When that happens, we don't throw up our hands and say, "This is too hard." We just resume the cycle and keep going. Remember the wisdom of "baby steps" (from the hilarious movie, *What About Bob?* that also provides great insights for control freaks). Yes indeed, Bob was right: baby steps are the way to change.

I strongly recommend that you enlist a coach to assist in the change process. Many corporations have realized this, and they are providing coaches to their senior leaders and emerging leaders, specifically to help them grow. They recognize that even those who have been highly screened will have some problem areas. This acknowledgment of the need for growth in even the best leaders is refreshing to the culture, because it brings a degree of reality, transparency, and even humility.

If you don't have the luxury of a corporate-sponsored coach, find someone who can fill that role. The main criteria are that they be objective and that they really care about you. The role of the coach is not to give direction or even give advice but to help the individual see areas in which changes are needed and then help that person design and implement strategies that will result in new attitudes and new behaviors. The coach can be anyone who is able to be objective and encouraging and provide ideas and friendly accountability.

What are the rewards of change?

The reward of positive change is growth, and that means you will become better equipped to deal with every aspect of life. Performance improves, you are more effective, you are a better teammate, and all your work relationships improve. You can also expect less stress, which means better health and a more enjoyable life.

The kind of personal growth we've been talking about also means that you could unload some baggage and maybe even receive some more unconditional acceptance. And think of the increased self-confidence that can come from a closer alignment of who you want to be and who you really are. With all that going on, you could gain freedom from some of the shame and guilt hiding in the dark rooms.

Let's not overlook the home front. For starters, how about less conflict and a reduction in having to say, "I'm sorry." Better yet, remember how a change by one person can break a power struggle. As you change, you'll free others to change also. There's a good possibility that even the most difficult conflict in your family could be turned into the kind of relationship you want it to be.

If you want to give your family a reward, if you want to give them a blessing like nothing you've ever done before, then walk this road of change and personal growth. The third law of planting says that the harvest comes in multiples. Thus your changed behaviors will have a ripple effect that will keep going even as a legacy to the third and fourth generations.

There is a principle that God laid out with Abram (later called Abraham) that I believe operates today in all our lives. By faith, Abram left his home behind and moved to a new land. God honored his faith and actions and promised him, *"I will bless you and you will be a blessing to all people."*[7] When we let go of and leave behind our old negative behaviors and baggage, we are blessed and others are blessed in the process.

Now, that's a reward that keeps on coming and enables us to keep on giving.

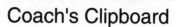

Coach's Clipboard

Key Point: Personal change is the most effective way to improve your leadership and teamwork.

Action Items

1. What changes do you need to make that you are denying? Why are you in denial? What will it take for you to act?

2. What would be the benefits from your changes and personal growth? To you? To your teammates? To others?

1. Ronald A. Heifetz and Marty Linsky, *Harvard Business Review,* "Managing Yourself: A Survival Guide for Leaders" (June 2002), 72.

2. Terry Anderson, *Den of Lions,* (TMS Corporation, © 1993, NY: Ballantine Books, 1994), 139.

3. Romans 7:15 NIV.

4. 2 Corinthians 12:6–10 NASB.

5. Shakespeare, *Hamlet.*

6. Dr. Linenger spoke at the Southern Company, Topazi Spring Forum, Point Clear AL, April 16, 2002. His courageous story is documented in *Off the Planet,* Dr. Jerry Linenger (NY: McGraw Hill, 2001).

7. Genesis 12:2–3.

❖

EPILOGUE

Gap analysis

The term "gap analysis" has become one of those buzz expressions that makes the rounds in corporate America. It means comparing where you really are with where you ought/want to be and developing plans that will close the gap. In retrospect, this material could be considered a manual on how to do gap analysis for human capital management and leadership development.

In the early chapters, we analyzed how people are matched to positions and saw that there is still a gap in the way we manage people and choose careers. The basic principle of matching talents to the task is clearly the solution to close this gap. When we talked about objectivity, it was to give a gap analysis of how we see ourselves compared to how we see others. We have to get a clear and balanced view of ourselves before we can see others accurately.

The section on personality was intended to fill in the gaps you might have in your knowledge about individual differences. A better understanding will hopefully equip you to lead a variety of talents and better manage your relationships with others. Likewise, the sections on teamwork and leadership were intended to help you analyze key issues in those areas and gain insights to maximize your performance and that of your team.

The final section on personal growth was the most painful gap analysis because we took an honest look at who we are compared to who we want to be. Perhaps like me, you discovered that this gap was much bigger than you had ever imagined.

Closing the gaps

One of the unique aspects of my experience as a POW was the opportunity to do a personal analysis. Since there was not much new input for several years, much of my time was spent reviewing the past. It was there that I first became aware of the gaps between what I wanted to be as a person and what I really was.

Since then I've grown in some areas, but I recognize that I'll never get to where I want to be. I am immutably flawed and will always be inadequate to achieve the mark. This ongoing awareness could be overwhelming if it were not for a spiritual understanding that I don't have to achieve perfection. Thankfully, the grace of God covers the gap between what I can do and what I can't.

I have found that spiritual perspectives are especially helpful when trying to understand human nature and the challenges of personal growth. For example, there are many examples of gap analysis in the actions of Jesus. To those who were aware of their gaps and were sad about them, He gave hope, encouragement, and grace. For those who were proud of their piety and perfection, He exposed their hypocrisy and showed them their gaps. He understands our shortcomings; and, ultimately, His love stands in the gap to provide sufficient grace to cover us all. This knowledge comforts and sustains me when I know I'm falling short of what I'm called to be.

Love is the killer app

In Chapter 23, we talked about another gap that we all

have: a lack of unconditional love and acceptance. After writing that chapter, I ran across an article from *Fast Company* magazine entitled "Love Is the Killer App."[1] The author, Tim Sanders, chief solutions officer at Yahoo, asserts that love is the most powerful force for your company and your career. I totally agree, because if there were one buzzword that would tie everything we've talked about into one small four-letter word it would be *love*.

Love is not only powerful, it is irresistible. Leaders and teammates who demonstrate love (the tough and soft sides) have inordinate influence over others. They are able to inspire people to high achievements and great results, and they build relationships that develop and retain people.

Earlier I mentioned that the most-listened-to radio station is WIFM (What's Init For Me). When people know that you care about them, that you are *for* them, you get clear channel FM communications with them because they know that "this person is For Me." Genuine caring is the channel to all our hearts: and, ultimately, it cannot be blocked. For leading talents and teams, we all need to remember that love can cover a multitude of faults, and it never fails to close the gaps.

---

1. Tim Sanders, "Love Is the Killer App," FastCompany.com, as published in *Fast Company*, February 2002, issue 55, page 64. Book by the same name released February 14, 2002 (Crown Business).

❖

APPENDIX A
RightPath Poem

The RightPath in Life

When starting out to find their way
Many people tend to stray,
Never seeking—never knowing—
Never looking where they're going.

Others follow others' dreams,
Doing what their father deems,
Or filling mother's expectation,
But having little motivation.

No thoughts of interests or of skills,
But only work that pays the bills.
No thought of values they hold true,
But only titles when they're through.

Then ulcers come and headaches grow.
Frustration, tensions begin to show.
What happened? It seemed so right at first,
But now no passion, hunger, thirst.

May we suggest you stop to seek
Your pattern for living that's quite unique?
Take time to learn how you are made.
Then take that path and never trade.

What you can be, or think, or do,
For what others may expect of you,
What fills the coffer, promises ease,
Swells the ego, or tends to please.

Don't lose your way and wander far
From how you're wired and who you are.
But discover your talents—to them be true.
They show the path that's right for you.

© Sue Clark 1/22/97
Modified 8/19/2002
All rights reserved.

APPENDIX B
Relationship Among the Personality Factors

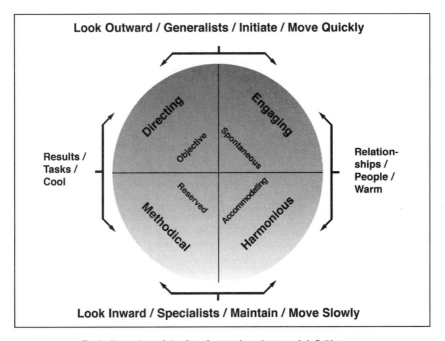

Each dimension of the four factors is unique and definitive.
However, the factors also share some common traits.

DIRECTING AND ENGAGING

- **look outward** to observe, engage, and challenge their environment
- **generalize** to see the big picture
- **prefer to initiate, make changes, pursue new ventures**
- **move quickly (physically) and from one idea/project to another**

DIRECTING AND METHODICAL

- **results and tasks oriented**
- **come across as cool and detached**

METHODICAL AND HARMONIOUS

- **look inward** to process, analyze, organize and understand
- **specialize** to see the details
- **prefer to maintain, operate, and refine**
- **move slowly (physically) and from one task to another** - bringing each to a conclusion

ENGAGING AND HARMONIOUS

- **relationship and people oriented**
- **come across as warm and friendly**

© 2002 RightPath Resources, Inc.
All rights reserved. Used with permission.

APPENDIX C

RightPath®4 Blended Profile Summaries
Sixteen Blended Profile Graphs

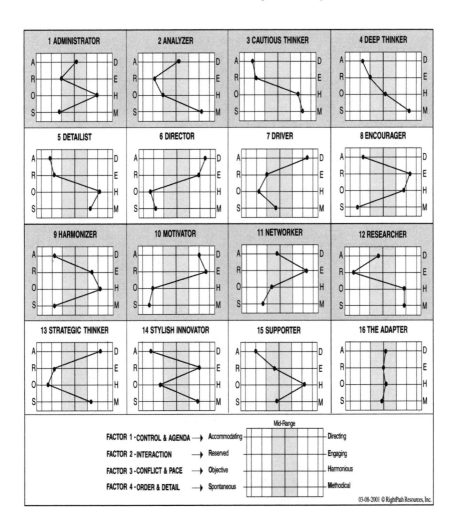

RightPath®4 Blended Profile Summaries

Brief Explanation of Blended Profiles

1
ADMINISTRATOR

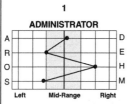

Left   Mid-Range   Right

UNIQUE BLEND: Factor three is on the right side and factor one is mid-range or to the right side.

ADMINISTRATORS combine the ability to get along with people with the determination to reach goals and accomplish tasks. This blend of personality strengths makes them well suited for situations where consistency, reliability, and persistence are important.

STRENGTHS: Administrators are persistent, goal-oriented people who promote team effort among employees in order to complete tasks. They also make good leaders by blending patience with firmness.

STRUGGLES: Administrators may not say what they really think. Sometimes they appear to agree but really don't and then backpedal. Can be stubborn, inflexible to new alternatives, and slow to change. Can be sensitive and take things personally.

RELATIONSHIP KEYS: Low key, unemotional relationships are what they like. Give them a challenge and basic guidelines, then let them do it their way. Recognize their achievements. Respect their privacy and earn their friendship over time.

2
ANALYZER

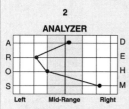

Left   Mid-Range   Right

UNIQUE BLEND: Factor four is on the right side and is greater than factor one, which is mid-range or on the right side.

ANALYZERS are very task-oriented and seek to balance the desire to obtain results with the desire for perfection. They are very competitive individuals who excel at evaluating the work setting and initiating changes to produce better results.

STRENGTHS: Analyzers tend to be analytical, logical, direct, confident; and they like new challenges. They excel at seeing the larger vision, creating efficient methods and procedures, and listening carefully for the facts.

STRUGGLES: Analyzers may lack sensitivity to the feelings or efforts of coworkers. In addition, they may come across as critical, curt, and impatient.

RELATIONSHIP KEYS: Deal with specifics and facts and avoid emotional expressions. Honor their need for structure and give them time to analyze and prepare.

3
CAUTIOUS THINKER

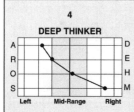

Left   Mid-Range   Right

UNIQUE BLEND: Factor four is greater than factor three, both are on the right side and factor one is on the left side.

CAUTIOUS THINKERS take great care to be accurate and thorough in their work, preferring to contribute by being precise and systematic and using careful reasoning.

STRENGTHS: Cautious Thinkers are organized, logical, analytical, thorough, and accurate in their efforts. They strive to be dependable, well-prepared, and informed. They typically enjoy assisting others and using structure, reason, and analysis in their work.

STRUGGLES: Cautious Thinkers sometimes are too picky. May overanalyze and delay making decisions. Can be pessimistic about outcomes and critical of others who don't meet their standards.

RELATIONSHIP KEYS: Give them time to process information and time to get it "right." Encourage them to share their ideas. Protect them from pressure and minimize risks.

4
DEEP THINKER

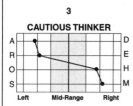

Left   Mid-Range   Right

UNIQUE BLEND: Factor four is the only one on the right side and factor one is on the left side.

DEEP THINKERS are analytical, logical, and philosophical in their search for meaning, truth, and purpose in their work. They are particularly adept at drawing incisive conclusions from data and research.

STRENGTHS: Deep Thinkers tend to be logical, organized, conscientious, thorough, analytical, prepared. They are focused workers who strive for high standards, precision, and integrity in their work.

STRUGGLES: Deep Thinkers may come across as distant or cold in relationships. They often underestimate themselves. May not express disagreement and go along with a decision, then later resent it.

RELATIONSHIP KEYS: Encourage their input. Give them logic, details, and facts. Avoid surprises. Give them time to prepare and time to process changes.

RightPath®4 Blended Profile Summaries

Brief Explanation of Blended Profiles (continued)

5

DETAILIST

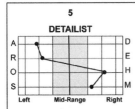

Left   Mid-Range   Right

UNIQUE BLEND: Factor three is greater than four; both are on the right side, and factor one is on the left side.

DETAILISTS are very attentive to details often overlooked by others. As a result, they are typically very organized, self-disciplined, and recognized at work for being both dependable and accurate.

STRENGTHS: Detailists typically are conscientious, cooperative, dependable, organized, thorough, analytical, cautious, patient, steady, understanding, and harmonious.

STRUGGLES: Detailists may be too cautious, unassertive, and may put off making tough decisions. May spend too much time on details and not keep pace on key projects.

RELATIONSHIP KEYS: Draw them into the discussion and encourage their input. Slow down the pace and be an active listener. Avoid intense or harsh expression and minimize conflict.

6

DIRECTOR

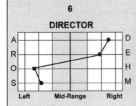

Left   Mid-Range   Right

UNIQUE BLEND: Factor one is greater than two and both are on the right side.

DIRECTORS usually have a unique blend of confidence, initiative, and people skills. They typically are able to see the larger vision and then use their superior communication skills to motivate others toward accomplishing it.

STRENGTHS: Directors are typically outgoing, bold, optimistic, fun-loving, competitive, confident, and assertive. They motivate others to accomplish tasks. Directors excel by having the freedom to define organizational goals and by influencing others to reach those goals.

STRUGGLES: Directors are impatient and usually poor listeners. May talk too much and can be judgmental and harsh. May have inflated egos and unrealistic optimism. They often struggle at finishing what they start.

RELATIONSHIP KEYS: Speak directly, challenge them, and expect them to challenge your ideas. Offer them options and then help them prioritize so they can get closure on their many projects.

7

DRIVER

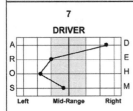

Left   Mid-Range   Right

UNIQUE BLEND: Factor one is the only factor on the right side.

DRIVERS are people who create activity and set the pace within an organization. Due to their desire to lead, they quickly take charge of work settings by defining goals and delegating tasks. They are not afraid to take risks or strong action in order to achieve the desired results.

STRENGTHS: Drivers are bold, direct, confident, competitive, often pioneering, assertive, frank, independent, responsive to new challenges, and capable of creating a direction focused on results.

STRUGGLES: Drivers tend to be poor listeners, opinionated, blunt, and distrustful of others. Highly independent, they have difficulty accepting and carrying out someone else's ideas.

RELATIONSHIP KEYS: Keep communications short and to the point. Give them bullets and options. Let them reach their own conclusions. Help them remember details and commitments by putting them in writing and getting sign-off.

8

ENCOURAGER

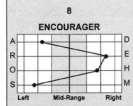

Left   Mid-Range   Right

UNIQUE BLEND: Factor two is greater than three and both are on the right side.

ENCOURAGERS are naturally relational and seek to be responsive to the needs of others. They make excellent listeners who respond to the challenge of helping others in practical ways, including solving personal problems.

STRENGTHS: Encouragers are typically energetic, friendly, encouraging, patient, understanding, loyal, steady, dependable, and are very versatile in the workplace.

STRUGGLES: Encouragers have a strong need to be liked and may delay making decisions, waiting for a consensus of opinion. Also have trouble saying "no." May neglect work objectives trying to meet the needs of others.

RELATIONSHIP KEYS: Remember their need for fun and excitement. Keep them involved with people and give them opportunities to be in the limelight. Help them set boundaries.

© RightPath Resources, Inc. 7/11/01

RightPath®4 Blended Profile Summaries

Brief Explanation of Blended Profiles (continued)

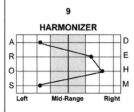

9

HARMONIZER

UNIQUE BLEND: Factor three is greater than two and both are on the right side.

HARMONIZERS excel at promoting harmony and cooperation within an organization. Their natural inclination is to help and support others to carry out a task and to build team-work in the process.

STRENGTHS: Harmonizers foster a cooperative team effort in their work by seeking ways to help, carrying out directives, completing tasks, negotiating, and delivering encouragement in practical, tangible ways. They relate well to people and excel at conveying care and compassion. They are also very versatile at work.

STRUGGLES: Harmonizers usually have difficulty setting boundaries. May avoid taking action or speaking up if conflict is anticipated. May lack confidence and not express good ideas.

RELATIONSHIP KEYS: Lower the intensity and avoid harsh, direct talk. Acknowledge feelings (yours and theirs) and seek their input. Acknowledge their contributions to others.

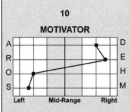

10

MOTIVATOR

UNIQUE BLEND: Factor two is greater than one and both are on the right side.

MOTIVATORS excel at blending their high energy and enthusiasm with the desire to achieve goals and results. Their superior communication skills enable them to motivate effectively an audience or workforce and mobilize it to action.

STRENGTHS: Motivators typically are passionate, highly interactive people who love to achieve, influence, and relate with others, especially large groups. They thrive on variety, changes, new challenges, and opportunities to convince others of their viewpoints. They point to the future with great optimism.

STRUGGLES: Motivators may dominate conversation and not notice that others are not in-terested. May exaggerate. Are sometimes overly optimistic and impulsive. May get emotional under pressure.

RELATIONSHIP KEYS: Help them channel their energy and enthusiasm. Encourage oppor-tunities for high-profile exposure. Help them focus their talent for influencing others.

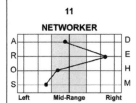

11

NETWORKER

UNIQUE BLEND: Factor two is the only one on the right side.

NETWORKERS enjoy new people, new situations, and new environments. They use their people skills to build relationships and interact with an ever-widening circle of contacts. Net-workers enjoy using their verbal skills and wit to be very engaging and persuasive.

STRENGTHS: Networkers are normally strong communicators. They are outgoing, en-gaging, lively, optimistic, gregarious, persuasive, fun-loving, enthusiastic, and inspiring.

STRUGGLES: Networkers may talk too much, be too emotional and too optimistic. May struggle with organization and details. Tend to overcommit and have difficulty finishing a task.

RELATIONSHIP KEYS: Include them in the group. Get their opinions and ideas. Accept their need for things to be fun. Help them transfer talk to completed action.

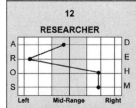

12

RESEARCHER

UNIQUE BLEND: Factors three and four are on the right side, factor two is on the left, and factor one is mid or right side.

RESEARCHERS are very task-oriented people who like to see the job completed efficiently, accurately, and on time. Capable of resisting distractions, they stick to the as-signment until it is completed.

STRENGTHS: Researchers are typically very productive people in the workplace. They blend their desire to accomplish goals with their desire for accuracy. They are motivated to become competent experts in their fields.

STRUGGLES: Researchers can come across as cold, blunt, and rigid perfectionists. Highly task oriented and independent, they typically dislike socializing and may be judgmental of those who operate through relationships.

RELATIONSHIP KEYS: They prefer written over verbal communications. Keep conversations brief and to the point. Respect their expertise, and build your credibility over time to develop the relationship.

© RightPath Resources, Inc. 7/11/01

RightPath®4 Blended Profile Summaries

Brief Explanation of Blended Profiles (continued)

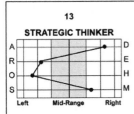

13

STRATEGIC THINKER

A — D
R — E
O — H
S — M

Left Mid-Range Right

UNIQUE BLEND: Factor one is greater than or equal to four and both are on the right side.

STRATEGIC THINKERS excel by blending their strong drive to reach goals with a desire for precision, accuracy, and quality. As a result, they are equipped to be strategic leaders in situations where achieving results in a challenging environment is a priority.

STRENGTHS: Strategic Thinkers are goal-oriented, precise, analytical, assertive, confident, and prepared; and they insist on high standards. They have a good eye for detail and push to get the job done right.

STRUGGLES: Strategic Thinkers can be picky, pushy, and controlling to get result. Quick thinkers, they are typically impatient, critical, and poor listeners. They have difficulty accepting input from others and stubbornly hold on to their ideas.

RELATIONSHIP KEYS: Keep it short and to the point. Give them options rather than contradict them or tell them what to do. Feed them the facts and let them reach their own conclusions.

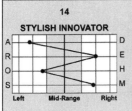

14

STYLISH INNOVATOR

A — D
R — E
O — H
S — M

Left Mid-Range Right

UNIQUE BLEND: Factors two and four are both on the right side.

STYLISH INNOVATORS are motivated to create lasting and favorable impressions by using precise, technical information and skills that inform, train, influence or persuade people. Achieving these impressions requires developing both an area of expertise and access to groups of people.

STRENGTHS: Stylish Innovators excel at promoting new ideas, stirring up high energy and enthusiasm of new projects, and drawing on their wide base of knowledge to successfully promote their agendas

STRUGGLES: Stylish Innovators may lack focus, take on too much, then try to do it all perfect and, in the process, get overwhelmed. Can be emotional and critical under stress.

RELATIONSHIP KEYS: Include them in the group and be sure to get their input before making decisions. Look for "limelight" opportunities where they can express their creative ideas and gain public recognition.

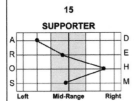

15

SUPPORTER

A — D
R — E
O — H
S — M

Left Mid-Range Right

UNIQUE BLEND: Factor three is the only one on the right side and factor one is on the left side.

SUPPORTERS naturally thrive when given the opportunity to help, encourage, or cooperate with others. They make loyal friends and employees and gain fulfillment by helping make others successful.

STRENGTHS: Supporters typically are excellent team players, due to their desire to cooperate, help others, and listen. They desire to be patient, loyal, and steady and to support the efforts of those in charge.

STRUGGLES: Supporters may delay tough decisions or actions to avoid conflict. May have difficulty in saying "no" or setting boundaries for others. Typically resist changes and are slow to initiate.

RELATIONSHIP KEYS: Remember their need for stability and harmony. Lower the intensity level and soften the tone of communications. Encourage their input and then actively listen. Acknowledge the value of their support.

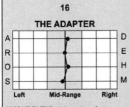

16

THE ADAPTER

A — D
R — E
O — H
S — M

Left Mid-Range Right

UNIQUE BLEND: At least three factors are in the Mid-Range. No factor is on the right side.

ADAPTERS typically have the ability to adapt to the needs of their environment. They are very versatile and can be very good team players.

STRENGTHS: Adapters have a natural ability to evaluate the situation and adjust their style to work well with others. They usually have a strong desire to please and so they are quick to devote their skills wherever they are needed to get the job done.

STRUGGLES: Adapters may be indecisive when there are conflicting opinions. May have difficulty in setting boundaries for others and self. May get overwhelmed and not tell anyone.

RELATIONSHIP KEYS: Recognize their contributions. Encourage them to share their opinions and ideas. Help them prioritize and develop systems and work relationships that reduce stress.

© RightPath Resources, Inc. 7/11/01

❖

APPENDIX D
Due Diligence for Hiring

Suggestions to enhance the RightPathing® process

None of these suggestions are intended to supercede your company's human resources' policies and procedures.

Common methods to gain insights **into an individual's potential for success in a particular position**

- Résumé
- Behavioral assessments (and other types of testing as appropriate)
- References
- Recommendations by people you don't know
- Recommendations by people you do know or are known to someone you know
- Past work history
- Education and training patterns and results
- Achievements of the past
- Interview
- Interview by someone in the company of the opposite sex from the primary interviewer (Women and men often discern very different insights in an interview.)
- Current life situation, such as willingness to relocate
- Expressed goals for the future
- Attitude and other intangibles
- Trial with a short-term project, contract, or temporary basis

*Note: *Although RightPath Resources, Inc. believes very strongly in the use of behavioral assessments to facilitate interviews and gain insights into potential employees, we caution that they should be used as only one of many sources of information for making hiring decisions.*

Some key factors to consider in the hiring process: (These are not intended to be interview questions. They can serve as a general guide to help you evaluate the potential match.)

1. **Passion**
   - What does the person really want to do?
   - How strong is the desire?
   - What are the motivating factors?

2. **Natural Talents (behavioral strengths, personality, temperament)**
   - How closely do the candidate's strengths and struggles match what is most commonly found in those who succeed in this or similar positions?

   Remember, you are not looking for average talents for the key functions of the position. For those areas, the individual should be using his or her best talents—those that have the highest potential for immediate use, as well as further development. Also, these talents should be ones that the person is highly motivated to use. For instance, corporate trainers usually love to prepare and then perform by presenting material to a group. A trainer who does not have a passion for communicating information to a group is likely to be a boring and unmotivated speaker.

3. **Character and integrity**
   - Is this person reliable?
   - Is this person ethical?
   - Is his or her work ethic compatible with the job, mission, and organization?

4. Experience

- What type of work has he or she done in the past?
- How much of his or her experience will transfer into the position you are filling?
- What has been the level of achievement?
- Are you considering the candidate more for now or later?

5. Job related

- Based on past performance, has the candidate demonstrated the skills that are needed in the position?

6. Chemistry and Diversity

- How well will this person fit the work team?
- Can he or she quickly become part of the group?
- Is it likely that he or she will accept others on the team and be accepted by them?
- Caution! Don't make the common mistake of seeing "different as wrong." Diversity is essential to a competitive workplace. Also, remember that first impressions can be biased by our past experiences.

7. Values

- Will your organization's products, services, and culture be complementary to the values of the individual and vice versa?
- Will there be conflicts? If so, how significant are the potential conflicts?
- Can everyone on the team accept the conflicts and still be good teammates?

8. Retention and career progression

- Consider how long you would like to keep this person in this position.

- Try to determine how long the candidate would want to stay in it. Evaluate in your own mind how much growth potential the person has.
- How strongly is the candidate motivated toward career progression versus stability? Is this person looking for a stepping-stone or a long-term relationship?

APPENDIX E
Building Blocks of Leadership

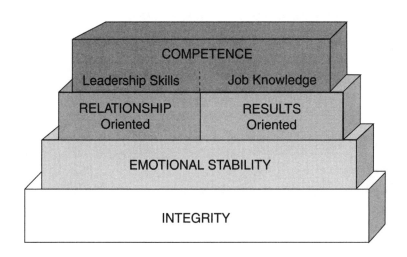

© 2002 RightPath Resources, Inc.
All rights reserved. Used with permission.

TOP LEADERSHIP ATTRIBUTES

✳	#1	**GOOD LISTENER**
▲	#2	**HONEST, TRUSTWORTHY, HAS INTEGRITY**
✳	#3	**CARED, CONCERNED ABOUT ME**
◆	#4	**MOTIVATES SELF AND OTHERS**
✳	#5	**TRUSTED ME TO DO THE JOB**
✳	Tie	**SUPPORTIVE, LENDS A HELPING HAND**
✳	Tie	**RESPECTS OTHERS AND ME**
▲	#6	**FAIR/TREATS OTHERS FAIRLY**
❏	Tie	**SEES BIG PICTURE, VISIONARY, STRATEGIC**
◆	#7	**KNOWLEDGEABLE, INTELLIGENT**
❏	Tie	**STRAIGHTFORWARD, GIVES CLEAR EXPECTATIONS**
❏	#8	**STRONG WORK ETHIC, GOOD PROBLEM SOLVER**
❏	Tie	**DECISIVE, GAVE DIRECTION, FIRM (BUT FLEXIBLE)**
◆	Tie	**EMPOWERS/CHALLENGES EMPLOYEES**
▤	#9	**POSITIVE, GOOD ATTITUDE, LOYAL**

Legend

✳ Relationship Oriented
❏ Results Oriented
▲ Integrity
▤ Emotional Stability
◆ Competency

© 2002 RightPath Resources, Inc.
All rights reserved. Used with permission.

LEADERSHIP ATTRIBUTES

from

My Greatest Leader/Manager Exercise 2001

Listed below is a compilation of the responses from 300 supervisors to the question: "What were the qualities that you most admired and respected in your greatest leader/manager?"

(Note: RightPath arbitrarily assigned the heading of items to provide groupings as a conceptual framework for discussion after the data was collected.)

PEOPLE ORIENTED

Good listener

Cared, concerned, cared about me

Trusted me to do the job

Supportive, lends a helping hand

Respects others and me

Approachable

Friendly

Priority was people first

Got to know me

Gave me regular feedback, reinforcement

Thoughtful, had a kind word for everyone

Observant and responded well to your needs

Had time for me, had time to teach me

Wanted person to succeed, looked for strong points

Allowed me to develop, learn, grow

Talked to the little people, treated me like a person

Compassionate

Easy to talk to

People person

Understanding

Team approach, helped me achieve my goals

Treated me as an individual

(PEOPLE ORIENTED continued)

Very encouraging
Likeable
Concerned about others
Served people
Valued me as an employee
Showed interest in what I was working on
Patient, took time to understand
Able to relate
Wanted and acted on my suggestions
Cared about my career

RESULTS ORIENTED, TASK FOCUSED

Straightforward, direct
Clear expectations
Strong work ethic
Decisive, gave direction
Good problem solver
Firm (but flexible)
High expectations of self and others
Very focused (on the mission, goals, tasks)
High standards, set high goals
Results oriented
Takes action, initiates, proactive
Created and expected accountability
Stern but fair
Desire to be the best
Committed to excellence
Paid attention to detail
Single-minded focus on customer service

INTEGRITY/ STRONG CHARACTER

Honest, trustworthy, integrity, does what he or she says will do
Fair/treats others fairly
Dedicated to the company

(INTEGRITY/STRONG CHARACTER continued**)**

Wise, good judgment
Accountable
Took personal risks to support people and organization
Willing to stand up to superiors
Strong family values

EMOTIONALLY MATURE/STABLE

Loyal
Positive, good attitude
Confident
Balanced, good perspective
Good humor, made work fun
Stable
Consistent
Genuine
Respected by peers
Got along well with others
Transparent
Calm
Diplomatic
Open-minded
Clear thinking, rational
Did not jump to conclusions (without facts)
Kept an even keel
Levelheaded
Down to earth
Maintained objectivity
Energetic
Enthusiastic
Flexible
Knew how to deal with others
Remembered his or her roots
Loved his or her job
Never quit
Person of faith

COMPETENT IN LEADERSHIP SKILLS

Was a motivator of others and themselves

Big picture, visionary, strategic

Knowledgeable

Intelligent, smart

Led by example

Empowered employees, allowed me to do my job with minimum
   supervision

Good communicator, shared knowledge

Challenged me within my capabilities

Competent, effective

Delegated

Provided resources to do the job

Organized and well prepared

Good judge of people, assessed capabilities

Asked questions, solicited and valued input

Professional—even under stress

Not too political

Creative, innovative, thinks outside the box

Trusted my decisions

Gave both positive and negative feedback

Gave recognition for a job well done

Experienced, record of high achievements

Matched people to tasks

Planner

Able to resolve conflict

Guided but did not control

Put effort into supervisory relationship

Provided environment for success

Able to prioritize among departments

Could navigate through information glut

Shared information

Able to filter politics

Was able to lead and follow

Knew when to listen and when to take action

Willing to teach

Believed we could make a difference

❖

APPENDIX F
Summary of
Coach's Clipboard Items

KEY POINTS

Chapter 1. The key to most of your talents is in your natural behaviors—your natural bent.

Chapter 2. Expect a struggle for every strength. Remember that it's the struggles that stress relationships.

Chapter 3. No one is totally objective, but objectivity is essential to managing self and others. We must have the courage to honestly face reality.

Chapter 4. Talents (natural behaviors) are measurable, so behavioral profiles can be used to predict strengths and struggles with a high degree of accuracy.

Chapter 5. Directing/Dominant people should keep in mind that success is a team effort and that it is important to hear what others have to say. *Listen up and give more respect to others' opinions.*

Chapter 6. Accommodating /Compliant people need to realize they have a tendency to hold back and that many of their best ideas never get heard. *Speak up.*

Chapter 7. Engaging/Extroverted people should remember that an effusive nature can be offensive to introverted friends. *Button up, tone it down, and share the limelight with others.*

Chapter 8. Reserved/Introverted people need to remember that extroverted friends take it personally when you are unresponsive, distant, and closed to their enthusiasm and craziness. *Open up, lighten up, and give others some attention.*

Chapter 9. Harmonious/Compassionate people must remember that a sensitive nature and patient style does not always yield the best results. *Toughen up, speed up, and speak up.*

Chapter 10. Objective/Detached people should remember that people are not machines; they do have feelings, and feelings are important. Also, quick action is not always the best policy. Or, as General Eisenhower often said, "Don't hurry to make a mistake." *Soften up, show more patience and kindness, and don't be so critical.*

Chapter 11. Methodical/Structured people should remember that perfection is not always needed and that rules and schedules are to enhance success—not preclude it. Analyze, but don't get paralyzed in the process. *Loosen up.*

Chapter 12. Spontaneous/Unstructured people should remember that details and structure can be powerful allies for success. Advanced planning and preparation will also help. Limit distractions and stay on task until the job is done. *Tighten up, get closure.*

Chapter 13. Matching the talents of the person to the needs of the job gives the greatest likelihood for success. With current employees, if a position change is not possible, try to realign some of their duties to better match their talents.

Chapter 14. Trust is an essential that must be cultivated through acceptance, understanding, and respect. Capitalize on diversity by accepting and valuing differences.

Chapter 15. A commitment to common goals and each other brings a spirit of togetherness—a powerful unity.

Chapter 16. Don't assume trust is in good shape. Develop a strategy to build it on your team.

Chapter 17. Individual behavioral traits shape team dynamics and are a good predictor of the team personality.

Chapter 18. Integrity and emotional stability are the bedrock that supports any leadership effort. Stay straight and keep an even keel.

Chapter 19. Relationships and results are both important, and you are probably good at one but will have to work on the other.

Chapter 20. Good leaders learn how to be intentional about reading self, others, and the environment and then acting appropriately.

Chapter 21. At the root of control is insecurity and fear. Exercise your best judgment and then allow faith, hope, and love to cover the things you can't control.

Chapter 22. Leaders must constantly be checking on themselves, lest they get off the path. Use markers and checkpoints to guide your course.

Chapter 23. Feelings of inadequacy and inferiority are the source of our problems. When we give unconditional acceptance to each other, it makes things better for everyone.

Chapter 24. Everyone has baggage. To improve your leadership and teamwork, identify yours and unload it.

Chapter 25. Personal change is the most effective way to improve your leadership and teamwork.

❖

APPENDIX G
Contact Information for RightPath

RightPath Resources
500 Highbrook Dr NE
Atlanta GA 30342-2319

Tel: 404.843.0367
Fax: 404.843.0051

1.877.THE PATH (843.7284)

contact@rightpath.com

www.rightpath.com

❖

APPENDIX H
Accessing the RightPath 4 Profile

Follow these instructions to take the free profile.

1. **Set your browser.**
   If you are using Internet Explorer browser, please adjust your browser as follows to print the reports: On the IE browser, go to **Tools > Internet Options > Advanced**. Scroll down to **Printing** and check the box that says **Print background colors and images** then **Apply**. This small adjustment allows the shaded areas of your graphs to print.

2. **Take the profile.**
   To access the profile, go to the site below and click on the link to the book. Log in with the unique ID from the book and the Password below.

   > **Assessment site (URL)** //:www.rightpath.com and click on the link for *Leading Talent, Leading Teams*. This will take you to the Login button.
   > **Login ID:** Use the unique login ID that came with your book for the free profile.
   > **Password:** *talents*

   Complete the profile.
   *Note: You'll be able to see your results and print them immediately.

3. **Print the report.**
   First view your results and then use the **Print Full Report** button to print your report. You may need to maximize your window to see this button.

   When you click on **Print Report**, it will open a report window. When the report has completely loaded (browser logo quits spinning and window says, "Done"), use the print button on your browser to print your report. **If you print before the report has completely downloaded, it will not print a complete report.**

   Use this same Login ID and Password to revisit your results at a later time if you choose.

IF you are interested in information about other books written from a biblical perspective, please write to the following address:

Northfield Publishing
215 West Locust Street
Chicago, IL 60610

an imprint of Moody Publishers
The Name You Can Trust
www.moodypublishers.com

LEADING TALENTS, LEADING TEAMS TEAM

ACQUIRING EDITOR:
Greg Thornton

COPY EDITOR:
Adeline Griffith

BACK COVER COPY:
Julie-Allyson Ieron, Joy Media

COVER DESIGN:
Smartt Guys Design

INTERIOR DESIGN:
Ragont Design

PRINTING AND BINDING:
Quebecor World Book Services

The typeface for the text of this book is
Sabon

Accessing the RightPath 4 Profile

Follow these instructions to take the free profile.

1. Set your browser.

   If you are using Internet Explorer browser, please adjust your browser as follows to print the reports: On the IE browser, go to **Tools > Internet Options > Advanced**. Scroll down to **Printing** and check the box that says **Print background colors and images** then **Apply.** This small adjustment allows the shaded areas of your graphs to print.

2. Take the profile.

   To access the profile, go to the site below and click on the link to the book. Log in with the unique ID and the Password below.

   Assessment site (URL) //:www.rightpath.com and click on the link for *Leading Talents, Leading Teams.* This will take you to the Login button.

   Login ID: *RCGP1840*

   Password: *talents*

   Complete the profile.
   * Note: You will be able to see your results and print them immediately.

3. Print the report.

   First view your results and then use the **Print Full Report** button to print your report. You may need to maximize your window to see this button.

   When you click on **Print Report,** it will open a report window. When the report has completely loaded (browser logo quits spinning and window says, "Done"), use the print button on your browser to print your report. **If you print before the report has completely downloaded, it will not print a complete report.**

   Use this same Login ID and Password to revisit your results at a later time if you choose.

If you have any questions or problems using the RightPath 4 Profile, contact:

RightPath Resources, Inc.
500 Highbrook Dr NE
Atlanta GA 30342-2319

877.866.9109
Fax: 404.843.0051

contact@rightpath.com

MOODY
PUBLISHERS
THE NAME YOU CAN TRUST®